"With rich historical and cultural insight, Dale Kuehne tells the story of how the sexual revolution emerged. He convincingly demonstrates that the shifts are not inconsequential. Sadly, he is right—our very lives and the well-being of society are at stake. *Sex and the iWorld* is a great apologetic for God's designs."

—**Dennis Hollinger**, Gordon-Conwell Theological Seminary

"Gracious, astute, courageous, authentic—Dale Kuehne's book offers just the kind of biblically formed ethical wisdom our generation desperately needs if it is to be led out of its current sexual darkness and pain into the light and healing of the Creator-Redeemer, whose own deepest desire is the fulfillment of all our deepest human desires."

—**Jonathan Chaplin**, Kirby Laing Institute for Christian Ethics, Cambridge, UK

"Erotic longing and its relationship to individual happiness and social stability have been the subject of serious thought at least since Plato wrote twenty-four centuries ago. Dale Kuehne's modern examination of this topic reminds us that many of the great philosopher's insights about the relation of physical sensation and the longing of the human soul to individual happiness are as applicable today as they were in ancient Athens."

—**Henry Olsen**, National Research Initiative, American Enterprise Institute

"In *Sex and the iWorld*, Dale Kuehne combines the micro-level sensitivity and spirituality of a pastor with the macro-level range and relevance of a politics professor. The link between these two—and between the traditional tWorld and the (post)modern, individualistic iWorld—is a robust relational theology and sociology. Kuehne offers this relational approach as a way to deal publicly with the most personal issues of identity and sexuality in Western societies. His approach is rooted in the Christian tradition but avoids alienating those not in tune with it by listening sensitively to the wider culture, particularly popular culture. You too may discover the relevance of U2 to the sexual anarchy of our age."

—**Gordon Preece**, Ridley College, Melbourne

Sex and the iWorld

Rethinking Relationship
beyond an Age of Individualism

Dale S. Kuehne
Foreword by Jean Bethke Elshtain

Baker Academic
a division of Baker Publishing Group
Grand Rapids, Michigan

Published by Baker Academic
a division of Baker Publishing Group
P.O. Box 6287, Grand Rapids, MI 49516-6287
www.bakeracademic.com

Printed in the United States of America

Library of Congress Cataloging-in-Publication Data
Kuehne, Dale S., 1958–
    Sex and the iWorld : rethinking relationship beyond an age of individualism / Dale S. Kuehne.
      p.   cm.
    Includes bibliographical references (p.) and index.
    ISBN 978-0-8010-3587-6 (pbk.)
    1. Sex—Religious aspects—Christianity. 2. Christianity and culture. 3. Christians—Political activity. I. Title.
BT708.K84 2009
261.8′357—dc22
                                                          2009014913

To E. F. Schumacher, who restored my sanity when I was perplexed

To Walker Percy, who helped me find my place in the cosmos

To Paul, David, Larry, and Adam, who reminded me I had a soul

To my wife, Rachel, whose tears help me find my soul

To Henri Nouwen for helping me understand the soul

To the Benedictines of the Saint Anselm Abbey,
who taught me the rule of the soul

To the church at the New Hampshire state prison (Concord),
who restored my soul

To my brother, Ross, who helped make all of this happen

We are unknown, we knowers, to ourselves. . . . Of necessity we remain strangers to ourselves, we understand ourselves not, in our selves we are bound to be mistaken, for each of us holds good to all eternity the motto, "Each is the farthest away from himself"—as far as ourselves are concerned we are not knowers.

Friedrich Nietzsche, *On the Genealogy of Morals*

And you may find yourself living in a shotgun shack
And you may find yourself in another part of the world
And you may find yourself behind the wheel of a large automobile
And you may find yourself in a beautiful house, with a beautiful Wife
And you may ask yourself—Well . . . How did I get here?

Talking Heads, "Once in a Lifetime"

Whoever it was that brought me here will have to take me home.

Martyn Joseph and Stewart Henderson

Contents

Foreword

JEAN BETHKE ELSHTAIN

Laura Spelman Rockefeller Professor of Social
and Political Ethics, The University of Chicago,
and Leavey Chair in the Foundations of American
Freedom, Georgetown University

We speak of "hot button" questions or "wedge issues." Television talk shows feature shouters representing the extremes on such issues, displaying thereby that "never the twain shall meet." We lament this—or many of us do. At the same time, we tend to shy away from attempts to discuss many of the issues we may care about deeply, including the culture of "hooking up," abortion on demand, the definition of marriage, because we know just how difficult it is for people to engage such questions in a fair-minded, civil manner. The upshot is political stalemate and discursive collapse.

Dale Kuehne, in this important new work, appreciates the dilemma. He himself was dragged kicking and screaming, so to speak, to the subjects he takes up. He understands just how difficult they are to discuss, how easy it is to distort one's position, how isolated are the voices that aim to illumine and understand rather than to condemn. That said, it is important to take the measure of issues one would rather avoid because they are critical to our understanding of the human person and of the sort of society we live in or hope to live in. This is the responsibility of a political figure, a pastor or priest, a teacher—indeed, of all of us in our capacities as citizens.

Kuehne examines the place of sexuality in our relationships. Contemporary America is continually depicted as "Puritan" by sexual libertines and liberals, as if our biggest problem is the stifling of sexual acting out. This is risible. We prate endlessly about sex, and nearly all boundaries have fallen. On those that remain—for example, sex acts between adults and children—we oscillate between a kind of horrified voyeurism and a rush to harsh condemnation that violates simple justice. Consider the cases a decade or so ago, conducted in an atmosphere of accusatory hysteria, that sent many innocent people—whose only crime was to tend to the children we do not care for ourselves, our own children—to jail, many with life sentences.

How to explain this simultaneous preoccupation with sex and ludicrous insistence that we are a "sexually repressed" society: that is the question. Kuehne examines the issue of lost boundaries and how these might be recovered. He tells us he avoided the so-called culture wars as he did not want to antagonize around "hot button" issues and because neither the left nor the right positions suited. Still, he determined he had something to say, something that needed to be spoken in a language of thoughtful critique rather than lofty moralism. To this end, he raises the issue of consent, our cure-all for every touchy sexual problem: was there consent? If so, enough said. Consent is our touchstone and talisman. But does it really suffice?

A narrowly legalistic approach to the vast and fraught arena of contemporary sexuality is a way to avoid deep and troubling matters, for persons and for the society as a whole. Kuehne traces the sea change in sexual attitudes with the "sexual revolution," the phenomenon of "hooking up" that aims to sever sexual acts from emotion. The result is sad emotional consequences, especially for young women. On this the evidence is considerable. What about out-of-wedlock births? Here, too, we possess solid data that children do better in two-parent households than in single-parent homes. Whole families rather than family fragments are more competent by far in the formation of the young. The biological, two-parent household is a child's best protection against child abuse, for example. Children at risk are children in homes that feature transient males, mom's boyfriends, if you will. Yet ideologies of family diversity make no such distinction, as if all children are equally at risk no matter what the structure of intimate relations. What about the explosion of pornography and the exploitation of children, the "final frontier" of illicit sexuality? The internet is rife with this ugly, repugnant stuff. Add the high incidence of promiscuity, the often ugly debate about homosexuality, and you see troubles enough to go around.

Kuehne reminds us that marriage historically was not just a personal relationship designed to fulfill the insatiable "me," but a foundational institution essential to the formation of society. He helps to bring the wisdom of the West to bear here, a wisdom we are in peril of losing. He examines our options and helps us to understand why the dominant modality of utilitarianism offers only a series of ad hoc pragmatic adjudications as we move from the unthinkable to the acceptable. There seems no principled place to "stop." The upshot is "Sheilaism," religion as "whatever I want it to be." (Sheila, as Kuehne later points out, is the name of an interviewee in Robert Bellah's *Habits of the Heart*, one of the many expressive individualists the researchers encountered in their studies.) This is a world of feel-goodism where once-crucial distinctions do not pertain: there is no difference between being married or shacking up, no difference between emotionally engaged sexuality and emotionless hooking up, on and on. Kuehne calls this the iWorld, where freedom of the individual reigns—this by contrast to the rWorld, a place based on the belief that homes are made for human beings understood in a capacious sense, worlds in which we live within and are engaged with the full constellation of healthy human relations.

How do we reinstitutionalize boundaries, resurrect forgotten wisdom? Kuehne finds natural law arguments inadequate. We just don't find these compelling any longer, he insists. No, what Christians, even more than others, should do is to live lives of love, to endure through thick and thin, rich and poor. The anti-Nazi German theologian Dietrich Bonhoeffer called Christ "the man for others," and that is what we should aim to emulate. Males and females are mutually constituted, relational beings. The existence of two such distinct human "types" requires that we respond to difference at the deepest level. To reject the "other" because she is female or he is male is to deny deep relationality of a very fundamental level.

What we require at this point in our society's life is a powerful and compelling narrative. And if we "really believe" that we "have something to add to the argument" about human sexuality, we should say it, knowing others will label us and categorize us in ways we ourselves would not have chosen. Kuehne takes up Christians who disagree with his approach, many of them indebted to psychological theories and models that accept uncritically the assumptions of the iWorld—offering no alternative narrative thereby.

It takes a good bit of faith to enter the lists in behalf of reasoned argument and critique. No "side" will find you an uncritical ally. That is precisely what recommends this challenging, well-written text. Kuehne is deeply immersed in popular culture: he listens to the music, goes to the films. He is utterly free from condescension. Kuehne appreciates that cultural critics are immersed in the culture they criticize. They cannot take up a lofty stance above the fray. As a teacher, a scholar, and a citizen, Kuehne offers in this volume a powerful example of what political theorist Michael Walzer calls "the connected critic." He is both American citizen and Christian. He is both inside and outside. He appreciates and he criticizes. Above all, he displays a stance that combines both compassion and judgment, reminding us thereby that the God Christians worship is a God of judgment and of mercy. All who read this volume will find much in it to engage, to criticize, to savor.

Preface

I shall be telling this with a sigh
Somewhere ages and ages hence:
Two roads diverged in a wood, and I—
I took the one less traveled by.

Robert Frost,
"The Road Not Taken"[1]

This is a book about sex, love, religion, and politics—all of the things our parents warned us to avoid in conversation. More precisely, it's about the ways our individual and collective choices about sexuality affect us both personally and relationally. It examines the place of sexuality in our lives and its role in relational fulfillment. At a time when contemporary culture, societal structures, and many Christian denominations are seeking to relax traditional restrictions and sanctions on sexual behavior, this book goes against the tide and argues that there are merits in resisting such attempts and in working to restore a number of the boundaries now being relaxed. What's more, it seeks to do so without resorting to a "Chicken Little" approach that has dominated much of the current debate. The aim of the book is simply to try to help keep us all from getting lost on a never-ending quest for acceptance, love, and fulfillment while looking in the wrong place.

1. Robert Frost, "The Road Not Taken," in *Mountain Interval* (New York: H. Holt, 1916).

There—I said it.

This is not a topic that I ever wanted to engage. Indeed I have spent the better part of my adult life avoiding it. Even though I am a pastor and a professor of politics, I have been content to sit on the sidelines and let the hotly contested social issues of the day be fought by others. The culture war being waged over the proper boundaries of human sexual behavior and the definition of marriage is a nuclear conflict disguised as a debate. In this conflict I would much prefer being the undertaker who collects carcasses on the side of the road or the physician who tends to the victims, rather than being a combatant on either side.

I like to think of myself as being a nice person. The Myers-Briggs personality test tells me that I am driven to try to make people like me and, if necessary, even to lie to help others feel good about themselves. It also tells me that I will attempt to avoid a debate like this at all costs—and on this point Myers-Briggs is right.[2] But the culture war came to my doorstep, and even though thoughts about deserting had a lot of appeal, I discovered that doing so was something that circumstances wouldn't allow. I live and work in New Hampshire, and one day, when I wasn't particularly paying attention, the Episcopal Church ordained as bishop one of my neighbors, the Reverend Eugene Robinson. Others, however, were paying attention. Since Robinson is open and unapologetic about being in a homosexual relationship, his ordination ignited a worldwide controversy in the Anglican Communion. Then as I was trying to formulate a way to avoid discussing homosexuality and ordination, the supreme court in neighboring Massachusetts decided the state constitution allowed for same-sex marriage.

Being one of the only, if not the only, ordained politics professor in New England, I found it nearly impossible to hide from these issues. The press, my parishioners, my students, and my fellow citizens came to me and asked, "What do you think about all of this?" They genuinely wanted help in sorting through these issues and wanted to know what I professed. "Is it theologically acceptable for Christians to support the ordination of those who support and/or practice homosexual behaviors?" "Is it theologically acceptable for Christians to agree with

2. For more information about the Myers-Briggs Personality Inventory, see www.myersbriggs .org/.

same-sex marriage?" "If we leave religious reasoning out of the discussion, are there any compelling nonreligious reasons to oppose same-sex marriage?" And finally, "Should Christians, or anyone for that matter, be trying to use the political process to outlaw same-sex marriage, or should they simply be content not to practice it themselves and let others make their own choices?"

As I began to think about these questions, I realized that they were the point of departure for a much broader and deeper inquiry into the meaning of human relationships and sexuality. They introduced a host of other questions I felt equally inadequate to address, such as: "What's your best advice for finding a rewarding and fulfilling relational life?" and "To what degree are love, sexuality, marriage, friendship, intimacy, and human fulfillment linked?", along with many others. It immediately became obvious that these questions involve us all, not merely a few of us.

When I understood this, I looked to the left and to the right and saw there was no dignified path of escape. I realized, like Robert Frost, a fellow citizen of New Hampshire, that I had come to a fork in the road and had to make a choice. I had to either respond directly or deny my chosen professions, for it would be impossible for me to continue in pastoral ministry, teaching, or politics if I chose to give stones to those who asked me for bread. All eyes were on me. But when I opened my mouth and took my first verbal steps on the road less traveled, I found that nothing I said was helpful.

At that moment I committed myself to write this book. I felt I owed my students, parishioners, family, and fellow citizens my best thinking about these issues rather than just the passing thoughts of a converted undertaker. In doing so, I have been fortunate to find support from a number of institutions. Saint Anselm College granted me a sabbatical. The Jubilee Centre in Cambridge, England, supplied extraordinary financial, intellectual, and spiritual support. The Monastery of Christ in the Desert in Abiquiu, New Mexico, provided me the solitude to pray, think, and write. The Emmanuel Covenant Church in Nashua, New Hampshire, gave me more sabbaticals in five years than most pastors receive in a lifetime.

I have also received the assistance of many individuals. Michael Schluter, Jason Fletcher, John Ashcroft, Guy Brandon, Femke Maes, and Jonathan Burnside have read and commented on countless drafts. James Skillen, Elizabeth Ossoff, Montague Brown, Gordon Preece, Mario Bergner, Chris Clark, Auriel Schluter, Brant and Emily Menswar, Howard Burgoyne, David Matta, Carolyn Larson, Jennifer Donahue, and my editors, James Ernest and Brian Bolger, have each given generously of their time and expertise. My son, Ryan, gave his twenty-first summer to revising this manuscript, and my daughter Naomi and Brant Menswar performed heroic feats in securing music permissions. Pat Ford guided me to new music, and Cathy Ford opened my eyes to dimensions of spirituality of which I was ignorant. I borrowed from Walker Percy the Nietzsche epigraph that opens the book, and gladly use it as a tribute to him, and from Mark Regnerus the Yeats epigraph that introduces the eighth chapter.

At Saint Anselm College, President Father Jonathan DeFelice, OSB, Academic Dean Father Augustine Kelly, OSB, and my department colleagues have supported me so profoundly that I have never been concerned that writing a politically incorrect book will harm our relationship. I am unaware of a better example of academic freedom. For the last fifteen years my Politics of Diversity students have interacted with me as I constructed the arguments that form the foundation of this book, and they have honored me with an honesty and authenticity that has instructed me profoundly.

My parishioners at Emmanuel Covenant Church have honored me in a deeper way. This topic is not merely academic but touches the deepest part of our lives. At Emmanuel Covenant we do not all agree on these issues, but it has mattered little. Our relationship with God and one another is more important than our opinions. To discover a congregation in which this is a lived reality has been one of the greatest gifts I have ever received. If it is indeed true that the best theology comes out of a pastoral context, and if this book reflects that in any way, it is a tribute to the men and women of Emmanuel Covenant.

Finally, this book comes out of a lifetime of learning from others about relationships. For that I thank childhood friends Scott Russell, John Nichols, and Ruth Hovland. I also must thank adult friends Patricia Sayre and Nelda and Darrell Godfrey. I offer deeper thanks to my parents, Norman and Janet; my brother, Ross, and his wife, Bonnie; and my in-laws James, Eleanor, Eric, Sue Beth, Lee, and Heidi. My deepest thanks are due to my children, Naomi, Leah, and Ryan, and especially my wife, Rachel.

Solomon wisely observed that "there is nothing new under the sun," and the reader will soon discern that this is true of this book. Being multidisciplinary in scope, each section relies heavily on the expertise of others for its content and authority. Indeed, at points it may be more true to say that I am the editor of this book than to say that I am its author. Nevertheless, it is a book I have been compelled to compile. I am grateful to the many who have instructed and challenged me and who will continue to do so in the future.

It would be foolish to publish anything on these issues unless I was convinced I had something worth saying. I do believe that is the case. Nevertheless, I present these ideas in the spirit of dialogue; I want to discuss them with people of all persuasions. I am not one who possesses the wisdom or authority to merely make pronouncements. I am well aware that these issues, while political and social, are also intensely personal. This book questions behavior practiced by my friends, my family, and myself. Those who have felt the condemnation of others for choices they have made, as well as guilt concerning impulses they cannot help but feel, will also read it. Moreover, given the cultural context from which positions like mine are usually proclaimed, it will be easy for the reader to infer that I write as a way to cast the first stone.

Nothing could be further from the truth. I will cast no stone, and I pray that all who read this will drop the stones from their hands, minds, and hearts. The question that drives this book is, "How can we live the best and most fulfilling lives as individuals, families, extended families, and communities?" My purpose is not to condemn but to consider seriously and deeply what human happiness and fulfillment require. I am convinced Paul is correct in Romans 3:23 when he says, "All have sinned and fall short of the glory of God." Repentance is demanded not of some, but of all. Forgiveness is needed not by some, but by all. Grace is needed not by some, but by all. It is life, not death, that is the driving passion of this book.

So what is the life to which we are called, and how can we experience the fulfilling life for which we yearn? Sexuality matters to human relationships, human happiness, and human fulfillment. But how, why, and in what ways? It is to these questions that we now turn.

Introduction

What were once vices are now habits.

The Doobie Brothers[1]

In the movie *Raiders of the Lost Ark*, Indiana Jones peers into the cave into which he would go in search of the lost Ark of the Covenant and sees it is teeming with snakes. He sighs deeply and groans, "Snakes? Why does it have to be snakes?" In real life, then-Senator Joseph Biden chaired the United States Senate Judiciary Committee during the Clarence Thomas Supreme Court confirmation hearings. The committee spent many days hearing testimony concerning Anita Hill's allegations of sexual misconduct by Clarence Thomas. It was an unpleasant ordeal for everyone involved. While it may be apocryphal, Senator Biden is said to have remarked at the end of the first week of hearings, "No matter what we do, we look bad, and I can't figure out what we can do so that we don't look bad." I approach the writing of this book with the same trepidation and misgivings of Indiana Jones and now–Vice President Biden. "Sex! Why does it have to be sex? No matter what I say, I am going to look bad."

---

1. The Doobie Brothers, *What Were Once Vices Are Now Habits* (Warner Brothers Records, 1974).

Human Sexuality in the Twenty-First-Century West

There is no topic in Western culture more contentious, more personal, more divisive, and more prone to cause hurt than human sexuality. The bitter battle over abortion has so deeply divided our culture that one can sense exhaustion whenever the topic is raised. Yet the issues raised in this book not only match but potentially exceed the emotional and intellectual intensity of the abortion debate. In this book we will look at the meaning of human life and identity as well as the purpose of human relationships and sexuality. We will spend considerable time examining two questions on which our culture is currently fixated:

1. Ought adults be able to engage in any form of sexual relations so long as it is consensual?
2. Will we be denied the best of human fulfillment and intimacy if we are not allowed freedom to engage in consensual sexual relationships outside that of a marriage between a man and a woman?

As I reflect on these two questions and see the faces of friends and students who are asking them, I wonder if there is any way to avoid writing this book badly. But, according to G. K. Chesterton, "If a thing is worth doing, it is worth doing badly."[2] So I have decided to venture ahead in the belief that addressing these questions is a thing worth doing even if I'm not able to do it well. If it inspires someone else to do so, it will have been worth doing.

The debate surrounding these questions is very complex, but one dimension of it is relatively new. Until the sexual revolution of the 1960s, there was a general and widespread agreement that the answer to both these questions was no. Today an increasing number of people are answering yes. This shift in public opinion on sexual morality is without precedent in the history of the West. It is not new that men and women practice a wide range of sexual behavior, but what is new in the past forty years is the significant erosion of the accepted belief that the moral boundaries of a sexual relationship should be confined to a marriage between a man and a woman.

2. G. K. Chesterton, *What's Wrong with the World* (New York: Dodd, Mead, 1927), 320.

While many factors have led to this profound shift in moral under-standing, the defining event was the sexual revolution of the 1960s. In the United States it was a movement of mostly young people who came together over opposition to the Vietnam War, and in addition to being a peace movement, sexual freedom was central to their politics.[3] While their antiwar efforts had some success, their sexual politics have changed the world.

In the first chapter we will examine why the sexual revolution oc-curred, and we will see that its impact has been truly revolutionary. What has changed is not merely our understanding of sexuality but also our conceptions of marriage, family, gender, friendship, and the nature of human happiness and fulfillment. We are living at a time of tremendous transition in our understanding of morality. The Doobie Brothers summed up this transition extraordinarily well in the title of their album *What Were Once Vices Are Now Habits*. Behavior that was once regarded by our society as vice is increasingly regarded as acceptable.

When I was born in 1958 the traditional family was a solid social unit, and its status as the ideal institution for procreation and child rearing was unrivaled and largely unquestioned. Since then a dramatic change has occurred in societal attitudes toward marriage and the ap-propriate boundaries for sexual behavior. Whereas before the sexual revolution it was widely understood that the proper place for a sexual relationship was between a husband and wife, since the sexual revolution marriage has lost its status as having an *exclusive* on sexual relations. Sexual relations are now governed by consent rather than a covenant. An increasing number of couples are opting for cohabitation instead of marriage, divorce has become unexceptional, and sexual relations no longer require the sanction of marriage to be seen as legitimate. Moreover, the definition of marriage as being between one man and one woman is becoming a historical artifact with same-sex civil unions and/or same-sex marriages legal in much of Europe and even in parts of the United States. Indeed, at this point, the relaxation of traditional sexual boundaries does not stop with cohabitation and same-sex re-

---

3. Stephan Ridgeway, *Sexuality and Modernity: The Sexual Revolution of the 60s* (Annadale, Australia: Isis Creations, 1997), www.isis.aust.com/stephan/writings/sexuality/revo.htm.

lationships since a movement toward the legalization of polygamous relationships is gaining traction.[4]

Some may be surprised at the speed with which the legalization of same-sex unions and marriages is occurring in Europe and the United States, yet when one considers the magnitude of the change in sexual morality that has occurred since the 1960s, the pace of this transformation is less surprising. It is a sad irony that at the same time same-sex couples are winning the right to marry, marriage as an institution is disintegrating. As David Popenoe writes in the 2007 Rutgers University study on *The Future of Marriage in America*:

> There can be no doubt that the institution of marriage has continued to weaken in recent years. Whereas marriage was once the dominant and single acceptable form of living arrangement for couples and children, it is no longer. Today, there is more "family diversity": Fewer adults are married, more are divorced or remaining single, and more are living together outside of marriage or living alone. Today more children are born out of wedlock (now almost four out of ten) and more are living in stepfamilies, with cohabiting but unmarried adults, or with a single parent. This means that more children each year are not living in families that include their own married, biological parents, which by all available empirical evidence is the gold standard for insuring optimal outcomes in a child's development.[5]

Accommodation and Impotence: Christianity and the Sexual Revolution

What I've just described is not just the story of Western culture; it is also the story of twenty-first-century Christianity in the West. The impact of the sexual revolution on the Christian community is enormous. Even as the culture has deviated from the traditional understanding of sexual ethics and marriage, so have Christians. While it is difficult to get accurate polling data on sexual behavior due to the propensity of

4. "Dutch 'marriage': 1 man, 2 women: Trio becomes 1st officially to tie the knots," *World Net Daily*, September 30, 2005, www.worldnetdaily.com/news/article.asp?ARTICLE_ID=46583.

5. David Popenoe, "Essay: The Future of Marriage in America," in *The State of Our Unions 2007: The Social Health of Marriage in America*, National Marriage Project at Rutgers State University, 2007, http://marriage.rutgers.edu/Publications/SOOU/TEXTSOOU2007.htm.

people to prevaricate about such matters when speaking to pollsters, there is good reason to believe the sexual revolution has more profoundly impacted the behavior of twenty-first-century Christians than has the Bible. George Barna and other social scientists provide abundant evidence concerning the degree to which the sexual revolution has affected the church in terms of the sheer quantity of adultery, fornication, and use of pornography by professing Christians. Remarkably little difference can be found between the sexual behavior of Christians and that of non-Christians in the United States.[6]

Barna identifies a cause for this in his book *Think Like Jesus*, stating that relatively few Christians allow their lives to be shaped by the Bible. "Only 14 percent of born-again adults—in other words, about one in seven born-again adults—rely on the Bible as their moral compass and believe that moral truth is absolute."[7] The statistics for people who attend church but are not born again are even more telling. Barna finds of this group, which represents about half the church-going population, that "just 2 percent . . . have the foundations of a biblical worldview."[8] Not surprisingly, as Christians have lost faith in biblical teaching, their behavior has come to mirror the culture. For instance, there is little difference in the rate of divorces among Christians and the broader culture. All this has led Barna to the inescapable conclusion that given their behavior, many Christians do not know the historic teaching of the church on these issues, or they don't seem to care, or both.[9]

Given the rapid shift in the sexual behavior of Christians, it should come as no surprise that when the church attempts to respond to the questions posed by the sexual revolution, it does so with mixed messages, a muted voice, and little impact. The indecisiveness of the church extends to the entire landscape of sexual relations and mar-

6. Barna Group, "American Lifestyles Mix Compassion and Self-Oriented Behavior," *Barna Update*, February 5, 2007, www.barna.org/FlexPage.aspx?Page=BarnaUpdate&BarnaUpdate ID=249. See also Lauren Winner, *Real Sex: The Naked Truth about Chastity* (Grand Rapids: Brazos, 2005), 16–19; Mark D. Regnerus, *Forbidden Fruit: Sex and Religion in the Lives of American Teenagers* (Oxford: Oxford University Press, 2007).

7. George Barna, *Think Like Jesus: Make the Right Decision Every Time* (Nashville: Integrity, 2003), 21.

8. Ibid., 21–22.

9. Barna Group, "Born Again Christians Just As Likely to Divorce As Are Non-Christians," *Barna Update*, September 8, 2004, www.barna.org/FlexPage.aspx?Page=BarnaUpdateNarrow &BarnaUpdateID=170.

riage. Equivocation and cultural accommodation is nothing new to Christianity. The letters of Paul demonstrate that the church has struggled with issues such as adultery, fornication, divorce, and remarriage throughout its history. Yet even though the church has turned a blind eye toward some sexual behaviors at various points in history, what is unique presently is the degree to which the historic orthodox understanding of sexual morality and marriage is being ignored or revised by clergy and laypeople alike. The extent to which the church is changing its interpretation of biblical teaching in a manner that conveniently accommodates, justifies, protects, and even sanctions the behavior of the sexual revolution would probably surprise even the Doobie Brothers.

Hypocrisy angers everyone. While some have consistently called the church to uphold the entire orthodox Christian teaching concerning sexual morality and marriage, many, if not most, have employed a double standard when it comes to homosexual behavior. The gay and lesbian communities are correct to accuse the church of hypocrisy and bigotry when for decades many Christians have turned a blind eye to adultery and sex between men and women outside of marriage while vigorously condemning homosexual behavior. When those inclined to same-sex sexual relations asked the church for the same blind eye that had been extended to others, many churches responded hypocritically and hatefully by ushering them to the exits. This response is simply unacceptable. Any criticism by Christians of gay and lesbian sexual relationships without correspondingly rigorous standards for all sexual relations between a man and a woman outside a marriage is both hollow and hypocritical. The inconvenient truth is that many Christians chose not to acknowledge the significance of the sexual revolution until it began to manifest itself in the public debate about the legal status of homosexuality and same-sex unions and marriages. By inconsistently applying the orthodox teaching on sexual conduct and marriage, Christians have minimized their ability to speak to the broader culture about all aspects of sexual ethics, including same-sex marriage.

While this book is not written specifically to Christians, I want to speak to Christians for a moment. The Bible teaches that all humans are made in the image of God and are deserving of respect and love.

That we have given less to anyone is inexcusable. Insofar as we have withheld love and respect from anyone, we need to confess our sin and ask forgiveness. We then need to reconsider what we stand for, practice what we profess, and only then re-engage the culture in a respectful dialogue about all aspects of human sexual behavior as well as the meaning of marriage. The issue of same-sex marriage is one of many topics that can and should be addressed from a Christian viewpoint. Centuries of bigotry toward homosexuals, while undeniably wrong, ought not to reflexively guilt-trip the church into silence on issues of sexual politics. Indeed, the church should ignore no issue related to sexual ethics. The presence of same-sex marriage in our contemporary ecclesiastical and political debates is an illustration of the extent of the sexual revolution's impact on the church and society. In this instance, something that has been inconceivable for virtually the entire history of the church—namely the moral approval of same-sex marriage—has in the past decade become not just conceivable but, for more and more Christians, acceptable.

The question is, "Why?"

Christendom is changing. The ordination of the Reverend Eugene Robinson as bishop of the Episcopal Diocese of New Hampshire in 2003 is not an isolated event. In 2007 the United Church of Christ became the first mainline denomination in the United States to support same-sex marriage, and it will not be the last.[10] While movement in this direction has been anticipated among more liberal denominations, what is more surprising is the relatively mild opposition to such moves from the laity. While American Catholic and evangelical leaders such as Boston Archbishop Sean O'Malley, James Dobson, Chuck Colson, and Eugene Rivers have taken strong stands against homosexual practice and same-sex marriage, they have not received the level of support from their ecclesiastical base that would have been expected just ten years ago. It is clear that the fallout of the sexual abuse crisis in the Catholic Church has marginalized its ability to provide leadership on this issue, yet the relative lack of response from evangelicals, especially those younger than forty, helps to explain why a majority of Americans

10. "Resolution in Support of Equal Marriage Rights for all for General Synod 25 of the United Church of Christ," United Church of Christ, www.ucc.org/synod/resolutions/RESOLUTION-IN -SUPPORT-OF-EQUAL-MARRIAGE-RIGHTS-FOR-ALL-FOR-GENERAL-SYNOD-25.pdf.

support same-sex unions and an increasing number support same-sex marriage.[11]

The question is, "Why?"

The serious discussion among Christians concerning the ordination of practicing homosexuals, as well as the decline in opposition to the legalization of same-sex unions and marriages, is without precedent in the history of Western society and the church. What is even more unprecedented is the speed at which this change is taking place. That we are on the verge of the legalization of same-sex marriage in Europe and the United States is beyond what most gay and lesbian activists dared imagine in the 1980s.

The question is, "Why?"

It is almost always an exaggeration to say that Christendom ever spoke with a unified voice on any issue, but if ever there were issues on which there was theological consensus, it was on sexual ethics and the definition of marriage. John Boswell argues that there may have been a time in premodern Europe when clergy blessed some same-sex unions and that there have been times when the church and culture turned a blind eye toward same-sex couples.[12] Nevertheless, until recently the orthodox Jewish and Christian teachings opposing same-sex marriage have remained constant; it has not even been a subject of serious debate. Yet since the sexual revolution, and especially in the past decade, this issue has become one that a growing number of Christians in the West seem ready to concede without a meaningful debate.

The question is, "Why?"

For the first time in the history of the church there is significant disagreement among church leaders, denominations, and the laity over many issues related to human sexuality and marriage. Unfortunately, it has proven difficult to talk in a civil and meaningful way about these

11. David Kinnaman and Gabe Lyons, *UnChristian: What a New Generation Really Thinks about Christianity . . . and Why It Matters* (Grand Rapids: Baker Books, 2007), chap. 5; "Gay Marriage," Pew Forum on Religion and Public Life, http://pewforum.org/gay-marriage/; "Same-Sex Unions and Civil Unions," Religious Tolerance.org, Ontario Consultants on Religious Tolerance, www.religioustolerance.org/hom_marp.htm.

12. See John Boswell, *Christianity, Social Tolerance, and Homosexuality* (Chicago: University of Chicago, 1980); John Boswell, *Same-Sex Unions in Premodern Europe* (New York: Villard, 1994); Andrew Sullivan, ed., *Same-Sex Marriage: Pro and Con; A Reader*, rev. ed. (New York: Vintage Books, 2004), 7–21.

issues. Even in this, the church mirrors the culture. There are theologians and church leaders on all sides of these issues who employ modes of argumentation that are uncivil, ineffective, unpersuasive, and self-defeating. Others have allowed themselves to be intimidated into public silence. There are precious few who cast more light than heat into the public discourse.

The question is, "Why?"

There are those, such as David Wells, who have foreseen the coming of this moment. He predicted decades ago that we were entering a post-Christian era, and he was right.[13] While there is a perception that the United States is a Christian nation, if it is, it is not a practicing one. Average weekly church attendance in the United States in 2005 slumped to just 17.5 percent.[14] The church as an institution has lost enormous credibility and is in danger of becoming culturally irrelevant.[15]

The question is, "Why?"

What we are witnessing on the issue of same-sex marriage is simply the logical extension of the same sexual ethic that our culture has applied to other sexual behavior since the 1960s. The sexual revolution occurred decades ago, and Christians are now presented with another opportunity to challenge it. Yet in challenging it, Christians must understand that at its heart the sexual revolution is not about homosexuality or same-sex marriage but about human sexuality and relational fulfillment. The primary reason Christians have not had the political fortitude and conviction to challenge our culture on the issue of same-sex marriage is that a growing number of Christians now doubt the traditional Christian teaching on human sexuality and feel it is wrong to condemn consensual sexual behavior. Since the 1960s a profound disconnect has occurred between the teaching and the practice of Christian sexuality among both the laity and the clergy, and this disconnect has played a strong role in causing the political and social laryngitis of the Christian community when it comes to challenging the behavioral implications of the sexual revolution. As George Barna has shown, the

13. See David F. Wells, *God in the Wasteland* (Grand Rapids: Eerdmans, 1994); David F. Wells, *No Place for Truth, or, Whatever Happened to Evangelical Theology?* (Leicester, UK: Inter-Varsity, 1993).

14. David T. Olson, *The American Church in Crisis: Groundbreaking Research Based on a National Database of over 200,000 Churches* (Grand Rapids: Zondervan, 2008), 29.

15. This is the thesis of Kinnaman and Lyon, *UnChristian*.

sexual behavior and attitudes of many Christians deviate so significantly from traditional Christian teaching that it is no wonder an increasing number of Christians have been unwilling to hypocritically impose different standards on practicing homosexuals. Hence the halfhearted and guilt-tinged silence that permeates the present debate.

The question is, "Why?"

What is occurring in the West is nothing less than the collapse of the Judeo-Christian worldview, a crisis of confidence in *modernity*, and the emergence of a new but undeveloped worldview that might be called "postmodern individualism" but that I will refer to as the "iWorld" and will define in the next chapter.

The challenge for Christians in the twenty-first century is not to use the same old arguments to try to persuade the West of the truth of the traditional teaching on sexual ethics. If these arguments were still persuasive, public opinion and behavior would not be what they are. Yet neither should Christians blindly or reflexively adjust theology to accommodate the sexual revolution without adequate scriptural support. Rather, the church needs to reexamine biblical teaching and orthodox theology in light of the challenges posed by the sexual revolution and see whether it is modification or rediscovery that is in order.

Questions That Face Us All

The questions facing us at this point in the twenty-first century are not merely for Christians but are for all humans. The meaning of human sexual relations and marriage and their role in human fulfillment matters to everyone. To make a decision about what future course is best for our world requires that we comprehend the nature of the astonishing change that has occurred in our world's understanding of sexual relationships and marriage.

In part 1 of the book we will examine the tWorld, the "traditional" world from which we came, and the iWorld, the "individualistic" world that is emerging. We will explore in depth what the iWorld is, what kind of society it seeks to create, and what it professes about the nature of human sexuality, relationship, and fulfillment, as well as the public policy implications of its positions.

In part 2 of the book we will use the Bible as a basis to help describe the rWorld (the "relational" world), a proposed alternative to both of these worlds, and we will explore what kind of alternative the rWorld provides concerning the understanding of human fulfillment and the place of sexuality, marriage, and relationships. Yet the Bible is not the only source text for the rWorld. Indeed, one may embrace the rWorld as a more constructive alternative to either the tWorld or the iWorld, or both, without being Christian or religious. The Bible, however, provides a coherent relational vision that will help in constructing an approach to life that can adequately contrast with the one currently offered by the iWorld.

The book will conclude by comparing and contrasting the iWorld and the rWorld and examining the contributions modern science can and cannot make to our deliberations. Finally, we will consider which of these "worlds" provides a more compelling vision of relational fulfillment in today's world.

Finding a way to live well is the purpose of this book. Even though my characterization of human history may appear unconventional, and even though dealing compassionately with the intensely personal issues surrounding sexuality provides a challenge, perhaps the biggest hurdle this book faces is whether people from very different faith and ideological perspectives can come together and converse about what it means to live together in today's world. Rather than create a veneer of faux objectivity behind which to hide my religious faith and write this book as though my religious convictions didn't matter, I have chosen to bring my faith into this conversation. In doing so it is not my intention to make this a *religious* conversation. I want to have a real conversation among real people about the real world, and I invite you to join me. I accept that there may be skepticism about whether this can be done, but because it is a thing worth doing, let's find out.

PART 1

From the tWorld to the iWorld

So I walk up on high
And I step to the edge
To see my world below.
And I laugh at myself
While the tears roll down.
'Cause it's the world I know.
It's the world I know.

Collective Soul,
"The World I Know"[1]

Making sense of the world we know is no small task given the staggering number of recent societal changes that just a few decades ago were inconceivable. In an effort to make this task manageable, I have divided the intellectual and cultural history of Western civilization

1. Ed Roland and Ross Childress, "The World I Know," Collective Soul (Atlantic Records, 1995).

into two eras by creating the terms "tWorld" and "iWorld." The tWorld (traditional world) represents the cultural worldview that developed in the West over centuries and that is drawn from Greek and Roman civilizations and Judaism, Christianity, and Islam. The iWorld represents the individualistic worldview that is rapidly replacing the tWorld throughout Europe, the United States, and urban centers worldwide.

I acknowledge that these categories inadequately reflect the complexities of intellectual and cultural history. My purpose in creating this terminology is only to provide useful referential designations to help discuss the changing understanding of the relationship between marriage, sexuality, intimacy, and human relational fulfillment. Despite the prevailing sense that society cannot have genuine dialogue about these matters in the present age, there is a conversation to be had. It is my hope that the use of this terminology enables and furthers this conversation.

1

The tWorld

The World from Which We Came

Toto, I have a feeling we're not in Kansas anymore.

Dorothy, *The Wizard of Oz*[1]

Buckle your seat belts, Dorothy, 'cause Kansas is going bye-bye.

Cipher, *The Matrix*[2]

The world is changing, and in order to get a sense of where we are and where we are headed, we need to recall where we have been. The movies *The Wizard of Oz* and *The Matrix* set the context for this chapter. *The Wizard of Oz* represents the values of a traditional world that precedes our present time, and Dorothy spends virtually the entire story seeking to get back to that world and home to her family in good old Kansas. In *The Matrix* the main character, Thomas Anderson, who

1. Frank Baum, *The Wizard of Oz*, screenplay by Noel Langley, Florence Ryerson, and Edgar Allan Woolf (Loew's Incorporated, 1939).
2. Andy Wachowski and Larry Wachowski, *The Matrix* (Warner Brothers Pictures, 1999).

goes by the computer alias "Neo," wakes up to discover that not only is the old world of his ancestors gone but so also is the modern world in which he thought he lived. Much to his amazement, he finds that he lives in the twenty-second century and the world has changed almost beyond his ability to comprehend and recognize. At the moment the above epigraph is spoken to him, Neo is about to find out just how much has changed and what, if anything, he can do about it.

The Relational Matrix of the tWorld

Since the sexual revolution, a profound change has occurred in the way we view and understand the world. This can be seen in the history of American television. When one regards the relational and sexual values represented by early 1960s shows, such as *Father Knows Best* and *Leave It to Beaver*, and compares them to the popular television shows of the early twenty-first century, such as *Sex and the City* and *Friends*, the contrast is clear.[3] Fifty years ago American television rarely showed significant physical affection between anyone who wasn't married, and even married couples were portrayed as sleeping in separate beds. In today's television shows sexual relationships are considered normal for virtually everyone—with the possible exception of married couples. In fact, contemporary television or cinema rarely portrays healthy marriages or sexual relations within marriage.

What has changed is not merely our understanding of sexual ethics but also the traditional relational order of Western society. The tWorld represents a way of ordering our relational life that grew up over millennia in the West and is the product of many philosophical and religious traditions. While each of these traditions has its own distinctiveness, there is a common understanding among them about the nature of marriage, the extended family, and the local community. Marriage is considered the legal and covenantal basis for a lifelong relationship between one man and one woman. Marriage is also the one relationship in which sexual relations are deemed appropriate because children—the product of a sexual relationship—are best raised

---

3. Gordon Preece, "(Homo)Sex and the City of God," *Interface* 9, nos. 1 and 2 (May and October 2006), 187–216.

in a home with a father and mother. Yet marriage is about more than having sex and children; it also connects extended families, forming the foundation of community and the backbone of the tWorld, without which it could not exist.

If such a statement sounds exaggerated or overreaching, it merely illustrates how much and how quickly our culture has changed. Just a half century ago not only was this framework understood, but it was accepted as a foundational norm of Western civilization. David Blankenhorn makes an even more far-reaching claim. In his book *The Future of Marriage*, he states: "The evidence that marriage as defined here is a universal human institution is overwhelming. In fact, especially in light of the vastness of the human historical record and the variety of human sexual experience, the power and prevalence of this one sexual institution across time and cultures is so noteworthy and so empirically incontrovertible, that I am tempted to say 'all human societies.'"[4] Blankenhorn admits there are a few examples in human history where this statement may not hold, but in speaking of the West he regards it as a bold yet defensible statement.

Marriage and the extended family were the relational foundation of the tWorld. They were so important and so constant that whether you lived in the tWorld one hundred years ago or several thousand years ago, your identity and your life were rooted in a well-ordered relational structure. Your identity was inextricably connected to your nuclear family, your extended family, your local community, and your nation. Much of your life was determined at birth on the basis of your family relations and social class, to say nothing of genetics. Your situation at birth impacted your educational path, your place in society, your occupation, whom you could marry, and with whom you would interact. Moreover, all this transcended individual choice. It was a world composed of relationships that were for the most part determined by birth.

To use different language, the tWorld was constructed on relationships of *obligation*. Each person was born into a matrix of relationships in which there were mutual obligations and responsibilities. These included a child's relationships with parents, grandparents,

4. David Blankenhorn, *The Future of Marriage* (New York: Encounter Books, 2007), 105–6.

siblings, extended family members, neighbors, fellow citizens, and the religious community. These obligations were fixed at birth. One could be unfaithful to the obligations, but one could not change the obligations.

To an inhabitant of the West in the twenty-first century, this framework may appear extremely restrictive and stifling, but citizens of the tWorld didn't necessarily see it that way. Like us they craved healthy, fulfilling relationships. The tWorld's relational matrix provided men and women with a rich opportunity for relational fulfillment. The relational matrix was so important that citizens of the tWorld feared being cut off from it. To be an orphan without a family was not a source of freedom but in many societies resulted in almost certain slavery. When convicted of the charge of corrupting the youth of his city, the Greek philosopher Socrates opted to drink hemlock and commit suicide rather than endure the alternative of leaving Athens forever.

While the tWorld offered a rich opportunity for relational fulfillment, not everyone experienced healthy relationships. To the contrary, many people experienced loneliness, abuse, and all manner of relational hurt. The point here is not to describe the tWorld in utopian fashion but to describe the potential it offered. Throughout the book we will examine in detail the concept of relational fulfillment because, while it is something for which we all yearn, it is neither well understood nor commonly achieved in any of the worlds being explored. The task at hand is to attempt to assess which of these worlds provides for us the basis for the most fulfilling relational lives.

While this relational framework has vanished from the developed world, it is the framework on which Western society rested until the last few decades. Moreover, it is the product of many philosophical traditions and religions. It can be found with different expressions from Plato and Aristotle in Greece, through Roman authors including Cicero and Tacitus, and in the sacred texts of Judaism, Christianity, and Islam. The tWorld has an understanding of freedom profoundly different from the twenty-first-century West's understanding. Rather than seeing freedom as the absence of restraint and the quantity of individual choice, the tWorld believed freedom was discovered in the process of finding contentment and meaning within the matrix of relationships found in one's extended families and community.

Aristotle argues that humans cannot be understood independent of the relationships given to us at birth. He defines the good life by the quality of three fundamental relationships of *obligation* into which people are born: family, neighborhood, and city. A person cannot be fulfilled in the absence of these relationships and cannot be considered whole without all three relationships. Moreover, a human life can be categorized as *good* only if these relationships are healthy.[5] That these relationships are given to us by birth, rather than being the product of individual choice, neither marginalizes their importance nor restricts individual freedom. They provide freedom from a multitude of hazardous circumstances because they give us, when the relationships are healthy, a quality of emotional support and relational security that allows us to thrive. This relational framework is qualitatively different from what can be provided by an individualistic society based on relationships of choice. In Aristotle's vision your family, neighbors, and city are required to care for you and you them. Unlike contemporary culture, if the society functions in a healthy manner, no one can fall through the social safety net; everyone has a place with relational connections. Hence in the tWorld the key to relational fulfillment was not to find the people with whom we most wished to relate, but to love and engage with those we had been given. Aristotle viewed family as irreplaceably beneficial because it was the place in which we learned the most important lessons about life, and there was no other institution that could teach those lessons as well. To be without a family was to be robbed of something needed for wholeness and happiness. Family taught us how to live with others, how to be citizens, and what it means to live in a community. At its best, the tWorld did not stifle a person, but instead provided the relational security, support, nurturing, and moral compass needed to develop ourselves in ways independent living could not provide.

According to Aristotle, however, there is a relationship of choice that enriches one's life: friendship. Unlike all the other relationships of obligation, friendships are freely chosen and are for the good of each person involved.[6] Since friendship is entered into without obligation, it

5. Charles Lord, *Aristotle: The Politics* (Chicago: University of Chicago Press, 1984), bk. 1.
6. Aristotle, *Nicomachean Ethics,* trans. Terence Irwin (Indianapolis: Hackett, 1985), bks. 8–9.

gives us a quality of love that adds depth and richness to our life. In the tWorld, friendship was not merely an appendix to a good life; it was an important aspect of the relational matrix. As C. S. Lewis observes, "To the Ancients, Friendship seemed the happiest and most fully human of all the loves; the crown of life and the school of virtue."[7]

Relational health is far more important to Aristotle than material standard of living. He recognizes that we must have our needs met to live a good life, but one of the greatest dangers to society and personal relational health is materialism: a belief that human happiness is dependent on financial wealth and the accumulation of possessions. Since we presently live in an age that equates material standard of living with quality of life, Aristotle's argument requires some explanation. To demonstrate, follow along with this brief experiment. Imagine your ideal car. Drive your ideal car for three years. Is it still your ideal car? Imagine your ideal house. Live in your ideal house for three years. Is it still your ideal house? We could go on with any object we possess or wish to possess. Will any of this, once we acquire and consume it, provide us with the happiness for which we yearn? No. As much as we may operate with these assumptions, we will never actually find the happiness for which we strive in the things we possess. We invariably grow tired of what we have and want more and different possessions. Yet ultimately we will tire of everything we acquire. In the pursuit of happiness, materialism is a dead end. Why? Aristotle understands that there is no material thing we can desire that won't eventually bore us if we possess it. Hence, if we wish to live a fulfilling life, the quality of our relationships matters much more than our standard of living.

In the tWorld *happiness* was deeply connected to the quality of our relationships. If we lived in a good family, a good neighborhood, and a good city and had good friends, we had most of what we needed to be happy. Human happiness and fulfillment was primarily dependent on the health of this relational matrix. Plato provides an illustration of this in his brief description of the healthy and "minimal" city in book 2 of *The Republic*. In the following excerpt, in which Socrates begins to explain his ideal life and city, one can see it is the relationships that matter and not the accoutrements:

7. C. S. Lewis, *The Four Loves* (New York: Harcourt Brace Jovanovich, 1960), 87.

First let us consider what manner of life men so provided for will lead. Won't they make bread, wine, clothing, and shoes? And, when they have built houses, they will work in the summer, for the most part naked and without shoes, and in the winter adequately clothed and shod. For food they will prepare barley meal and wheat flour; they will cook it and knead it. Setting out the noble loaves of barley and wheat on some reeds or clean leaves, they will stretch out on rushes strewn with yew and myrtle and feast themselves and their children. Afterwards they will drink wine and, crowned with wreathes, sing of the gods. So they will have sweet intercourse with one another, and not produce children beyond their means, keeping an eye out against poverty and war.[8]

The phrase here translated "will have sweet intercourse with one another" would in contemporary English be "will take pleasure in each others' company" or "enjoy their life together." According to Plato, the quality of our relational life, which he does not identify with sexual gratification, is an essential aspect of our happiness.

Plato and Aristotle understood, however, that there is still another dimension to happiness and the good life. To carry the previous exercise in thought one step further, imagine your ideal friend. After relating to him or her closely for three years, would he or she still be your ideal friend? Imagine your ideal spouse. After living with your ideal spouse for seven years, would he or she still be your ideal spouse? No and no. What Plato and Aristotle recognize is that a fulfilling life requires something beyond having our material needs met and enjoying healthy human relationships. In their view the only thing that can truly fulfill us is being able to spend our life contemplating that which is higher than ourselves, attempting to understand it but never fully being able to. So just what is this thing that is higher than ourselves? Since we can never fully know it, it cannot be fully explained. Plato and Aristotle refer to it as "the good," "the best," "the ideal," and "the prime mover," and understanding this is the very purpose of philosophy. Since this is transcendent, theologians might refer to it as God. For Plato and Aristotle, contemplation of that which is beyond us is foundational for the best life possible.

8. Plato, *Republic* 2.372b, in *The Republic of Plato*, trans. Allan Bloom, 2nd ed. (1963; repr., New York: Basic Books, 1991), 49.

To the contemporary world, which is so fixated on activity to the exclusion of the contemplative, such a statement sounds like abject nonsense. Yet Plato and Aristotle believe that the only thing that can truly satisfy us is to engage in a pursuit we can never finish because it is the only pursuit with which we will never grow bored. It is in this quest that human fulfillment is complete. In the tWorld, the happiest life requires that we be philosophical or theological (seeking to know that which is beyond us), and as we find fulfillment in this pursuit, we can find fulfillment in all our relationships. The best life possible comprises all these elements.

Sexual Relations and Relational Fulfillment in the tWorld

It is important to understand that in the tWorld sexuality was viewed as a drive and an appetite but not a means of fulfillment. Plato believed that appetites would enslave us if they were not controlled and governed appropriately. Sexual relations had a function and a purpose within marriage but were unnecessary outside of marriage. When our sexual impulses become our master, rather than producing happiness they enslave us and rob us of happiness. Plato may have stated this best in the first book of *The Republic* when Cephalus, who is of advanced age, speaks to Socrates about aging and the desires of the flesh, including sexuality:

> Now then, when they meet, most of the members of our group lament, longing for the pleasures of youth and reminiscing about sex, about drinking bouts and feats and all that goes with things of that sort; they take it hard as though they were deprived of something very important and had then lived well but are now not even alive. Some also bewail the abuse that old age receives from relatives, and in this key they sing a refrain about all the evils old age has caused them. But, Socrates, in my opinion these men do not put their fingers on the cause. For, if this were the cause, I too would have suffered these same things insofar as they depend on old age and so would everyone else who has come to this point in life. But as it is, I have encountered others for whom it was not so, especially Sophocles. I was once present when the poet was asked by someone, "Sophocles, how are you in sex? Can you still have intercourse with a woman?" "Silence, man," he said. "Most joyfully did I escape it,

as though I had run away from a sort of frenzied and savage master." I thought at the time that he had spoken well and I still do. For in every way old age brings great peace and freedom from such things. When the desires cease to strain and finally relax, then what Sophocles says comes to pass in every way; it is possible to be rid of many mad masters.[9]

For Plato and the tWorld, sexuality was a drive and appetite that had a function and purpose, but if not harnessed and channeled appropriately, it would enslave us.

In many Platonic dialogues, sexual relations outside of marriage were part of the landscape. It is not the case, however, that Plato regarded these relations as morally acceptable.[10] His discussion with Cephalus illustrates sexuality as an appetite rather than an agent of personal or relational fulfillment. Since sexual relations outside of marriage were not an aspect of the best life and could distract us from the pursuit of the best life, they were not virtuous outside of marriage. Virtuous behaviors contributed to the best life; vice was that which undermines our ability to enjoy the best life. Since Plato and Aristotle did not have a theological conception of sin, they did not attach stigma to sexual vice in the way Judaism, Christianity, and Islam do, but neither did they condone it.

It is not the case that sexual relations in the tWorld were always what they should be. Tacitus reports that every variety of sexual vice existed in Rome.[11] If it is true that "hypocrisy is the tribute that vice pays to virtue,"[12] then Rome paid a great deal of tribute. While over time Rome grew in corruption and its leaders came to ignore its moral code, Romans did not so much change their moral code to justify their behavior; instead they opted for hypocrisy over obedience.

Human happiness and fulfillment in the tWorld were directly related to the health of personal relationships and the ability to engage in a

9. Plato, *Republic* 1.329a–d, in Bloom, *Republic of Plato*, 5.
10. Thomas Pangle, trans., *The Laws of Plato* (Chicago: University of Chicago Press, 1980), 229–34. Some might argue that Plato contradicts himself in book 5 of the *Republic* when he describes the community of wives and children. Book 5, however, exists to help support his argument about justice and is not a normative description of human relational life.
11. Michael Grant, trans., *Tacitus: The Annals of Imperial Rome*, rev. ed. (London: Penguin Books, 1971).
12. Attributed to Matthew Arnold (1822–1888), British poet and critic.

contemplative life. Vice undermines all that is good, and the tWorld understood this.

Since a well-constructed and healthy extended family is the foundation of the tWorld, it is not surprising that sexual relations were sanctioned only in a marriage between one man and one woman.[13] Cohabitation, adultery, and illegitimate birth undermined the relational matrix of the tWorld. Once enough people, for whatever reason, found themselves living outside the framework or discarded commitment to their relationships of *obligation* for relationships of choice, sexual or not, the existence of the tWorld was threatened. One cannot have it both ways: if the relational matrix is no longer the rule, then the society created by it will give way. Indeed, by virtually any set of measures, this is happening to our own society at present. The tWorld is passing away before our eyes. The question then is, "What will take its place?"

---

13. David Blakenhorn does a good job of describing the way this ethic developed historically in Blakenhorn, *The Future of Marriage*, chaps. 2–4.

2

How in the iWorld Did We Get Here?

> The freedom of our day is the freedom to devote our-
> selves to any values we please, on the mere condition
> that we do not believe them to be true.
>
> Student response at Harvard commencement[1]

The world has changed dramatically in the past century. It requires no leap of faith to believe that the amount of technological change that has occurred in the last hundred years is greater than what has occurred in any similar period of human history. Yet the magnitude of this change is not limited to technology. During the past several decades we have witnessed a dramatic shift in our culture's relational framework and moral compass. Sexual behavior that for millennia was regarded as unvirtuous or sinful is not merely tolerated today but is often regarded as acceptable or healthy. A shift is occurring in the worldview on which Western civilization is based. We live in a time in which the nature of the way we think about the world and ourselves is changing. We are leaving an era that had a well-established way of

1. Robert N. Bellah, Richard Madsen, William M. Sullivan, Ann Swidler, and Steven M. Tipton, *The Good Society* (New York: Vintage Books, 1992), 44.

understanding humans, human relationships, and sexuality, and are moving to an era that has a very different perception. It is an era in which long-established boundaries are dissolving in the belief that individual moral and relational choice will yield the greatest level of happiness and fulfillment for which we yearn. We are leaving a world in which the epigraph that begins this chapter would have been nonsense and are entering a world in which it makes sense. We will now examine how things became this way and why.

Personal relational choice is replacing the tWorld's relational matrix as the preferred path to human freedom and fulfillment. The freedom to construct our own moral and relational world, as opposed to finding contentment within the moral and relational matrix we are given, is now seen as offering the greatest opportunity for human fulfillment. Mutual consent rather than a marriage contract between a man and a woman is the new moral foundation for sexual relations. As a result, sexual relations have been disconnected from marriage and procreation. The decision to have children is now a choice separate from having sexual intercourse. Even the personal health consequences of engaging a wide variety of sexual partners are regarded as an acceptable result of freedom of choice. The results of individual relational choice on children, parents, spouses, and third parties are considered of secondary importance to the happiness and autonomy of the individual adult. Marriage still exists, but only insofar as both marriage partners wish it to exist. Relationships with extended family may still exist, but only so long as all involved wish to stay interconnected. We may see a television show, such as the *Sopranos*, in which even in a flawed family loyalty is sacred and blood relations are thicker than any other relational bond, but such relational commitments are becoming increasingly uncommon in the West today.

This shift in the understanding of marriage, family, and human sexuality is of truly seismic proportions. It is not an exaggeration to say that we now inhabit a world with a completely new relational paradigm. This signals the onset of an unheralded and entirely separate era. The West is moving away from classical philosophy and revealed religion (Judaism, Christianity, and Islam) as the moral foundation of our lives and is transitioning into an era in which individual preference and choice reign supreme.

So how and why did this take place?

The difficulty in answering this question is in finding a way to understand and define the era into which we are moving. Since we are still in transition, there is no consistent, philosophically coherent way to describe the ethos that rules our current moment in history. It is reasonable to say that we are transitioning to a new world, but we are not yet there, and as we will see, it is not yet clear exactly where "there" is. As a result, I believe the best way to describe and understand our present moment is to call it the "iWorld." Steve Jobs and the people of Apple Inc. have brilliantly understood the spirit of our age—a spirit of unfettered individualism and freedom—by marketing many of their products by using the prefix *i*. The iMac, iPod, and iPhone are product names that capture the very essence of the age in which we live. In short, the tWorld is being replaced by the iWorld.

This transition constitutes a revolution in our understanding of freedom and fulfillment. The tWorld and the iWorld embrace both as essential aspects of the best life possible; the debate between them is over how each is understood and achieved. On this they disagree profoundly, but it is clear that the iWorld is presently winning in the court of public opinion due to a profound shift in the way we understand the world. Philosophically speaking, we are undergoing a shift in our cultural epistemology. By "epistemology" we mean "theory of knowing," or in other words, a particular answer to an underlying question of human existence: "How do we know what is true?" Every society or era is based on a particular epistemology—a particular answer to the question of how we know what is true. We rarely wake up in the morning questioning the very moral and social structures of our world. Along with millions of fellow travelers, we do not need to ask this question each day because we collectively share a common set of answers based on a shared epistemology (our collective answer to the question of how we know what is true). Without this, we could not function as a society. We are able to function in relative peace and harmony because we share a common answer that helps us each regulate our life.[2] The

2. Alexis de Tocqueville, *Democracy in America*, vol. 2, ed. Phillips Bradley (New York: Vintage Books, 1990), 8.

tWorld had its own epistemology, but as it was progressively rejected, the transition to a new world was inevitable. By exploring how this occurred, we will be able to answer the "Why?" questions raised in the introduction.

A Brief Overview of the History of Epistemology in the West

Different eras of history in Western civilization are notable for having different predominant epistemologies at the foundation of their thought. For instance, the classical world is noted for having certain strands of Greek and Roman philosophies at the foundation of its worldview and ethics. There was not a singular monolithic philosophical approach that dominated, but rather what defined the classical era was a commitment to a belief that the best way to understand reality was found through the manner of philosophical inquiry pursued by Plato and Aristotle. The generally accepted (although not universally held) belief was that philosophical inquiry, through studying the ends or the purpose of things, could yield moral truth that ought to govern human behavior.

Medieval thought had a predominant epistemology that differed from classical thought because it gave divine revelation (the Torah, the Bible, the Koran) an authoritative place in human moral inquiry. For the most part medieval thinkers did not regard divine revelation to be at odds with the best in classical philosophical thought. Instead it was believed that divine revelation both provided an important confirmation of many of the tenets of classical philosophy and added information concerning the purpose of this life and the afterlife. While Christians, Jews, and Muslims dispute which texts constitute divine revelation, each of the three religions incorporate some of the same texts or stories into their canon. All three also affirm the epistemological authority of divine relation, which provides an essential foundation for understanding the natural world and particularly the moral code for human life and relationships.

It is important to note that the moral code advocated by Judaism, Christianity, and Islam contains much in common regarding human sexual relationship and in particular the teaching about fornication, adultery, and homosexual relations.[3] What developed in the Middle Ages was not so much a break with the classical world as it was something understood to be in harmony with it. Hence the resulting emergence of what is referred to here as the tWorld—a civilization that was built in the West on the basis of Greek and Roman philosophy and these three revealed religions.

The Epistemology of Modernity

The shift to the iWorld commenced as scientists began to question the conclusions and assumptions of classical and medieval thinkers regarding the natural world. Galileo and other scientists found that the philosophers and theologians of previous eras had mistakenly asserted, among other things, that the sun revolved around the Earth. Galileo and his colleagues rebelled against the coercive measures the church used to enforce these mistaken opinions. It may not have been their intention to undermine classical philosophy and divine revelation as the epistemological framework of Western society, but that was the result. Since philosophers and theologians had misunderstood much about the natural world, and since natural science proved to be such a reliable way to get accurate information about it, modernity elevated natural science to the level of an epistemology—a new method to authoritatively establish what is true in all aspects of life.

The scientific method can be defined as an approach used to test the validity of a wide variety of truth claims, and its use has greatly advanced our understanding of the natural world. As Frank Wolfs, professor of physics and astronomy at the University of Rochester, explains:

The scientific method has four steps:

1. Observation and description of a phenomenon or a group of phenomena.
2. Formulation of an hypothesis to explain the phenomena. . . .
3. Use of the hypothesis to predict the existence of other phenomena, or to predict quantitatively the results of new observations.

3. Don S. Browning, M. Christian Green, and John Witte Jr., eds., *Sex, Marriage, and Family in World Religions* (New York: Columbia University Press, 2006), xxii–xxvii.

4. Performance of experimental tests of prediction by several independent experimenters and properly performed experiments.

If the experiments bear out the hypothesis it may come to be regarded as a theory or law of nature. . . . If the experiments do not bear out the hypothesis, it must be rejected or modified. What is key in the description of the scientific method just given is the predictive power (the ability to get more out of the theory than you put in; see Barrow, 1991) of the hypothesis or theory, as tested by experiment. It is often said in science that theories can never be proved, only disproved. There is always the possibility that a new observation or a new experiment will conflict with a long-standing theory.[4]

The scientific method is the epistemology of modernity, and it has provided us with many benefits. Scientists have corrected mistaken assumptions about the natural world made by philosophers and theologians. In addition, they have greatly expanded our knowledge of the natural world and enabled us to make enormous advances in multiple disciplines such as medicine and engineering. Modernity could have used science as an epistemological supplement to classical philosophy and medieval theology in much the same way medieval theology incorporated many insights from classical philosophy. Instead, it has used the scientific method as an epistemology to replace both classical philosophy and medieval theology. Philosophically, modernity makes no room for any way of thinking that is scientifically unreasonable.

It didn't have to be this way. There is nothing in the essence of natural science that requires the abandonment of philosophy or theology as ethical guides. For instance, many Christians have worked to demonstrate an essential harmony among science, reason, and revelation.[5] Instead, modernity came to be dominated by Enlightenment philosophers, such as Voltaire, who assert that Christian revelation is in conflict with modern scientific reasoning and as a result argues that Christianity must

4. Frank Wolfs, "Introduction to the Scientific Method," http://teacher.pas.rochester.edu/phy_labs/AppendixE/AppendixE.html. The Barrow reference is to John Barrow, *Theories of Everything* (Oxford: Oxford University Press, 1991).

5. Examples include G. K. Chesterton, *Orthodoxy* (Garden City, NY: Image Books, 1959); C. S. Lewis. *The Abolition of Man; or, Reflections on Education with Special Reference to the Teaching of English in the Upper Forms of Schools* (New York: Macmillan, 1955); Stanley L. Jaki, *Bible and Science* (Front Royal, VA: Christendom, 1996).

be discarded or significantly modified so the world can progress to a new world of freedom.

Eighteenth-century modernity abounds in optimism concerning the ability of science and reason to answer all questions about life and free us from the chains of history, tradition, and religion. Thomas Jefferson reflects such a view in his letter to Roger Weightman on June 24, 1826:

> May it be to the world, what I believe it will be (to some parts sooner, to others later, but finally to all), the signal of arousing men to burst the chains under which monkish ignorance and superstition had persuaded them to bind themselves, and to assume the blessings and security of self-government. That form we have substituted, restores the free right to the unbounded exercise of reason and freedom of opinion.[6]

There was great optimism in this era that if humans were free to reason without restraint, they would free themselves of religion ("monkish ignorance") and superstition and find truth and freedom.

The "revelation" of modernity is the scientific method. The belief in the power of science to conquer the natural world is so profound that the scientific method is employed in the hope of providing the human (or social) sciences with the same ability to conquer the prevailing limitations of humans. The social sciences (economics, psychology, sociology, anthropology, and political science) were developed in the twentieth century with the intention of systematically applying the scientific method to the study of human behavior. The goal was for the social sciences to expand our understanding of humans in a manner as revolutionary as science had been in our acquisition of power over the nature. This experiment in the social sciences—the Modern Project—was a systematic effort to use scientific reasoning to reexamine every belief concerning the world in order to enhance human power. Natural science would enable us to conquer the natural world in the name of freedom, and social science would allow us to conquer human nature for a similar end.[7]

6. Thomas Jefferson, *Selected Writings*, ed. Harvey C. Mansfield Jr. (1979; repr., Arlington Heights, IL: Harlan Davidson, 1987), 12–13.
7. Leo Strauss, "The Crisis of Our Time," in *The Predicament of Modern Politics*, ed. Harold J. Spaeth (Detroit: University of Detroit Press, 1964), 41.

Modernity is an era of scientific triumph during which the invention of the printing press, the Industrial Revolution, the application of electricity, and countless other discoveries enable science to conquer or harness nature and free us to use this knowledge for our own ends. The chief philosophical school of modernity is liberalism, and as its name indicates, its focus is on liberty and freedom.[8] Liberalism is an ideal political and philosophical companion to modern science insofar as, like science, it contends that reason can expand our freedom over the world of tradition and convention. It is here that we can see the seeds of the iWorld being planted. Hobbes, Locke, and other liberal philosophers reconceived human freedom in individualistic terms, and relationships in contractual terms. While there is still a prevailing belief in a natural order that includes political boundaries (human rights) and a moral code based on reason, modernity became an era synonymous with the expansion of human freedom. Whereas previously freedom was understood as living in accordance with our nature in the traditional relational framework, liberalism turns this understanding of freedom on its head by redefining freedom as living with as few boundaries and restraints as possible. In the same way that modernity seeks to use natural science to help humans overcome the boundaries of nature, so liberalism seeks to expand the boundaries of political and moral freedom.

Perhaps the best statement of liberalism's understanding of freedom comes from John Stuart Mill in the introduction to his essay *On Liberty*:

> The object of this essay is to assert one very simple principle. . . . That principle is that the sole end for which mankind are warranted, individually, or collectively, in interfering with the liberty of action . . . is self-protection. That the only purpose for which power can rightfully be exercised over any member of a civilized community, against his will, is to prevent harm to others. His own good, either physical or moral, is not sufficient warrant. He cannot rightfully be compelled to do or forbear because it will be better for him to do so, because it will make

8. "Liberalism," as a school of philosophy, has a different meaning than the use of "liberalism" in contemporary American politics. For instance, the Republican and Democratic parties, to the degree they espouse any consistent set of ideas, both have philosophical roots in liberalism. Their disagreements, to the extent they are philosophical, often represent a dispute about the meaning of liberalism.

him happier, because, in the opinions of others, to do so would be wise or even right. These are good reasons for remonstrating with him, or reasoning with him, or persuading him, or entreating him, but not for compelling him or visiting him with any evil in case he do otherwise. To justify that, the contact from which it is desired to deter him must be calculated to produce evil to someone else. The only part of the conduct of anyone for which he is amenable to society is that which concerns others. In the part which merely concerns himself, his independence is, of right, absolute. Over himself, over his own body and mind, the individual is sovereign.[9]

This may be the definitive liberal definition of individual freedom, yet Mill raises an important question concerning the meaning of morality in modernity. Individual freedom is important, but so are the limits he places on it. In *Utilitarianism*, Mill argues that moral behavior maximizes pleasure and minimizes pain and, therefore, the effect of our behavior on other people must be calculated before we can deem any particular behavior moral.[10]

Hume, Nietzsche, and the Fall of Modernity (and the Advent of Postmodernity)

Mill's equation concerning pain and pleasure, the "utilitarian calculus," does not provide us with moral certainty to the same degree natural science provides certainty in the laws of nature. Finding a definitive way to understand morality becomes a conundrum for liberal philosophers and the Modern Project. Can the scientific method and reason alone provide authoritative answers to moral questions? Early in the era, John Locke and others were optimistic that it would. The epitaph on the stone marking the grave of Locke at Christ Church Cathedral, Oxford, reads, "I know there is truth opposite to falsehood[,] that it may be found if people will[, and that it] is worth the seeking." Thomas Jefferson believed that it could, as can be seen in his devotion to reason. In his Bible, Jefferson removed the miracles and all that did not conform to the discoveries of natural science, but he

9. John Stuart Mill, *On Liberty*, ed. Elizabeth Rapaport (Indianapolis: Hackett, 1978), 9.
10. John Stuart Mill, *Utilitarianism* (Indianapolis: Hackett, 1979), chap. 2.

left the moral teachings of Jesus, which he regarded to be supported by enlightened reason.[11]

Yet even as Jefferson did this, doubt was beginning to grow among Enlightenment philosophers that the scientific method could provide the laws of morality that liberalism sought and modernity required. Philosophers such as David Hume saw that the modern scientific search for morality was doomed to failure. Hume and others realized that while the scientific method excelled at understanding aspects of the natural world, science could not determine moral truth. The scientific method could increase human power to control the natural world and even manipulate behavior, it could clarify the moral choices available to us, but science alone could not determine which moral choice was correct. Hume articulates this problem in his reflection on the "is-ought dilemma" in his *Treatise on Human Nature*, observing that one cannot derive an "ought" from an "is."[12] Science can tell us what *is*, but it cannot tell us how we *ought* to act. For example, science can teach us how to make an atomic weapon, but it cannot tell us when, if ever, that weapon ought to be used. Since morality is focused on the question of how we *ought* to behave and what we *ought* to do in any given situation, science, which can only describe what *is*, cannot resolve moral questions. Consequently, if the true epistemological basis of modern and liberal philosophy is the scientific method, then the logical problem confronting moral philosophy that Hume describes cannot be resolved.

Hume's observation has staggering implications for modernity. If Hume is correct, then *ought* is a morally meaningless word because there is no scientific way to evaluate competing *ought* claims. Since virtue, justice, goodness, and morals cannot be scientifically verified, science is effectively agnostic when it comes to answering moral questions. If Hume is correct that science is the only way to derive claims of truth, then the moral choices we make are dictated by feeling rather than by reason. Since feelings are personally subjective, they cannot be regarded as adequate guides for moral reasoning.

11. Thomas Jefferson, *The Life and Morals of Jesus of Nazareth: Extracted Textually from the Gospels, Together with a Comparison of His Doctrines with Those of Others* (St. Louis: N. D. Thompson, 1902).

12. David Hume, *A Treatise of Human Nature*, 2nd ed., ed. L. A. Selby-Bigge and P. H. Nidditch (Oxford: Clarendon, 1978), 469–70.

Hume is the great narrower in the modern understanding of the human being.[13] First, he subjugates reason, philosophy, and theology to scientific reasoning, thus rendering the practice of moral philosophy and theology as morally meaningless enterprises. Second, if the scientific method is the only correct approach to studying humans, then the only thing that matters is the material. The spiritual and any nonmaterial categories, such as love, become irrelevant to our study of humans because they cannot be verified by the scientific method. If Hume is correct, humans are solely material and our motivations are merely the product of our emotions. Accordingly, what we describe as love, spirituality, or a relationship with God is nothing more than a phantom—the illusory product of feelings produced by the biochemical reactions going on in our bodies as impacted by what we gather through our five senses. If Hume is right, there is no such thing as a nonmaterial (spiritual) sixth sense. If Hume is right, then this also means that nothing of value remains of the meaning of classical moral philosophy, not to mention revealed religion. And finally, if Hume is right, then the tWorld had been struck a blow from which it would never recover. This is indeed what happened, but it wasn't until the sexual revolution of the 1960s that the West fully realized it.

Carl Becker points out that there is often a delay between the time when philosophers formulate and grapple with ideas and when these ideas, if embraced, transform society.[14] This is precisely what occurred when liberalism, with its exultation of individualism and deconstruction of the traditional relational matrix, intellectually undermined the moral foundation of the tWorld. Yet the tWorld did not vanish immediately or even quickly. Even as the Enlightenment progressed, very little seemed to change in the West. Even as philosophers wrote treatises that, if seized on, would undermine the tWorld, it remained intact. Few people either understood or appreciated the moral implications of this liberalism, or those who understood did not persuade society to change accordingly. It is almost as though the philosophers went to the office in the morning and spent their day writing the books that would eventually

13. Montague Brown, *Restoration of Reason: The Eclipse and Recovery of Truth, Goodness, and Beauty* (Grand Rapids: Baker Academic, 2006), 106–11.

14. Carl L. Becker, *The Heavenly City of the Eighteenth Century Philosophers* (New Haven: Yale University Press, 1932), see esp. chap. 3.

undermine the tWorld, but at the end of the day they turned out the lights and returned home as though nothing had changed.

Hume is a great example of this because he never actually published his most cogent essay on the moral implications of modernity, *The Dialogues Concerning Natural Religion*. He left it unpublished in his desk drawer, and it was discovered only after his death.[15] It is almost as if he looked into the future but didn't like what he saw, so he left it to others to break the news.

Edmund Burke and Alexis de Tocqueville saw that profound change was on the way. In Burke's *Reflections on the Revolution in France*, he states the impact that this liberalism will ultimately have on society. In writing about the French Revolution, the fall of the French royal family, and Marie Antoinette in particular, he laments what this liberal revolution will mean for the future of the West in extraordinarily passionate and elegant terms.

> It is now sixteen or seventeen years since I saw the queen of France, then the dauphiness, at Versailles, and surely never lighted on this orb, which she hardly seemed to touch a more delightful vision. . . . Oh! What a revolution! and what a heart must I have to contemplate without emotion that elevation and that fall! . . . Little did I dream that I should live to see such disasters fall upon her in a nation of gallant men, in a nation of men of honor and cavaliers. I thought ten thousand swords must have leaped from their scabbards to avenge even a look that threatened her with insult. But the age of chivalry is gone. That of sophisters, economists, and calculators has succeeded; and the glory of Europe is extinguished forever. . . .
>
> This mixed system of opinion and sentiment had its origin in ancient chivalry; and the principle, though varied in its appearance by the varying state of human affairs, subsisted and influenced through a long succession of generations even to the time we live in. . . .
>
> But now all is to be changed. All the pleasing illusions which made power gentle and obedience liberal, which harmonized the different shades of life, and which, by a bland assimilation, incorporated into the politics of sentiment which beautify and soften private society, are to be dissolved by this new conquering empire of light and reason. All the decent drapery of life is to be rudely torn off. All the superadded ideas,

---

15. Ibid., 71–73.

furnished from the wardrobe of a moral imagination, which the heart owns and the understanding ratifies as necessary to cover the defects of our naked shivering nature, and to raise it to dignity in our own estimation, are to be exploded as ridiculous, absurd, and antiquated fashion.

On this scheme of things, a king is but a man, a queen is but a woman; a woman but an animal, and an animal not of the highest order.[16]

The French Revolution was a triumph for liberalism, and Burke could see that profound change was coming on a scale beyond the dreams of the French revolutionaries: the replacement of the relational matrix of the tWorld with liberal individualism.

Burke was not alone in this insight. Alexis de Tocqueville came to the United States in the 1830s to study the emerging liberal democracy and realized that change was coming. Tocqueville discovered that as citizens threw off the traditional relational and class framework of the tWorld and took seriously the liberal ideas of human equality and freedom, what was emerging was a new phenomenon in human history: the emergence of individualism hitherto unknown and unimagined.

I have shown how it is that in ages of equality every man seeks for his opinions within himself; I am now to show how it is that in the same ages all his feelings are turned towards himself alone. Individualism is a novel expression, to which a novel idea has given birth. Our fathers were only acquainted with egoism (selfishness). Selfishness is a passionate and exaggerated love of self, which leads a man to connect everything with himself and to prefer himself to everything in the world. Individualism is a mature and calm feeling, which disposes each member of the community to sever himself from the mass of his fellows and to draw apart with his family and his friends, so that after he has thus formed a little circle of his own, he willingly leaves society at large to itself. . . .

Selfishness blights the germ of all virtue; individualism, at first, only saps the virtues of public life; but in the long run it attacks and destroys all others and is at length absorbed in downright selfishness. Selfishness is a vice as old as the world, which does not belong to one form of society more than to another; individualism is of democratic origin, and it threatens to spread in the same ratio as the equality of condition. . . .

16. Edmund Burke, *Reflections on the Revolution in France*, ed. J. G. A. Pocock (Indianapolis: Hackett, 1987), 66–67.

Among democratic nations new families are constantly springing up, others are constantly falling away, and all that remain change their condition; the woof of time is every instant broken and the track of generations effaced. Those who went before are soon forgotten; of those who will come after, no one has any idea: the interest of man is confined to those in close propinquity to himself. As each class gradually approaches others and mingles with them, its members become undifferentiated and lose their class identity for each other. Aristocracy had made a chain of all the members of the community, from the peasant to the king; democracy breaks that chain and severs every link of it.

As social conditions become more equal, the number of persons increases who, although they are neither rich nor powerful enough to exercise any great influence over their fellows, have nevertheless acquired or retained sufficient education and fortune to satisfy their own wants. They owe nothing to any man, they expect nothing from any man; they acquire the habit of always considering themselves as standing alone, and they are apt to imagine that their whole destiny is in their own hands.

Thus not only does democracy make every man forget his ancestors, but it hides his descendants and separates his contemporaries from him; it throws him back forever upon himself alone and threatens in the end to confine him entirely within the solitude of his own heart.[17]

As Robert Bellah and others have pointed out, there is perhaps no one living today who has had as much insight into the nature of contemporary Western society as Tocqueville.[18] That he could recognize the future impact of liberal individualism with such clarity in the 1830s is an astounding achievement.

With prophetic clarity, Burke and Tocqueville saw that modernity was unleashing a way to think and live that would ultimately undermine the tWorld. Even though there was little evidence as we approached the twentieth century that the changes anticipated by Burke and Tocqueville would be realized, the seeds of this revolution were lying dormant and only waiting to be germinated. Friedrich Nietzsche succeeded in doing just that.

17. Tocqueville, *Democracy in America*, vol. 2, 98–99.
18. Robert N. Bellah, Richard Madsen, William M. Sullivan, Ann Swidler, and Steven M. Tipton, *Habits of the Heart: Individualism and Commitment in American Life* (Berkeley: University of California Press, 1985).

While many philosophers lived in denial of the threat to moral philosophy posed by Hume's observation concerning the is-ought dilemma, Friedrich Nietzsche not only saw it but utilized ruthless logic to expose the problem for what it was, and in so doing he opened the door to the iWorld. For Nietzsche the issue could be reduced to the following question: if modern science provides an inadequate basis for the development of moral thought, and if modern science has undermined the credibility of classical moral philosophy and theology, what is left for humans to rely on in their quest to find moral guidance for their lives? The answer, according to Nietzsche, is "nothing." Hence the name of his philosophy: "nihilism" (or "nothingism"). Nietzsche summarizes the problem succinctly when he says that the problem with any moral philosophy or theology is that "the why has no answer."[19] A young child who pesters an adult endlessly with the question "Why?" is either sent away in frustration without an answer or given an inadequate response such as, "Because I said so." In the same way, Nietzsche asserts that we find ourselves in the position of the young child asking philosophy, theology, and science why something is right or wrong. If we press the "Why?" question long enough, we will find that philosophy, theology, and science—like the frustrated parent—can provide no conclusive, objective answers (scientific proof) but ultimately only a subjective rationale (a belief based on feeling) for why one option should be chosen over another.

To understand the persuasive power of Nietzsche and the reason he is arguably the most influential figure in the twentieth century, let us see how his reasoning can be applied to the following example: On what basis can anyone ultimately say that the Christian moral code is superior to any other? Can its superiority be proved? Nietzsche argues that if the questioner replies "Why?" to every answer given by the Christian apologist, he or she ultimately will be forced to say "I don't know," or "Because I feel it," or "Because I believe it," thereby admitting the Christian has only a subjective basis for that belief. Yet this is not a problem just for Christianity but also for every moral philosophy or theology. Indeed, Nietzsche is an *equal opportunity* deconstructionist. Since he believes all moral philosophies and theologies are ultimately based on

19. Friedrich Nietzsche, *The Will to Power*, ed. Walter Kaufmann and R. J. Hollingdale (New York: Vintage Books, 1967), 9.

premises that are assumed and unproven, he argues that the only honest, rational conclusion we can draw concerning competing moral claims is that there is no rational basis on which to choose between them. If this is true, then there is no way to morally distinguish between the life choices of the infamous murderer-cannibal Jeffrey Dahmer and those of Mother Teresa of Calcutta.[20]

Nietzsche, however, doesn't stop with the philosophers and theologians. Social scientists face the same critique when it comes to their attempts to establish a defensible morality. Thanks to decades of rigorous research, natural and social scientists can provide us with reams of information about humans. Yet all that information concerning what *is* does not translate into what we *ought* to do and how we *ought* to behave. The scientists join the philosophers and the theologians who stand before Nietzsche stammering as they seek to formulate a reply to the question "Why?"

Nietzsche believes the basis of morality is not reason but feeling and will. Morally speaking, reason is of no consequence. In *Beyond Good and Evil*, Nietzsche proclaims that psychology is now "Queen of the Sciences" because it is feeling, not thought, that rules and our world needs to pay homage to the science of feeling—psychology.[21]

If Nietzsche is correct, the implications are chilling. He admits as much when he uses the word "pessimism" to describe the inevitable emotional reaction to realizing the truth of nihilism.[22] His philosophy of nihilism is based on this foundational assertion that there is no rational way humans can distinguish between moral claims. Nietzsche comes to the same conclusion as Hume, but unlike Hume, who doesn't want to be the one to expose the moral implications of modernity, Nietzsche does not hesitate to do so. If Nietzsche is correct, then there is no way for humans to discern a universal meaning of existence or a transcendent moral code.

If you have not previously encountered Nietzsche, you may be either protesting that he cannot possibly be correct or, alternately, perceiving that you have finally found your first commonsense philosopher. But

20. For a quick summary of the Dahmer case, see www.time.com/time/2007/crimes/16 .html.

21. Friedrich Nietzsche, *Beyond Good and Evil: Prelude to the Philosophy of the Future*, ed. Rolf-Peter Horstmann and Judith Norman (Cambridge, UK: Cambridge University Press, 2002), 32.

22. Nietzsche, *Will to Power*, 11.

regardless of whether we agree with Nietzsche, the reality is that we are living in an age in which Nietzsche's assertions have moved beyond mere philosophical speculation to becoming the edifice on which a new worldview—postmodernism—is being constructed.

Postmodernism is the philosophical movement and epistemology that arises from the acceptance of Nietzsche's conclusion. Postmodernity denies the possibility that any philosophy, theology, or scientific approach can provide a universally objective and moral account of the meaning of human life and relationships. It argues that every moral system and worldview is a subjective human construct; the search for truth is a multidirectional quest that can reach no final end. Instead of searching for truth, people are encouraged to focus their attention on constructing a meaningful life for themselves. Nietzsche describes this search as the "will to power." We identify what we wish to be and then use power to realize that wish.

Nietzsche identifies the "will to power" as a search for identity. Discovering or choosing our identity is one of the defining characteristics of the postmodern age. In no other age is identity so malleable. Previously, human identity was assumed to be a product of nature, religion, family, culture, class, and occupation—something given, not created. The human task was to live within the boundaries of one's given identity. From a postmodern perspective, however, humans are encouraged to discover or create their own identities, because their "given" identity is simply culturally imposed. In postmodernism one of the most fundamental human questions—"Who am I?"—can never be answered in a conclusive way. Therefore, the search for personal identity arguably becomes the single most fundamental human task, and a postmodern society seeks to remove as many obstacles and boundaries as possible for individuals on this quest. In this personal construction project there are, in principle, no limits other than those that we accept or that society imposes. So long as we have the power to do what we imagine, we can become or identify ourselves as whatever we desire. Under such a system, no one has the moral authority to make these choices for another person.[23]

23. For fuller and more nuanced explanations of postmodernism, please consult Heath White, *Postmodernism 101: A First Course for the Curious Christian* (Grand Rapids: Brazos, 2006);

The reader will no doubt understand the innate appeal of this aspect of postmodernism. Just as the tWorld provided humans with a secure relational structure and the means to find freedom within it, so quite to the contrary postmodernism finds freedom in a place in which the tWorld believed only harmful irresponsibility and bondage could be found. So if Nietzsche is the founder of nihilism and, by extension, of postmodernity, how can the iWorld be defined?

James K. A. Smith, *Who's Afraid of Postmodernism? Taking Derrida, Lyotard, and Foucault to Church* (Grand Rapids: Baker Academic, 2006).

3

The Brave New iWorld

I came upon a child of God
He was walking along the road
And I asked him where are you going
And this he told me
I'm going on down to Yasgur's farm
I'm going to join in a rock 'n' roll band
I'm going to camp out on the land
I'm going to try an' get my soul free

We are stardust,
We are golden,
And we've got to get ourselves
Back to the garden

Then can I walk beside you
I have come here to lose the smog
And I feel to be a cog in something turning
Well maybe it is just the time of year
Or maybe it's the time of man
I don't know who I am
But you know life is for learning

We are stardust
We are golden
And we've got to get ourselves
Back to the garden

By the time we got to Woodstock
We were half a million strong
And everywhere there was song and celebration
And I dreamed I saw the bombers
Riding shotgun in the sky
And they were turning into butterflies
Above our nation

We are stardust
Billion-year-old carbon
We are golden
Caught in the devil's bargain
And we've got to get ourselves
Back to the garden

Joni Mitchell, "Woodstock"[1]

One of the defining moments in the emergence of the iWorld was the Woodstock music festival held August 15–18, 1969, in Bethel, New York. This event drew half a million people from across the United States, successfully bringing together varying strands of the antiwar movement, the sexual revolution, and contemporary music into a new counterculture under the banner of "Peace, Love, and Music." Even though she didn't attend Woodstock, Joni Mitchell's song about the festival perfectly captures the zeitgeist. It describes the hope for a new world: the desire not just to end the Vietnam War, but also to turn weapons of war into butterflies so as to end all wars. Using biblical imagery, Mitchell expresses the longing to take back our world from the devil and find our way back to Eden or some semblance of it. Still, the biblical imagery is secondary to a more contemporary worldview. On her way to the festival she may have met a child of God who wanted to get back to the garden, but she

1. Joni Mitchell, "Woodstock," *Ladies of the Canyon* (Warner Brothers Records, 1970).

doesn't sound confident that this is either possible or even desirable. She expresses doubt about who she is, professes the evolutionary notion that we are created from carbon that is a billion years old, and yearns to overturn that which is evil. Yet it is not Eden to which she strives to return but to some imitation of it. While she does not say it directly, one might imagine the Eden of which she dreams as one we are to create together; after all, "life is for learning." The Woodstock festival, the peace movement, the counterculture, and the sexual revolution were about the creation of a new world. Inherent in this is the implication that what preceded us has not delivered on its promise so we now need to create a new garden, a new world, to realize that promise.

Graham Nash expressed this same optimism in his song "Chicago," which he wrote as a call to his fellow feuding band members, Stephen Stills and Neil Young, to go to Chicago in 1969 to protest the Chicago Eight trial and the war in Vietnam. His song captures both outrage and the optimism that together we can overthrow the "establishment" and create a new garden:

> We can change the world
> Re-arrange the world
> It's dying . . . if you believe in justice
> It's dying . . . and if you believe in freedom
> It's dying . . . let a man live his own life
> It's dying . . . rules and regulations, who needs them
> Open up the door
>
> Graham Nash, "Chicago"[2]

"Chicago" is a terrific anthem about revolution, but not just any revolution—this could serve as the de facto anthem of the new iWorld, the clarion call to a world of unbridled individualism: "Rules and regulations, who needs them/Open up the door."

Mitchell's and Nash's songs stand alongside hundreds of other songs, poems, and books that not only helped to shape this movement but still represent it. This new counterculture is about much more than a sexual revolution; it is about a transformation in the nature of society. Graham

2. Graham Nash, "Chicago," *Songs for Beginners* (Atlantic Records, 1971).

Nash captures its very essence: the triumph of individualism.[3] This is not Nietzsche's rather cold, pessimistic deconstruction of all truth claims. Instead it is an optimistic, exultant expression of individualism: "Rules and regulations, who needs them/Open up the door." This is not liberalism, because the liberal philosophers would never abide individualism without limits. But neither is it nihilism, because it does something the nihilists wouldn't condone: the positive affirmation of individualism as a value that ought to be embraced by all. It is nothing less than the birth of a new era. It is an announcement of the dawning of the iWorld—the "Age of Aquarius"—which is appropriate because no one is exactly sure where it will lead. Depending on the extent of one's optimism, the hope is that it will lead us to an altogether new garden.

Finding Freedom in the iWorld

The iWorld brings with it much more than a sexual revolution. As English scholar John Ashcroft of the Relationships Foundation points out, it is a world that seeks to claim three freedoms:

freedom from nature
freedom from authority
freedom from want

It seeks to claim these freedoms even if it does not presently possess the power to fully realize them. It is, however, fully invested in the procurement of such freedoms and will continually seek the power to do so.

These new freedoms have implications for every aspect of our lives. This includes a sexual dimension, since the development of increasingly reliable contraception combined with a relaxed moral framework that exalts individual choice allows people for the first time to decouple sexual intercourse from childbearing and marriage.

3. Australian Labour Cabinet Minister Lindsay Tanner describes the impact of this revolution on Australian society in Lindsay Tanner, *Crowded Lives* (Melbourne, Australia: Pluto, 2003), chap. 3. Kay S. Hymowitz describes the impact of this revolution on the United States in Kay S. Hymowitz, *Marriage and Caste in America: Separate and Unequal Families in a Post-Marital Age* (Chicago: Ivan R. Dee, 2006), chap. 1.

The freedoms, however, go far beyond sexuality to politics, economics, and religion. These freedoms tell us we can be free from the ethical
and religious constraints of others. They tell us to free ourselves from
the aristocratic stratification and economic inequity of the tWorld. Yet
the implications of these freedoms are even more radical. The iWorld
is based on a set of individualistic assumptions that are leading us in a
direction we as a species have never gone before.

Now if the iWorld is not liberal or nihilistic or even postmodern,
then what is it? Nietzsche may be a pivotal figure in its creation, but
he is not the only one. A host of other philosophers such as Jean-Paul
Sartre and Albert Camus expounded ideas similar to Nietzsche, including the death of God, the absence of objective morality, and the
need for humans to re-create themselves and the world in their image.
They argued that the existing power structure was neither sacred nor
just, and hence its overthrow was not only desirable but also necessary.
Their ideas became required reading in colleges and universities during
the 1960s, during which a generation of young people did more than
take notes, pass exams, graduate, and go to work within the existing
order; they took these ideas to heart and sought to create an entirely
new order. It was at this point that a generation faced up to the moral
deficit and hypocrisy of modernity. But rather than step back from what
looked to Hume like an abyss and to Nietzsche as a meaningless void,
they envisioned the possibility of a new garden and optimistically took
a leap into the unknown to commence its creation.

A hallmark of the iWorld is the optimism that a society of extreme
individualism is not only possible but good. This is a world that neither
John Stuart Mill nor Friedrich Nietzsche could support, nor would
they recognize it; yet ironically it is one they both helped to create. The
iWorld is a unique combination of the liberal yearning for freedom
coupled with postmodern deconstruction.

I recognize that students of history and philosophy may take exception to this rather unusual description of where we find ourselves at
the beginning of the twenty-first century and how we got here. The
most obvious criticism is that this depiction of the iWorld is logically
incoherent. It takes two schools of thought—liberalism and nihilism—
and fuses them with optimism to create a worldview that is not wholly
coherent and an individualism whose sustainability is in question. Nei-

ther liberals nor nihilists would accept that the optimism of the iWorld is justified. Alternatively, one could describe the iWorld as a product of the philosophical movement of anarchism—the belief that by tearing down the existing order, peace and fulfillment will reign. In many ways this conclusion would be philosophically convenient, though inaccurate. The iWorld bears the imprint of many currents of thought, including anarchism, Marxism, and Christianity, yet ultimately it is not a pure distillation of any of these. It is a hybrid, and it is unclear how long the individualism for which it stands can be sustained. It may end as quickly as it began.

As a consequence, it is possible this book may become dated remarkably quickly, but I believe this won't be the case. There is no question that a revolution is occurring, but genuine revolutions don't happen very often, and once people have embraced a new way of thinking about the world, it is not something they let go of easily. The undoing of the tWorld began centuries ago with the advent of modernity, but it took until the present day for the relational and moral framework to finally be discarded. Moreover, given the multiple philosophical and theological currents that created the tWorld, it is unclear whether it had deep, internal philosophical and theological consistency either. Yet although the iWorld may not be fully coherent, it is being embraced rapidly by Western society. Hence, it may be with us for a long time to come.

As such, the iWorld cannot be considered liberal, because liberalism wishes to affix rational limits to human behavior that the iWorld does not accept. For the same reason, it is important to understand why the iWorld cannot be fairly described as nihilistic or postmodern. In one respect it is very close; the notion that there ought to be no rules and regulations is the very essence of nihilism. What nihilism cannot support, however, is embracing individualism as a positive value, because Nietzsche could not support any conclusion as authoritative or normative. Indeed, nihilism and postmodernism can just as easily lead in a more totalitarian direction as in an individualistic one. Many will argue, with some merit, that Nietzsche provided the inspiration for twentieth-century Nazism and Fascism. He did believe in a world without boundaries, but that also applies to the boundaries of individualism. He supported the will to power of a Fascist who wishes to impose his or her will on the world as well as the anarchist who wishes to be left alone. The iWorld makes individual freedom its non-negotiable value; Nietzsche had no non-negotiable values.

The Core Commitments of the iWorld

Even if the iWorld is not philosophically consistent, its core commitments are, first, to provide space for the maximum legal amount of individual freedom through the expansion of individual rights and, second, to make sure that such an expansion does not violate the rights of others.

The Expansion of the Possibilities of the Self

In practical terms the iWorld can function like a mechanism that consistently attempts to determine and deliver the broadest possible extent of individual freedom. This manifests itself in continually challenging new and existing boundaries on individual freedom: when a restrictive boundary is identified it uses whatever means available—often the legal system—to secure either the relaxation of the boundary (providing choice) or its outright elimination. It then moves on to the next boundary that arises or is deemed an impediment to individual freedom. The iWorld is predicated on a foundational belief that the expansion of individual rights will lead to increased happiness and fulfillment.

The iWorld safeguards self-definition as the right of every person. Ideally, the only boundaries an individual will face in this quest will be what he or she is able to imagine and desire. Society assists in this task by identifying and deconstructing every possible boundary in order to provide the broadest range of options in each individual's quest to understand who he or she is and wants to be. The iWorld seeks to not promote any particular choice; rather, it seeks to expand the available choices.

The iWorld regards itself as the place in which human freedom triumphs. One can see its message in a multiplicity of advertising slogans:

Apple: "The power to be your best." "Think different."
Outback Steakhouse: "No rules, just right."

PlayStation: "Be whatever you want to be."
Burger King: "Have it your way."
Nike: "Just do it."

One might say that the iWorld is preaching a gospel that exhorts us to discover who we are or to make ourselves into what we want to be. Indeed, calling it a gospel is not hyperbole. Robert Bellah's book *Habits of the Heart* illustrates this in an interview his research team conducted with a woman named Sheila. She calls her religious faith "Sheilaism," explaining that "it is whatever I want it to be."[4] Sheilaism may be antithetical to revealed religion, but it is a religion well suited to the iWorld.

It is important to see that the iWorld is not merely about innovation. It has no problem with any individual who chooses a lifestyle that is consistent with the tWorld or one or more of the revealed religions. The iWorld does not dictate a set of behavioral choices but instead seeks to remove the cultural and social limits on behavior. What it will not abide, however, is any person or group seeking to impose ideas on someone else. This is what is meant by the student respondent at the Harvard commencement who said, "The freedom of our day is the freedom to devote ourselves to any values we please, on the mere condition that we do not believe them to be true."[5] This statement provides an extremely effective way to compare and contrast the iWorld with the tWorld. To anyone in the tWorld this statement is patent nonsense, yet it is a fundamental creed of the iWorld. To see the degree to which this statement captures the essence of our world one merely has to conduct the following experiment:

1. Go into any mixed social setting in which those in attendance don't know each other well.
2. Ask a moral question of anyone in the group.
3. After they've answered, ask them, in front of others, if they believe that those who disagree with them are wrong.
4. As soon as the word "wrong" is spoken you will see discomfort or even anger in the body language of each member of the group.

4. Bellah et al., *Habits of the Heart*, 221.
5. Bellah et al., *Good Society*, 44.

5. See how long it takes for the person to repudiate your assertion that his or her beliefs about morality are true, by explaining that their moral *beliefs* are merely *opinions*.

6. Watch everyone avoid you for the rest of the evening, and see if you ever get invited back.

You probably don't even need to imperil your social life by conducting the experiment. The Harvard student commencement speaker expressed a fundamental moral and social creed of our world, and it is practically settled law as far as polite society is concerned. The same is true in business settings, political gatherings, and most college and university situations. Even though institutions of higher education were founded to explore and discuss ideas, it is the rare professor and the rarer student who are willing to pronounce that they believe those who disagree with them on a question of morality are wrong. People in the iWorld are usually quite civil except when someone asserts a universal moral value. If Nietzsche were listening he might well be nodding in agreement, because the iWorld has been persuaded by his conclusions.

The iWorld is continually encouraging us to be ourselves, find ourselves, or create ourselves. It assists us by constantly pushing the boundaries of convention and even nature.[6] This is exemplified in the iWorld's understanding of gender. One of the single most significant pieces of information required for human interaction is knowledge of a person's biological sex. As long as that remains uncertain, our interactions are stifled. When it becomes known, our interactions can take shape. Knowledge of biological sex is so powerful that it can literally rule our lives, encouraging women to adhere to one set of behaviors and men to another. As a result, one might ask if historical gender roles do justice to the actual variations among humans. The iWorld maintains that they don't. Rather than categorizing humans as male and female by virtue of their genitals, the iWorld looks at humans as individuals. The iWorld allows people, if they choose, to free themselves from the cultural and historic expectations attached to their biological sex. Rosalind Barnett

---

6. Anthony Giddens is particularly adept at explaining the plastic and reflexive nature of the self and sexuality at this historical moment. See Anthony Giddens, *Modernity and Self-Identity: Self and Society in the Late Modern Age* (Stanford, CA: Stanford University Press, 1991).

and Caryl Rivers argue that not only is this possible but it is a better reflection of reality. In their book *Same Difference* they write:

> Of course there are difference between the sexes—how could it be otherwise? But more important is the size of difference *between* men and women compared to those *among* women and men. In most areas of life, the latter are much larger. If you are a woman named Sarah, you may be very different from Jessica, Elizabeth, or Susan in the way you tackle a math problem, deal with subordinates, relate to your spouse, soothe your child, feel about yourself. In fact, you are just as apt to be like Richard, Tom, and Seth in those areas as you are to be like other women.[7]

Barnett and Rivers conclude:

> Throughout this book, we have heard voices chanting that we must return women and men to a traditional past. This dated message belies the energy we see around us, as our society embraces new freedoms and discovers new tolerance, rejecting old stereotypes. No era is without its pressing social issues, but we are optimistic about the future of the sexes in a world of same difference. More freedom may indeed bring more anxiety; more choice may bring more confusion and less certainty. But it allows us to be more varied, complex, and unique than does a world shackled by the iron bars of a gender-difference culture.[8]

The iWorld agrees with the research of Barnett and Rivers and goes even further. Not only is it willing to allow people to ignore their genitals when seeking to understand who they are; it is also willing to allow people to change their sex to the degree it is scientifically possible. After all, if nothing is truly authoritative except individual choice, then neither is genetics, and to the degree that science develops methods to change ourselves genetically and biologically, the iWorld provides freedom and permission to do so.

There are many other examples that could serve to illustrate the extent to which the iWorld is willing to go in order to expand the boundaries of choice and individual freedom, but deconstructing gender itself effectively makes the point. Any boundary that can be moved or dissolved

7. Rosalind Barnett and Caryl Rivers, *Same Difference: How Gender Myths Are Hurting Our Relationships, Our Children, and Our Jobs* (New York: Basic Books, 2004), 13.
   8. Ibid., 254.

will be. Nature, authority, and want stand as the obstacles to freedom that can and should be overcome.

The Self in Relation to Other Selves

Even in the iWorld, however, there are limits to freedom. While the iWorld focuses on expanding the range of individual freedom, even it cannot allow complete individual freedom lest, as Mill fears, one person use it coercively over another. The iWorld embraces three taboos that serve to limit individual freedom if it affects another person's individual freedom:

1. One may not criticize someone else's life choices or behavior.
2. One may not behave in a manner that coerces or causes harm to others.
3. One may not engage in a sexual relationship with someone without his or her consent.

I call these "taboos" because they are regarded by our culture as primary rules of social engagement. They are taught to us by society from an early age and reinforced throughout our life. If you want to get along in the iWorld, adherence to each of them is essential. We still talk in somewhat reverential terms about the Ten Commandments, but we break them with impunity and, save for two or three, they are infrequently enforced or punished by government. These three iWorld taboos, however, command a much greater respect, and they are reinforced daily in schools, the workplace, the media, and so forth. If the government can't or won't enforce them, then citizens will. Indeed, the first taboo is the basis for the creed of political correctness.

The inspiration for these taboos can be found in John Stuart Mill's *On Liberty*. He grapples with the same questions as the iWorld: "How do we maximize individual freedom, and what are the fewest possible limits that must be imposed on individual freedom in order to protect it?" In many respects the iWorld owes a great debt to Mill, yet it is interesting that Mill's taboos are taken but not the utilitarian calculus he used to determine what is moral in any given situation. This is an effective illustration of how the iWorld has departed from liberalism. Gone is the desire and permission to define what is moral or even to study the consequences of our choices. It is freedom, not morality or virtue, that is the goal.[9]

Freedom of individual choice, the first taboo, is the highest ideal of the iWorld, but all three taboos are held in such esteemed regard that the person who breaks them is treated not with toleration or mere disdain but with strident anger. In the iWorld these taboos are held with the fervor of religious zeal, and those who challenge or are willing to entertain questions about their adequacy are usually treated as heretics.

As for how these three taboos are applied in practice, perhaps the best way to explore this is to examine their bearing on sexual and social relations in the iWorld.

9. Some philosophers may object to my characterization of the iWorld's procedural view of protecting freedom and doing justice as not being liberal. I acknowledge that what Robert Nozick and John Rawls sought to do in their respective scholarship comes close to this by proposing what might be termed procedural liberalism. It may be argued that it is they and not Mill who ought to be regarded as the political theorists of the iWorld. Yet I think Mill is the proper focus because he is the source of the taboos the iWorld embraces, and because Nozick and Rawls tried to save liberalism from the challenge of Nietzsche and existentialism, as opposed to replacing liberalism, which the iWorld is doing. Robert Nozick, *Anarchy, State, and Utopia* (New York: Basic Books, 1974); and John Rawls, *A Theory of Justice*, rev. ed. (Cambridge, MA: Belknap Press of Harvard University Press, 1999).

4

Love, Sex, Family, and Public Policy
iWorld Style

> If you can't be with the one you love, love the one you're
> with.
>
> Stephen Stills[1]

M ake love, not war" was a mantra of the Woodstock era, and while
the peace movement seemingly faded with the end of the Vietnam
War and the hippie counterculture ran out of energy in the 1970s, the
lovemaking kept right on going. The abiding legacy of Woodstock and
the counterculture is the sexual revolution, and its impact on human
relationships and sexuality has changed Western society through the
widespread embrace of the iWorld.

The iWorld's most significant impact has been on the relational structure of Western society. The driving force in the development of the
iWorld was the desire to champion the ideal of individual choice. While
the focus was not on sexual freedom per se, this has become one of its
most cherished freedoms. By challenging and changing our understand-

1. Stephen Stills, *Love the One You're With* (Atlantic Records, 1970).

ing of what it means to be human, the iWorld fundamentally altered our perception of human nature, the self, and the purpose of family, relationships, and sexuality.

For centuries the tWorld provided an established framework for human development and flourishing in which people functioned best when finding contentment and investing themselves in a constellation of healthy relationships. Freedom was found within this framework, and the greater the relational health of one's life, the greater the freedom. Ideally the nuclear family, extended family, community, and society provided everyone with a place to love and be loved, nurture and be nurtured, work, relax, celebrate, and even find friendship. It was understood and accepted that the full extent of intimacy in all its dimensions was found in this matrix, and sexual relations were not considered an essential component of a fulfilling life. Sexuality was regarded as a drive and an appetite but not an end in itself.

Yet in the past forty years the relational structure and understanding of human life that had served the West for centuries has been turned upside down. Relationships of obligation have been replaced with relationships of choice, and sexual intercourse has been transformed from being valued primarily for its role in procreation and in cementing a marriage relationship to being a pleasurable and typically essential component of intimate adult romantic relationships. The definition of intimacy in the iWorld has narrowed to become more sexual, and sexual freedom among consenting adults has been elevated to a place reserved for inalienable rights. The two fundamental elements of relational fulfillment in the iWorld are sexual and relational freedom.

Sexual and Relational Freedom in the iWorld

In the 1980s when I was in graduate school at Georgetown studying politics, I engaged a colleague in a discussion about the question, "What matters most to Americans?" I made the case that financial well-being was the number-one concern of Americans and that nothing else came close. After letting me drone on for several minutes he simply replied, "Sorry, you're wrong. Sexual freedom is the number one issue to Americans. Any politician who seeks to restrict sexual freedom will die a very painful political death." In the years that have since transpired I have come to profoundly agree with this view.

Sexual freedom enjoys a privileged position in the iWorld. People are free to do and be whatever they wish, and provided they don't violate the three taboos, they are entitled to value whatever they desire. There is no specific obligation or requirement for anyone to engage in sexual relations or even to value them. People can and do prioritize anything—including material wealth, power, or status—into their highest aspiration. They can converse with others for no other reason than the intrinsic joy of conversation. They can find meaning in solitude and meditation as their highest ideal. People can choose a life of celibacy or a single, lifelong, monogamous relationship. They are free to decide on whatever lifestyle or values they choose, but ever-increasing numbers are embracing unfettered sexual freedom in an unprecedented way.

Since in the iWorld independent living is the goal of human existence, a significant level of individual wealth is a prerequisite. The iWorld also promotes a desire for the immediate; we prefer not to wait for anything. This can be seen in the unprecedented levels of consumer debt and the growth of the fast-food industry. Yet nowhere is the transformational power of the iWorld clearer than in its impact on relationships and the place of sexuality in them. It is difficult to find a dimension of the iWorld that does not have a relational consequence, and sexual relations are no exception. For example, the iWorld's impulse of immediacy has introduced sexual relations more quickly and casually into even the earliest stages of romantic relationships.

In the tWorld you didn't need to be independently wealthy or live for the immediate moment because you could expect that your family and relational community would be there for you from the cradle to the grave. In the iWorld, however, we have no such expectation. We need to take care of ourselves, which requires that we each have independent means of doing so. We also need to continually seek or reevaluate relational attachments because there is no certain way to secure them. Money and material wealth matter greatly in the iWorld, but relational and sexual freedom matter even more.

Supporting evidence is all around us. Pornography was the first profitable industry on the Internet. Advertising demonstrates daily that sex appeal sells. You want to sell beer? Snow covered mountains are good;

a woman in a bathing suit is even better. You want to sell a car? The proper lighting and camera angles matter, but you can seal the deal if you have the right woman in the right dress and the right shoes driving the car and saying, "The question is, when you turn your car on, does it return the favor?" You want to sell magazines? Good writing helps, but George Clooney on the cover helps even more. You want to sell furniture? You want to sell anything? Sex sells and the iWorld is buying. Just look at the cover of *Cosmopolitan*.

You want to sell yourself? Wealth helps; sex appeal helps even more. Vanity does not come close to explaining how much money people spend on makeovers and cosmetic procedures. Breast enhancement or reduction, nip and tuck facial surgery, Botox, cosmetic dentistry, weight reduction, liposuction, hair transplant, hair removal—the list of enhancements goes on and on, and as technology progresses it will extend even further. The motivation for all this is not comfort but confidence. We know that if we are going to "sell" ourselves on the open market of relationships, it's good to have money, but it's even better to have head-turning looks. Moreover, when it comes to looking good it's not enough to have a pretty face; these days a chiseled physique with all the right proportions is an essential part of the package.

Of this I'm convinced. You've probably never met me, and you probably never will. Yet if I want to go out and successfully promote myself, I better hit the gym, lose some weight, and find a hair stylist who is willing to make the best of a bad situation. I grant that a million dollars won't turn me into a sex symbol, but if I want to sell myself in person, how I look matters, and I'm going to need more than just an Armani suit. Sex appeal matters, and while appearance isn't everything, it is the key that opens doors in the iWorld. One might ask, "Why is it that sex and sex appeal are so highly valued in the iWorld?" The compound answer is: the desire for popularity and the fear of loneliness.

There is no question that the tWorld often fell well short of its relational potential. While it offered a lot of security, there is no question that some people found themselves stuck in miserable relationships from which they couldn't escape. Not every family was a good family, not every marriage was healthy, not every extended family was supportive, and not every community was friendly. The tWorld was a great place if your relationships were mature, healthy, and supportive, but if the opposite were true it could be something like purgatory or worse. Some who have read this far may yearn for a return to the tWorld, but I am confident in saying the vast majority prefer the iWorld despite its apparent flaws. There must be good reason why so many people, Christians included, have rejected the tWorld for the iWorld. In the eyes of more and more people, the tWorld is no longer even competitive as a relational structure.

However, despite its triumph, the iWorld is not perfect. Two of the primary difficulties facing people in the iWorld are loneliness and insecurity. These are inherent by-products of individualism. If individual freedom is the goal and the means of achieving this freedom is replacing relationships of obligation and responsibility with a world of relational choice, then a certain amount of loneliness and insecurity will result. There will be more for some than others, but the fear of loneliness and insecurity will affect everyone.

If the new standard of relational commitment is that people will relate for as long as they both desire, then there is no one who will possess long-term relational security. Even if people promise to stay related until death do them part, the iWorld does not have the political will to enforce it. If people hope to stay in relationship until they die, they will not have certainty of achieving this until their own death. There is a perpetual haze of relational insecurity that lingers in the iWorld. There is also the ever-present, nagging question, "How will I ever know if I might be happier with someone other than the one I'm with?" The answer is that we can never be certain. In the tWorld these problems were moot since the ethos was to find contentment and fulfillment in the relationships we were given. In the iWorld the question lingers not far from the hearts and minds of everyone. Citizens of the iWorld need to look out for themselves. They need to get the most they can from their current relationships and be open to future relational possibilities. This is not to say that the people who lived in the tWorld were inattentive to pleasure and intimacy in romantic relationships; they certainly were attentive to them. What is different is that in the tWorld it was normal to take a more long-term view of relationships.

So how do people in the iWorld most effectively deal with this latent relational insecurity? By seeking to get everything they can, as soon as they can, from their romantic relationships. "Everything" often means sexual relations. In a world of relational insecurity, people seek to maximize their current pleasure and intimacy because it may be fleeting. Many, if not most, people in the iWorld believe that intimacy and relational fulfillment are enhanced by a sexual relationship, and there are good reasons for this. Science tells us that we come loaded with a sex drive and that we are hormonally structured to desire sex, not just because of the emotional release involved in intercourse or an orgasm but because it triggers biochemical and hormonal reactions that enhance our sense of well-being. Hence, there are physiological reasons to have a sexual relationship whenever possible. Sex is pleasurable.

There are also psychological reasons. If, as we saw in chapter 3, modernity is correct in its assumption, based on the scientific method, that we are comprised only of mind and body, then what is intimacy? The tWorld believed intimacy had a spiritual dimension and that humans could enjoy intimacy in a wide variety of nonsexual relationships in addition to marriage. But if humans are composed only of mind and body and do not have a soul, then what is the nature of intimacy? It must then be either physical, mental, or some combination of the two. Given the physiological and psychological power of a sexual relationship, it is not surprising that many in the iWorld have equated sexuality with relational intimacy.

An example of this is the way in which the iWorld uses the word "intimacy" and the phrase "sexual relationship" synonymously. In one context we might tell people we are having a sexual relationship and they understand that we are enjoying an intimate relationship. In another context we might tell people that we are enjoying an intimate relationship and they assume we are having a sexual relationship.

In the iWorld if you find yourself romantically inclined toward someone of the same gender, there are no longer insurmountable obstacles to prevent you from engaging in a sexual relationship with that person. As we have seen, the iWorld deconstructs gender and makes it less important relationally. What's paramount is that you find intimacy and fulfillment in your relationships. If you find someone of the opposite gender with whom to partner, great. If you find someone of the same gender with whom to partner, great. So long as you do not violate the three taboos, however you find intimacy and fulfillment is your prerogative. Since the iWorld is a by-product of the age of the scientific method, experimentation is believed to be a good thing. If you need to experiment sexually with people of both genders to discover what brings you the greatest fulfillment, that freedom is your right.

Romantic relationships, intimacy, and sexuality are so connected in the iWorld that it is widely accepted that if you want to have genuine intimacy you need to have sex. Moreover, if you aren't in a sexual relationship, then many will assume you are lonely and unfulfilled. Money matters, but intimacy and personal fulfillment matter more. If a sexual relationship is the most direct avenue to intimacy and fulfillment, and if no one has any certainty of being in a lifelong, committed relationship, then it only stands to reason that sexual freedom will have a greater value than will money. This will be true for those who are married as well as those who are not. Given the lingering insecurity that is latent in the iWorld, even if you are in a good marriage, the freedom to keep your options open is important. There is, after all, no certainty about what will happen to your marriage in the future. As a result, sexual and relational freedom are broadly embraced as the highest ideals of the iWorld.

I accept that one may object that the picture I have painted of the iWorld is a caricature that overstates the importance it places on sexual freedom. It may be percceived that I am making day-to-day life in the iWorld sound like we live in something akin to the Playboy Mansion. I recognize that is not the case. There are many people in long-lasting, monogamous relationships who wish to remain so. There are also people who are single and practicing chastity. A longer and more nuanced discussion would consider the many values of the iWorld, including financial well-being, power, and health. Moreover, it is almost certainly the case that sexual freedom does not have the same significance for the elderly as it does for the younger segment of the population. The iWorld depicted here represents a picture of where things are headed if we continue to value individual freedom to the degree we presently do, and it is my thesis that from among all the options, sexual and relational freedom will be the most highly valued.

We may not be there yet, but our culture's increasing commitment to individual freedom and a materialistic worldview ("we are . . . billion-year-old carbon")[2] has led to the creation of new attitudes

2. Mitchell, "Woodstock."

and approaches to sexual and relational behavior that are becoming norms. We may not each choose to act promiscuously today, this month, this year, or ever; nevertheless, sexual promiscuity is increasing. It is becoming the story of our culture in which we find increasing fascination and excitement. We see it in magazines, novels, television shows, and movies. The sexual and relational freedom of the iWorld is now our story. If this were not true, we would be spending our time and money on a different story. Whether we are promiscuous or not, we find reassurance in the freedom and opportunity to be able to be so. Many people may find partners with whom they spend their entire life, but since they now live in the iWorld, they will not feel the security in their partnership that they would have had in the tWorld. Today fewer people find permanent partners, and more decide they do not necessarily want one. Many want to keep their options open or reserve the right to escape if their partner ceases to fulfill and satisfy them at any point. The reality is that when all the activity and noise of the world is filtered out, what one hears is the drone of relational insecurity and ennui endemic of the iWorld. That is why the citizens of the iWorld treasure the freedom to pursue sexually intimate relationships at will. Even if we never find what we are looking for relationally, we want the freedom to search elsewhere if we find ourselves alone or, worse, unfulfilled in a marriage or similar relationship. Karla Bonoff's song "Someone to Lay Down Beside Me," which was made famous by Linda Ronstadt, sums up this sentiment beautifully.

> There's somebody waiting alone in the street
> For someone to walk up and greet
>
> Here you are all alone in the city
> Where's the one that you took to your side
> Lonely faces will stare through your eyes in the night
> And they'll say—woman sweet woman please come home
>   with me
> You're shining and willing and free
> But your love it's a common occurrence
> Not like love that I feel in my heart
> Still you know that may be what I need

Is someone to lay down beside me
And even though it's not real
Just someone to lay down beside me
You're the story of my life

Well morning is breaking the street lights are off
The sun will soon share all the cost
Of a world that can be sort of heartless
Not like love that you feel in our heart
Still you know that may be all you get

Is someone to lay down beside me
And even tho it's not real
Just someone to lay down beside me
You just can't ask for more[3]

The citizens of the iWorld desire more, but they at least want freedom to have a relationship of convenience.

Friendship and Family in the iWorld

So what of the other relationships in the iWorld such as friendship and family? In one sense, friendship is the relationship that changed the least between the tWorld and the iWorld. This is not surprising given the fact that friendship was the one relationship of choice in the tWorld. What does change in the iWorld is that friends are entitled to have a consensual sexual relationship. In some fashion every relationship in the iWorld can bear a resemblance to friendship, since every relationship outside of parenting is a relationship of choice. It is not surprising that the television show *Friends* resonated so strongly in the late twentieth and early twenty-first centuries.

Relationships of obligation, however, are now in crisis. The traditional three-generation or extended family (hereafter referred to as 3GF) has become a relic in the iWorld. The cause for this rests with many sociological factors related to the transition from an agrarian to an industrial society and the corresponding demand for a mobile labor

3. Karla Bonoff, "Someone to Lay Down Beside Me," *Karla Bonoff* (Sky Harbor Music, 1976).

force. Mobility has changed our world dramatically, and while there have been benefits, it has been devastating for the 3GF. Very few people live in the same place all their life, and when children turn eighteen and leave home, they usually return only to visit. About the only segment of society for which the 3GF model is still practiced is that of recent immigrants, though it usually takes only a generation for their children raised in the iWorld to become acculturated, mobile, and, as a result, make 3GF disintegration their story as well.

The iWorld is also undermining the nuclear family unit. Having removed the legal restrictions on divorce and remarriage and the moral restriction confining sexual relations to a husband and wife, the nature of the family is being profoundly altered. In the United States in 2006 nearly 40 percent of children were born outside of marriage,[4] yet the changes are not limited to the United States. According to the British Social Attitudes 24th Report (2008), 66 percent of people in the United Kingdom think there is little difference socially between being married and living together.[5] Marriage rates in the United Kingdom are at their lowest since records started being kept 150 years ago,[6] and a majority of babies of British-born mothers are now born outside of wedlock.[7] Societies throughout the West no longer live in the tWorld.

Also gone is the idea that children are a natural or necessary by-product of marriage. Having children is now seen as a choice, and science and law have made this choice possible for almost everyone. Replacing the notion that marriage between a man and a woman is the gold standard for child rearing, the belief now is that a committed and loving adult, or two, or more, can raise children as effectively as the traditional family. In the iWorld children can be obtained via intercourse, adoption, or artificial means depending on the desire of those involved. Moreover, there is no expectation that if you are married you ought to have children. The reliability of modern contraception has given many the choice not to have children. Because the iWorld individualizes not only the pursuit of happiness and the conduct of relationships but also

4. Popenoe, "Future of Marriage in America."

5. www.natcen.ac.uk/natcen/pages/news_and_media_docs/BSA_24_report.pdf.

6. "4% Fall in UK Marriages," National Statistics, www.statistics.gov.uk/CCI/nugget .asp?ID=322.

7. "An Illegitimate Argument," *Spectator*, December 12, 2007, www.spectator.co.uk/ coffeehouse/399431/an-illegitimate-argument.thtml.

parenting, it is now believed to be more a *personal* obligation on the part of each parent rather than a *relational* obligation shared between the biological mother and father. In the iWorld children are raised in a wider variety of circumstances by a wider number of people than ever before. Moreover, in the iWorld society will have to assume a greater role in the care of children. Economics will make it less likely that people can afford to stay at home to raise their children. In addition, some people will find that they are unable or unwilling to shoulder the responsibility of parenting should their relational circumstances, desires, or needs change.

This constitutes a profound shift from the model of the tWorld, but the iWorld does not regard it as inherently problematic for the children or parents. It believes the only damage done to children occurs in families or partnerships that turn physically, emotionally, or verbally abusive or neglectful. Although these certainly cause the greatest harm to children, the iWorld gives no credence to the loss experienced by the absence of a traditional family. The focus of the iWorld is making sure those in the household are engaged in loving relationships, which is good for both parents and children. In this view, keeping children in the care of loving adults is what is important, not the number of adults, the type of relationship(s), or even the gender composition of the relationship(s).

The Politics and Public Policy of the iWorld

The emergence of the iWorld impacts politics and public policy in a number of different ways. Democracy is a political system ideally suited for the iWorld since it can adapt to the constitutional and legal apparatus of Western democracy. In this instance the term "adapt" is used because the iWorld's approach to governance is, by nature, different than had been anticipated by those who created democracy in England and the United States. The English and U.S. Constitutions were founded on a conception of natural law—the belief that there are truths that are self-evident and that cannot be changed.[8] In the

8. It should be noted that the English Constitution, unlike the U.S. Constitution, is not formally written and is the result of centuries of informal development and precedence.

iWorld, natural law does not possess the same constitutional status. Instead the Constitution is viewed as a framework of procedures that provides society with rules concerning lawmaking and with rights that are based on public opinion rather than a permanent notion of right or wrong. As public opinion changes, laws and rights change accordingly. Thus there are no permanent boundaries or limits to what individuals and societies legally can or cannot do, nor are there any defined boundaries on the role and scope of government. The presence of a Constitution may delay social change but cannot forestall it indefinitely. For instance, in the United States there is no practical way one can argue that the original authors of the Massachusetts state constitution intended to provide a right to same-sex marriage. Nevertheless, the Massachusetts Supreme Court interpreted the law in such a way as to "discover" that right within the constitution. It would not be surprising to have the United States Supreme Court make a similar finding at some point during the twenty-first century. However, even if it does not do so, should public opinion continue to shift on this issue, then a legal statute or constitutional amendment legalizing same-sex marriage could effectively accomplish the same ends. Constitutions and established law in the iWorld are as malleable as societal attitudes.

In the iWorld, not only can laws and constitutions become increasingly malleable, but the underlying absence of legal dogmatism will also seep into public political discourse. In the iWorld politics gives every appearance of becoming less about the free discussion and debate of ideas and more about protest and activism. As Alasdair MacIntyre argues in *After Virtue*, in a world that ceases to believe in truth, it is no longer possible to debate ideas because there is no commonly accepted standard to resolve debate.[9] Consequently, politics becomes what Nietzsche envisioned: an exercise in will and power rather than dialogue and debate. If reason or discussion cannot resolve political disagreements, then the most effective political tools that remain are protest, manipulation, demagoguery, and coercion. If ideas and character are not the relevant political currency, then people will almost certainly need to use

9. Alasdair MacIntyre, *After Virtue: A Study in Moral Theory*, 2nd ed. (Notre Dame, IN: University of Notre Dame Press, 1984), see esp. chap. 2.

money to create it. Accordingly, in the iWorld money will only increase its value as a political currency.

Accepting that the one constant of politics in the iWorld is change, what can be said about public policy? So long as individualism remains its core commitment, one can gain a sense of what the nature of law and public policy may become. This cursory exploration of the iWorld suggests that there are seven public policy directions that could reasonably be expected to emerge and develop in the foreseeable future. One cannot speak with certainty about the precise legal framework that will emerge, but the contours of emerging policies show signs, on examination, of many initiatives already being fleshed out by Western democracies. Since the rationale and philosophical basis of these policies has already been presented, they need not be summarized again here.

Government Support for the Widest Variety of Sexual Lifestyles

The iWorld does not discriminate between various sexual lifestyles, and it will require that citizens not discriminate either. Politically, the issue of sexual orientation is moot. The purpose of government is not to proscribe orientation but to protect rights of behavior. Public policy in the iWorld will seek to protect all sexual behavior and relationships so long as the three taboos are not violated. Such protections would be promoted through educating citizens to accept the behavior of those who behave differently. Therefore one can expect the government to mandate the design and dissemination of educational curriculum to educate children accordingly, teaching children to observe the three taboos and emphasizing the importance of extending tolerance to different behaviors and lifestyles. The sexual education curriculum will be focused on public health and the health of each child, teaching children the use of contraception, and making them aware of the health risks and consequences associated with the variety of sexual behaviors. In addition, educators will be responsible to help children understand and consider their gender, and counseling will be made available to help students understand their preferences and grapple with their options. Educators will be required to adopt a strict code of moral neutrality in relation to the various options.

Decriminalizing Consensual Sexual Relationships

Consent is the primary ethical issue concerning sexual relationships in the iWorld. The three taboos provide the basic guidelines for sexual relationships of all types. Unwanted sexual advances or contact are regarded as criminal and are dealt with harshly. Protection is increasingly being extended to all types of consensual sexual relationships, with the only exception being those involving children. Public policy will continue to relax existing laws restricting consensual sexual behavior among adults, even those such as sodomy. A significant legal question facing the iWorld will concern the nature and age of consent. Presumably if someone is mature enough to be capable of giving consent, then he or she ought to have the right to engage in sexual relationships. Hence, public policy in the iWorld will likely lower the age of consent, seeking to replace age with a different standard by which to measure the validity of consent.

Two related public policy questions to be addressed by the iWorld concern incest and bestiality. If individualism is the highest good, if birth control can successfully disconnect sexual relations from reproduction, and if genuine consent can be established, we can expect public policy will relax or eliminate laws that restrict sexual relations between various family members. And there is reason to believe that if the laws of consent are adequately retooled to apply to all possible sexual relationships, specific laws prohibiting incest, sodomy, and bestiality eventually could be eliminated. To summarize, if genuine consent consistent with that of an adult can be established, we can expect that the iWorld will provide protection to the corresponding sexual relationship.

Transforming Marriage into a Contractual Relationship of Consent

The iWorld will end the exclusive understanding of marriage as a permanent arrangement between a man, a woman, and their extended families. From a legal point of view, virtually nothing of the historic covenantal nature of marriage in which "what God has joined together, let no one separate" remains. Given the legal embrace of no-fault divorce and the increasing use of prenuptial agreements, this change in public policy is already being implemented. Increasingly, marriages will be regarded as a contract between individuals, regardless of gender and flexible as to the number of people in the marriage. Any of the people involved with the contract will be able to terminate it at any time, thus giving individuals the maximum freedom to be connected to whomever they desire, whenever they desire, for as long as they desire. A man and a woman who wish to be married, have children, and spend their life together will be free to do so, but the umbrella of marriage will be broadened to include whatever terms are desired so long as the three taboos are not violated. The iWorld will almost certainly allow polygamy, though whether it would allow animals to be part of the arrangement remains to be seen.

One of the more difficult questions will be what to call this legal partnership: a marriage, a civil union, or either. Since the word "marriage" is so invested with traditional and religious meaning, the iWorld may be reluctant to use it if it cannot redefine it sufficiently. If so, it will likely jettison the use of the words "marriage," "husband," and "wife," replacing them with "civil union" and "partners." It is clear that the historic marriage relationship with all the rights and privileges sanctioned by the state will be expanded to include all adults who wish to enter into this relationship.

Redefining Family

The first three areas of public policy reform are relatively straightforward and easy to understand if one comprehends the ethos of the iWorld. Understanding family, however, is a conundrum for the iWorld; the problem concerns the responsibility for the nurture and care of children. In this the tWorld was straightforward: the mother and father were responsible for the care of the children, and if for some reason they could not perform their duties, the responsibility passed to the extended family, and in the last resort, to the state. In the iWorld the responsibility for the care of children is much more complex. As we move away from requiring the biological mother and father to assume the primary, lifelong responsibility for their children, the lines of responsibility in their care can become blurred. As a result, the iWorld is dealing with issues concerning the care of children that humanity has never faced before.

We are already familiar with custody issues for children whose parents divorce, even if custody is assigned and the parents remarry several times. While there is certainly an emotional toll for all involved, the courts can resolve custody and child support issues even if the geographic distance between the original parents grows. We are also familiar with the more complicated issue of children born out of wedlock and the challenges they face when their parents migrate to other relationships. Again, while resolving and enforcing custody and child support arrangements is difficult in these situations, the courts can do so as long as they are able to sort out paternity and maternity.

What is less clear is how to assign responsibility for individuals or couples who use artificial insemination. Since so many people consider parenting a right and an important part of personal fulfillment, public policy in the iWorld already supports the acquisition of children as a right that individuals and couples possess regardless of whether they are in a legal union. What will need to be addressed in the future are the rights and responsibilities of the biological parents, who may not be the legal custodians or parents, as well as the rights of children. To illustrate the difficulty, consider a recent legal case in Britain in which a lesbian couple contracted with a man to have his sperm impregnate one of the women. When the two women separated, however, the woman who did not have custody of the child claimed that she did not owe any child support since it was not her child. The court agreed and required the man to pay child support instead.[10]

We could go further to describe more complicated entanglements, but we will leave that to politicians, geneticists, and lawyers. The point is that one of the most significant contrasts between the tWorld and the iWorld is in the area of family and, in particular, the nurturing of children. The whole concept of adult responsibility for child care doesn't easily fit into the iWorld framework. The iWorld functions effectively with responsible adults, but is less adept at dealing with children and

10. "Why Fireman Sperm Donor MUST Pay to Raise Our Children, by Lesbian Mother," Mail Online, November 4, 2008, www.dailymail.co.uk/news/article-499342/Why-fireman-sperm -donor-MUST-pay-raise-children-lesbian-mother.html. See also a similar ruling in the United States: Elizabeth Marquardt, "When 3 Really Is a Crowd," New York Times, July 16, 2007, www .nytimes.com/2007/07/16/opinion/16marquardt.html?adxnnl=1&adxnnlx=1185202864–E43y MY4/Iit5/TTsWQlPZA.

others who are economically vulnerable and do not have the cognitive ability to be free.

Children pose the biggest challenge because, while parents can nurture them well, some may come into the care of adults who find parenting too challenging or not personally fulfilling and so do not wish to continue. Children may also be an unintended consequence of sexual intercourse by people who do not wish to be parents. The conundrum the iWorld faces is what to do with adults who have children but do not wish to care for them. Coercion would be problematic since it violates the essence of the freedom for which the iWorld stands, and it is hard to imagine parents performing their responsibilities well under the threat of coercion. Consequently, it seems inevitable that the state in the iWorld will increasingly take responsibility to care for more and more children.

Aside from the cost, which will be enormous, there is concern about whether a government-based child-rearing model can provide the quality of care and nurture that children need. As we have seen, Aristotle regarded the family as the fundamental, irreplaceable nurturing unit of society that was critical for the creation of responsible, ethical, caring citizens. Plato constructed a thought experiment in *The Republic* in which he postulated the communal raising of children, but it is not clear whether he believed it would work. Anthropologists have identified societies in which the tribe or clan takes more responsibility for child rearing than the biological parents. Even Marxists, who regard the nuclear family as a creation of the capitalist order, have been reluctant to do away with the family out of concern over what institution can adequately take its place. The iWorld, with its commitment to individualism, takes child rearing into a brave new world. Can an individualistic conception of society find a way to rear children effectively and affordably? That is a challenge for the iWorld.

Expanding Child Creation Capacity

While we cannot yet tell what new arrangement the iWorld will create for effective child rearing, we can foresee that the iWorld will pioneer new ways to create children. The iWorld will need to account for the increasing number of couples who cannot have children biologically but who want children of their own or who may want greater latitude and control in the creation of their own children. There is no question that many infertile couples are more than willing to adopt. But with the advances in cloning and genetic selection, there is also no question that more people will demand that the government increase the capacities of the scientific and medical institutions to enable them to order with some precision the child they desire. This will include the selection of gender and race as well as the whole array of engineering geneticists can provide. It will also include the demand for human cloning. Governments of the iWorld will almost certainly grant these requests. While these developments will cause political controversy, so long as individual choice remains the highest ideal of the society and people continue to believe that humans are merely physical, rather than also spiritual beings, it is hard to imagine any of these developments being stopped. It may take time for them to be fully accepted by society, but in the iWorld all things capitulate to the demand of individual choice and freedom.

Facilitating Change of Sex and Genetic Traits

Accordingly, the iWorld will grant the right for individuals to go to the furthest extent allowed by science to change their sex and genetic traits. Government will fund the medical and scientific research to accomplish this and provide its citizens the freedom to avail themselves of it. If the iWorld is willing to do this for embryos not yet born, it will certainly allow it for men and women past the age of consent. People who make such changes will be given legal protection against discrimination, and similar protection will be provided for transgendered individuals. Public policy in the iWorld is dedicated to helping humans do and be what they want to do and be and to help expand the choices and possibilities available, so long as doing so does not violate the three taboos.

Neutering Humanity

One further related area of public policy development will be how the iWorld ultimately deals with gender-distinct activities and facilities. While the public policy emphasis up to now has focused on fostering equality *between* the sexes, the next focus will be equality *among* the sexes. As the boundaries between genders become blurred, the rationale for existing boundaries will become more difficult to sustain. For example, if a male were to change his sex to female, ought she be entitled to play professional women's sports? In the case of Dr. Rene Richards the answer was yes. Should a woman be exempt from the more financially lucrative world of male sports merely because she is a woman? In golf the fact that Annika Sorenstam and Michelle Wie were allowed to compete in men's PGA events demonstrates that existing boundaries are becoming porous. Another example can be found on many college campuses where men and women now live in the same dorm, on the same floor, and in some cases in the same room. In the 1970s the Equal Rights Amendment failed in Congress largely over the fear of social changes on the order of the creation of unisex bathrooms. Defeating the amendment was clearly not the long-term solution to this public policy issue.

While these seven public policy issues are not the only ones the iWorld will face in matters related to sexuality, gender, and family, they do highlight the major issues. There is, however, another issue that cuts across them all, and that concerns the degree to which the entire society will be required to adhere to these policies or whether nongovernmental institutions, particularly religious institutions, will have the right to opt out. For instance, will religious organizations be able to exercise autonomous selectivity (i.e., discriminate) in hiring and in enforcing discipline of its members based on their particular moral or religious frameworks? This raises a fundamental question concerning the extent to which government in the iWorld will adjudicate the primacy of citizens as individuals. Will it allow the existence of private, voluntary associations whose members may wish to adhere to different standards? Charles Taylor provides an excellent examination of this dilemma in his book *Multiculturalism*.[11] While various societies may choose to approach this differently, it seems that if the iWorld is indeed the triumph of individualism then it stands to reason that ultimately the authority of each group to regulate itself will erode until only individuals and their individual rights and the three taboos remain.

11. See Charles Taylor et al., *Multiculturalism: Examining the Politics of Recognition*, ed. Amy Gutmann (Princeton, NJ: Princeton University Press, 1994).

Concluding Thoughts on the iWorld

In the book's introduction I stated that there are two questions of fundamental significance being asked by our society:

1. Ought adults be able to engage in any form of sexual relations so long as it is consensual?
2. Will we be denied the best of human fulfillment and intimacy if we are not allowed freedom to engage in consensual sexual relationships outside that of a marriage between a man and a woman?

The iWorld has clearly answered yes to each.

These questions are not new, nor are the sexual behaviors that we are discussing. There is a lot of sexual déjà vu in the history of the West. What is new, however, are the answers that we as a culture are giving to these questions. Since the sexual revolution, more and more people in the West are saying that to be fully human, to be fulfilled, to enjoy true relational depth and intimacy we ought to have the maximum freedom to do and be whatever we wish, and that this freedom allows for a consensual sexual relationship to extend beyond marriage between one man and one woman, to any relationship. So many people have come to embrace this set of beliefs that we now live in an age that would have been inconceivable even fifty years ago. The iWorld is upon us.

It is important to note that the transition from the tWorld to the iWorld has been one of the few truly peaceful revolutions in human history. It has not come about by the sword; to the contrary, it has happened because many people are persuaded that the iWorld offers a way of life superior to any that preceded it. While there are many points at which Christianity and other religions find themselves unable to endorse the iWorld, insofar as any religion supports human freedom it must acknowledge that the iWorld offers much that is good. Moreover, for those whom the tWorld trapped in toxic relationships, the iWorld provides a welcome release. The question is whether the iWorld offers the best response to these issues. It is a question we will have the opportunity to engage as a culture sooner than later.

Even though the point of departure for this book was the election of the Reverend Eugene Robinson as Episcopal bishop of New Hampshire and the legalization of same-sex marriage in Massachusetts, it should be clear by now that the driving issues of our day are not same-sex marriage or the ordination of practicing homosexuals. These are merely examples of life in a world in which the rules and regulations are being rewritten for everyone. Indeed, we now live in a world that is beyond what even Aldous Huxley envisioned in 1932 when he published *Brave New World*. We are only beginning to perceive where all this is leading, and we do not yet understand all its implications for human life. We do not even know if the personal freedom the iWorld promises is sustainable or if the attempt to deliver an unprecedented amount of individual freedom will lead to a breakdown of order such that a more Fascist or totalitarian political regime will arise to restore order.

More could be said about virtually every aspect of the iWorld: its hope, its promise, its challenges, and its insecurities. Whether the reader agrees with every aspect of this caricature, the iWorld's spirit of individual freedom animates the West at present. Regardless of whether we are sympathetic to that spirit, this is the world in which we now live, and we need to take account of it. Moreover, there is a reason we have come to this point: the decline and fall of the tWorld. The tWorld had its chance, yet for a variety of reasons, we live in the generation that rejected the tWorld and replaced it with something new. The iWorld represents the hopes and dreams of millions if not billions of people who see in it their best hope for freedom. The question before us is whether there is an alternative that more fully satisfies the longings of the human heart.

Considering the rWorld

I got a puzzle in my head
Spend a lifetime finding pieces
It will take forever to put together
the square and the round

Dada, "Puzzle"[1]

Given the swiftness with which the iWorld is emerging, one might ask if there is any reasonable or compelling alternative. I believe the answer to that question is yes, and the purpose of the second part of this book is to present that vision. The alternative proposed here is one I refer to as the "rWorld." Whereas the iWorld is a place in which freedom of the individual reigns, the rWorld is based on the belief that humans are made for relationship and that we find our deepest fulfillment not when seeking self-fulfillment but when living and engaging in the full constellation of healthy human relationships. After presenting

1. Dada, "Puzzle," *Puzzle* (Blue Cave Records, 1992).

this vision of the rWorld, the book's concluding chapter will compare and contrast the iWorld and rWorld, examining the merits of each.

The choice of the term "rWorld" to describe this position may strike the reader as curious and therefore warrants some explanation. Since I have already revealed that I am a Christian and a pastor, one might expect that I would call any proposed alternative the c(hristian)World. Or perhaps the reader might suppose that I'd call on society to return to the tWorld, since it was clearly influenced by Christianity.

So why suggest an alternative rather than just a return to the way things had been? The tWorld was based on the traditional, relational framework that grew up in the West out of a multiplicity of philosophical and religious traditions but that did not adequately encapsulate any one of them. Like anything that exists in the real world, it possessed an organic quality that reflected the influences that created it, but it didn't accurately reflect any of those individual influences. There is much about the tWorld that Greeks, Romans, Jews, Christians, and Muslims could support, yet there are aspects of the tWorld with which each would disagree. For instance, Greek philosophers would not have the same objections to homosexual behavior that Muslims do. Hence I am not advocating a return to the tWorld, because first, I don't fully agree with it, and second, at this point it would be impossible to resurrect it. It developed in a time and place that had a particular context, but the social and economic conditions that created and sustained it no longer exist.

So why not call it the cWorld instead of the rWorld? Since I am a Christian and since it is my belief that the rWorld is consistent with biblical thinking, it may strike the reader as natural for me to do so. I elected not to do so for four reasons. First, while I believe the rWorld is consistent with Christian faith, I do not presume to take on the burden of laying out *the* Christian position. My description of the rWorld will be too brief to even approach a fully defensible theology. In declining to adopt the term "cWorld," I am making it clear that I do not claim the mantle of the authoritative interpretation of the Christian faith. I'm a politics professor, not a biblical scholar.

Second, I do not believe you need to be a Christian, or even a person of faith, to find merit in the relational framework and societal benefit the rWorld can provide. As I indicated in the introduction, I freely use biblical references to construct and support the argument because doing so is the best way I know to explain the rWorld. Nevertheless, I believe there may be many who do not accept the authority of the Bible but are open to considering the rWorld as an intriguing alternative to the iWorld. If that sounds like you, I welcome you as a fellow traveler on this journey. Understanding the rWorld is like putting together a puzzle, and even as I describe my thoughts on how the pieces fit together, I do not consider mine to be the final word on the subject. I would encourage all who read this book, whether or not they are people of faith, to continue to consider for themselves how the rWorld might manifest itself in their own relational paradigm. Christians are not the only ones interested in relationships, and as is clear from history, neither do they have a monopoly on understanding relational health.

Third, I hope to provide a means of thinking about relationships that transcends the boundaries of any particular religion. If I propose an rWorld that aspires to be a better alternative to the world we know, then it must be so for all humans, not just those of a particular religious persuasion. There have been times in history when Christians controlled the culture and used power to dictate morality and enforce conformity in unjust ways and toward unjustifiable ends. Not only did this approach fail, but it also discredited those who engaged in it. Autocratic coercion is not an approach Christ embraced. He modeled relational living and taught that the greatest commandments are to love God and to love one another. Those faithful to Christ do not dictate but instead, like Christ, engage the world truthfully and with respect. When Christians have approached governing in a dictatorial fashion it has not served society or the faith well. If Christianity is a relational religion, then that should be reflected in its politics. If the rWorld is viable it will not be implemented by fiat, but everyone will be invited to participate in its creation; it will be advanced through conversation and formed by the consent of those who are persuaded.

Finally, we need to look forward, not backward. Because of the historical foundation of the Christian faith and its affiliation with the tWorld, it would be easy for readers to infer that embracing a relational framework consistent with the Bible will lead us back to the tWorld. I do not want to return to the tWorld, and this book does not recommend we try. The tWorld contained much that was good and that is consistent with my faith, but unfortunately it also contained many evils, including slavery, autocracy, sexual hypocrisy, relational dysfunction, and the legal subjection of women—all of which I earnestly hope never return. Instead I am arguing that in rediscovering the relational essence of Christianity and in seeking to live accordingly, society would actually be doing something that has never been done well. In short, I am asking you to be open to the possibility that what I am about to describe is something that has been often misunderstood and never fully lived.

Before we cast our gaze toward the rWorld, however, we must first have an imaginary conversation with Nietzsche, because if his critique of revealed religion is as decisive as millions have come to believe then there is no reason to explore the rWorld. If Nietzsche was right, even discussing it would be pointless. So before we go any further we must first discover if there is any plausible way to respond to Nietzsche's claim that God (and morality) is dead, because if not, we cannot find an objective answer to the question of whether there are moral boundaries beyond the three taboos.

5

Answering Why

Uno dos tres catorce!

Lights go down, it's dark
The jungle is your head
Can't rule your heart
A feeling is so much stronger than
A thought
Your eyes are wide
And though your soul
It can't be bought
Your mind can wander

Hello hello
I'm at a place called Vertigo
It's everything I wish I didn't know
Except you give me something I can feel, feel

The night is full of holes
As bullets rip the sky
Of ink with gold
They twinkle as the
Boys play rock and roll
They know they can't dance
At least they know. . . .

I can't stand the beats
I'm asking for the cheque
The girl with crimson nails
Has Jesus round her neck
Swinging to the music
Swinging to the music
Oh oh oh oh

Hello hello
I'm at a place called Vertigo
It's everything I wish I didn't know
But you give me something I can feel, feel

Check mated
Oh yeah
Hours of fun . . .

All of this, all of this can be yours
All of this, all of this can be yours

All of this, all of this can be yours
Just give me what I want and no-one gets hurt. . . .

Hello hello
We're at a place called Vertigo
Lights go down and all I know
Is that you give me something

I can feel your love teaching me how
Your love is teaching me how, how to kneel . . .

Yeah yeah yeah yeah

Bono with The Edge, "Vertigo"[1]

Nietzsche's Gauntlet

Nietzsche poses a profound challenge to Christianity as well as to every other philosophical or theological worldview. He argues that the "Why?"

1. Bono with The Edge, "Vertigo," *How to Dismantle an Atomic Bomb*, U2 (Island Records, 2004).

has no answer when it comes to morality. He asserts that if anyone questions a moral statement by asking, "Why is that true?" the person who attempts to defend the statement eventually will be compelled to say, "Because I feel it to be true," or "Because I believe it to be true." Nietzsche asserts that there is no intellectually definitive way to choose between competing moral claims rooted in desire or feeling. Consequently, theology and philosophy are unable to provide us with objective moral guidance because they cannot supply an objective answer to the "Why?" question. Given Nietzsche's belief that desire or feeling is the only way to differentiate between moral answers provided by various philosophers and religions, he would say they have nothing of value to tell us morally.

Nietzsche is not the first person to question the empirical case for moral truth,[2] yet he wrote at a time when the intellectual climate was open to seriously considering his position. As we have seen, philosophers during the Enlightenment adopted an epistemology that undermined the foundations of the tWorld, but the cultural impact of that epistemology took generations to be realized. Nietzsche asked the question, and he received enough attention from scholars that when they raised the same question with their students in the 1960s, the students responded with a collective "Why not?" It was as though the intellectual and cultural foundations of the tWorld were in such decay that when the students determined there was no answer to "Why?" they decided they were not going to live as if there were. Rather than accepting the framework in which the West had lived for millennia, students determined to create their own world—and thus came the sexual revolution and the iWorld.

Even though relatively few people have heard of Nietzsche, and fewer have read his works, he is a pivotal figure in the transition from the tWorld to the iWorld. Since the iWorld genuinely believes that "Why?" has no answer, it perceives that Christianity and every other moral philosophy and theology have been exposed as frauds and the concept of objective truth is of no moral importance. Philosophy and religion may have emotional or historical significance to individuals, but that

2. This is a discussion that has been ongoing since the dawn of the West. For an example, see Plato's *Republic*, bk. 1.

is where their relevance ends. The iWorld proclaims an ethic that allows everyone to be and do whatever they please so long as they do not violate the three taboos. While Nietzsche would question the authority of the three taboos, the iWorld ignores him at this point. The universe does not require philosophical or theological consistency to function; it merely requires that people live according to the same inconsistencies. The iWorld has effectively become the moral operating system of the early twenty-first century in the West.

Regardless of whether Nietzsche's argument is true, it has been persuasive. Society has embraced the iWorld, believing it has a more compelling understanding of human nature and fulfillment than any competing religious or philosophical system. Most believe it to be a worldview more in keeping with our nature and potential as a species, and on no issue is this more clear than that of human sexuality. While it does not specifically assert that sexuality is the primary avenue to maximize happiness, it consistently defends the ability of humans to engage in whatever consensual sexual relationships they choose, and based on the behavior of Western society, people have embraced this freedom as no other.

Bono, of U2, sings of the power of the iWorld's sexual creed in "Vertigo." He describes watching a band playing in a nightclub and being overwhelmed with the sensual nature of the experience. When he is ready to leave, the alluring beauty of a woman with red fingernails and a crucifix around her neck mesmerizes him. He faces the question of whether he ought to give in to the feelings that are encouraging him to take advantage of the moment and engage in a sexual liaison. Adding to the temptation is a voice that says, "All of this can be yours." What should he do and why? Decisions, decisions. The iWorld says, "If you want her and she wants you, say yes." The tWorld said no to casual sexual relations. Judaism, Christianity, Islam, and many moral philosophies would agree. Yet we live at a time when people are saying yes in remarkable numbers, including a growing number of people who identify with religions that tell them no.

What has changed? It is the moral question of our day. Since I cannot speak authoritatively for people guided by other religions or moral philosophies, let's use self-identified Christians as a case study. An increasing number of Christians are persuaded by Nietzsche's critique of moral reasoning. Having grown up in the iWorld and in an educational climate influenced by Nietzsche and other existential philosophers, many Christians have absorbed their way of thinking and are having increasing difficulty finding a compelling reason to say no. They may believe they should say no, they may say no, but increasingly they may not know why. They find it difficult to persuade others to say no, and they find it more and more difficult to deny themselves this pleasure. Why?

Intellectually the response of the church to Nietzsche and the iWorld has been ineffective. The problem is not that Christians are ignorant of orthodox Christian teaching on human sexuality but that Nietzsche, through the iWorld, has undermined their faith in the revelation on which the teaching is based, and clergy have offered the laity little help in dealing with Nietzsche's challenge. It is hardly surprising that the laity suspects that the reason their leaders don't give a compelling response is because there isn't one. There are Christian leaders who are telling their congregations to say no, but they are not explaining to their congregants why they should say no. Consequently, much of what has been written and spoken by Christian leaders attacking the decline of adherence to Judeo-Christian sexual morality has made no difference in changing behavior, public opinion, or public policy. In fact, what has been said is often so unpersuasive that it has damaged the credibility of Christianity. Many Christian leaders address the subject with rational arguments best suited for the tWorld, not the iWorld. When they sense they are not being heard, they increase the volume of their microphones but do not change the approach of their argument. Speaking the same words louder and more stridently is not an effective technique in persuasion.

It may be for this reason that other clergy don't even attempt to address the subject. Remaining silent, however, is hardly an effective response either. By saying little or nothing, it is as if many clergy are hoping that if they delay long enough, the iWorld and Nietzsche will just go away. Yet if they offer no credible response, it is not the iWorld and Nietzsche that will be going away. The absence of an effective rebuttal to the sexual ethic of the iWorld is responsible for the loss of confidence by Christians in the authority of Scripture and its teaching about human sexuality. Unless there is a credible response from those who claim to

lead them, nothing will change and the number of Christians who are
being absorbed into the iWorld will continue to increase.

What the world wants to know is whether this "Why?" has an answer.
Is there any transcendent basis for morality that we can discover, and if
so, how? Every response to the iWorld and Nietzsche must begin here or
risk being not only ignored but ridiculed. One of the problems with this
is that natural law arguments that many people of faith have used for
centuries to communicate their ideas to the broader culture no longer
have currency in the iWorld. "Natural law" refers to an approach to
ethics that can be traced from the stoic philosophers to Thomas Aqui-
nas to the present. It asserts, among other things, that morality can be
derived from the study of the natural world and the consideration of
an idealized human nature. To say that the iWorld is not persuaded by
natural law arguments is not to suggest that natural law is untrue, but
merely that the culture no longer finds it compelling. Using natural law
arguments in the iWorld is like trying to lecture on quantum physics
when the audience has lost faith in calculus. Without calculus, quantum
physics is incomprehensible. Without a belief in the possibility of moral
absolutes, natural law is incomprehensible.

A Reply to the "Why?" That Allegedly Has No Answer

So is there no credible response to Nietzsche? This is not merely a
question for Christians; it is a question for everyone. For example,
let's look at the question of whether or not humans have a soul. The
study of the soul is the quantum physics of humanity. Is there a credible response to such a question? Is there good reason to believe the
"Why?" has an answer? Speaking from within the Christian tradition,
the answer is still yes.

To respond effectively to Nietzsche's challenge requires that there
be a way to reaffirm the spiritual epistemology, the calculus, on which
Christian faith rests. Let's examine how this holds up. The primary
epistemological difference between Nietzsche and Christianity is that
Nietzsche accepted the modern scientific notion that everything is material and that humans are composed of nothing other than body and
mind. Christianity argues that there is a nonmaterial dimension to

humans called the "soul," and it is through this nonmaterial dimension that God communicates and relates with us. The fundamental question is whether we can make a plausible case that humans have a soul or even a spiritual dimension. If so, then the "Why?" can have an answer, because spirituality provides the possibility of connecting with an authoritative source of information outside of us, such as God.

Do humans have a spiritual dimension? What must be understood at the outset is that science cannot answer this question. Science can only evaluate material reality. If nonmaterial reality exists, the scientific method cannot detect it, and science, if it is intellectually honest, will remain agnostic on this point. Since science cannot resolve this question, we will have to answer it using an approach different from science—one that is open to the possibility of the existence of nonmaterial reality.

What argument is there for the existence of spirit and soul? Throughout history there have been many. Christianity, for one, teaches that humans are spiritual beings composed of body, mind, and soul. The body is the vehicle by which information is gathered through our five senses of sight, touch, taste, hearing, and smell. The Puritans articulated what Christians in general believe—that the soul is the spiritual faculty wherein our spirit resides and through which we are able to communicate with and receive communication from the spiritual world. The mind is the organ by which we gather all the information received by the body through the senses and the soul and then seek to make sense of it all. Right reasoning consists of integrating the insights that come from the body and the soul.

So if this is true, why is it not clear to everyone that we have a spiritual dimension? According to Christianity, pride complicates the task of reasoning and engaging spiritually with God. According to the book of Genesis, after Adam and Eve are expelled from the Garden of Eden, not only do they find themselves cut off from God, but they also find themselves strongly inclined to reason selfishly, without reference to God or to their soul and spirit. Insofar as their story is the story of the human race, it is here that we meet Nietzsche.[3]

Dismissive of the spiritual dimension of reasoning, and clearly in touch with subjective human reasoning, Nietzsche makes a compelling

---

3. In chapter 6 I will discuss at length the theology of the Garden of Eden.

critique of all existing moral systems. Rather than being threatened by his critique of reason, however, we can benefit from understanding and appreciating its honesty and depth. He argues that by using human reason alone there is no way to distinguish between moral claims. While the Bible does not support this conclusion, it provides an explanation for why Nietzsche and those who deny the existence of a spiritual dimension find it so compelling. In Genesis 3 Adam and Eve are warned not to eat of the fruit of the Tree of the Knowledge of Good and Evil, for if they do they shall become like God and know good and evil for themselves. Since they disobey, they are banished from the garden.

On the face of it, this seems to be a harsh punishment. One explanation for the prohibition of eating the fruit is to alert Adam and Eve that they are incapable of determining good and evil for themselves. Evidence for this is demonstrated by what follows after they are expelled from the Garden of Eden. Adam and Eve do not enter a world of their dreams based on their own conception of good and evil; instead they inherit a nightmare. Their son Cain kills his brother Abel, and the never-ending chaos of post-fall humanity is put in motion. Nietzsche, a keen observer of human history, looks at the entire post-fall record of humans and draws a reasonable conclusion: we are incapable of deciding good and evil for ourselves. As a race, we are lost, and if that is true then we must confront the fact that, like it or not, we live in a place beyond good and evil.[4] It is up to each of us to decide good and evil for ourselves, and we have no choice but to do so subjectively.

What Nietzsche does not allow is that men and women may have a soul and that as a result there would be a way for us to connect with a God who can spiritually inform us of all that is good and evil. Hence the question for Nietzsche and the iWorld is not "Why?" but "How?" How is it that humans can escape the merely subjective world of self and connect with that which is objective or transcendent? In this case, the answer is through the soul and spirit. Nietzsche makes a compelling case when he says that through mind and body we cannot escape the subjective, but his argument falls short in asserting that there is no possible way for humans to access truth. What Nietzsche, the iWorld,

4. Nietzsche, *Beyond Good and Evil*.

and a staggering number of Christians have lost sight of is the spiritual dimension of human existence.

Since the Enlightenment, the majority position has been that humans are creatures who are merely mind and body and whose only thoughts and emotions are those generated by the five senses. The elevation of natural science as the exclusive epistemology of modernity created the exclusivity of this perception. Since the scientific method can neither prove nor disprove the existence of nonmaterial reality, natural science can never access spiritually based information or understand how to account for its possible existence. Since the scientific method came to be seen as the only source of knowledge, the notion of the soul as a means of discernment and enlightenment was lost in the modern world. It was inevitable that someone as honest and perceptive as Nietzsche would blow the whistle on morality viewed through the lens of modern epistemology. When the application of empirical validation to moral philosophy was found to be impossible through the scientific method, it appeared to the modern world (which had grown increasingly doubtful of the existence of spirit and soul) that Nietzsche's nihilism and its rejection of the possibility of objective moral reasoning was the only rational conclusion. What is curious is that so many in the Christian community either forgot their own epistemology or started questioning it so deeply that, as if in a trance, they walked into the iWorld alongside Nietzsche. It is ironic that so many churches, in an effort to show themselves acceptably rational to the modern world, developed a sort of amnesia about the spiritual component of human existence—the very source of its existence and relevance.

Now it is important to be clear on what can and cannot be established. What we have established is that Nietzsche was wrong to dogmatically claim that the "Why?" has no answer. As we have seen, there is no way to make this claim with certainty because the "Why?" may at least have a spiritual answer. Yet we have not established with certainty that the "Why?" has an answer; we have merely established the possibility. So what is the answer? We will each have to decide for ourselves whether we have a soul and spirit and whether through these vessels God, discernment, and wisdom can be accessed and whether there is the possibility of any dimension of perception beyond the five senses we all acknowledge. Our personal answer will go a long way in determining the way we view the iWorld, the rWorld, or any other world.

A Christian response to Nietzsche's challenge is to seek to rediscover the spiritual calculus on which Christianity claims to be anchored. The Bible asserts that at the moment of conversion, the Holy Spirit enters us and re-establishes our spiritual connection with God. It is through this spiritual connection that our hearts testify to the truth of Christ (see Rom. 12:1–2). It is through this spiritual connection with God that our minds can once again be renewed and transformed. This conversion makes possible the recognition of moral truth since through the transforming work of the Spirit we are better able to keep our pride in check and look on the world not as we wish it were but as it truly is. Conversion does not completely remove the problem of pride, hence God provides us with multiple avenues to test the information we believe we have received through the Spirit. Among these avenues are the Scriptures, the community of faith (the church), the accumulated wisdom of the ages (tradition), and the knowledge available through all avenues of human learning. It is through all these working together that the Spirit of God can give us wisdom and moral instruction about how we should live. We are not left, as Woody Allen suggests, in a naked universe in which, in the absence of God, we have to take on the role of God and decide good and evil for ourselves.[5] Rather, we find ourselves in a universe in which we have a choice to continue to live as we are— as gods unto ourselves—or to (re)enter into a relationship with God wherein we take our instruction for life as revealed to us and in so doing discover that we live in a universe full of love, life, relationship, reason, and meaning. In short, Nietzsche's mistake in claiming authoritatively that the "Why?" has no answer is that he is unaware of or fails to acknowledge the possibility of truth being revealed to humanity through a spiritual dimension.

This Christian epistemology may appear novel, but it is certainly nothing new. It is merely a recovery of the historic Christian epistemology largely forgotten in modernity. It provides an answer that Christians have been seeking to the iWorld and provides a way to engage

---

5. *Crimes and Misdemeanors*, DVD, directed by Woody Allen, produced by Robert Greenhut (New York: Orion Pictures, 1989).

the iWorld in a dialogue about the meaning and purpose of life. This argument does not *prove* Christianity is correct or that we have a soul, but it gives reason to consider it.

Interestingly, it is this message that lies at the heart of U2's "Vertigo," for Bono says "no" in spite of being sorely tempted to surrender to the pleasures made available to him at the nightclub, even though he hears a voice reminiscent of Satan's temptation of Jesus in Matthew 4:9, "All of these I will give you, if you will fall down and worship me." "Vertigo" ends with Bono's repudiation of Satan by opting not for the love of the woman but for the love of God that is "teaching me how to kneel." The question facing all humanity is whether we will choose to please our senses in the name of love or kneel and reach out spiritually to relate to the God who is love.

The fundamental disagreement between Christianity and Nietzsche is epistemological. And while Christianity can't prove scientifically that humans have a soul and spirit, Nietzsche can't prove that we do not. This limitation in Nietzsche's framework has significance for everyone. It not only creates room that Christianity may inhabit, but it creates room for other religions and moral philosophies as well. What is significant is that the "Why?" may have an answer that is not discernable to the scientific method. Consequently, the issue of morality and the meaning of life is an open question. This confronts each of us with a question of faith: among all the options, which approach to understanding reality is most adequate?[6]

Having raised the question, the challenge is to find an answer. It is one thing to have created the intellectual space for the existence of spirit, soul, and God; it is another to determine if it is inhabited. This is a question for everyone. Let us first consider the rWorld by examining what the Bible says about the nature of human life and relationships. Then we can begin to determine if the rWorld can offer a compelling alternative to the iWorld's vision of life.

6. E. F. Schumacher expresses this in his chapters on *adequatio*. See E. F. Schumacher, *A Guide for the Perplexed* (New York: Harper and Row, 1977), 39–60.

6

The Nature of the rWorld

If God had a name, what would it be?
And would you call it to his face?
If you were faced with him in all his glory
What would you ask if you had just one question? . . .

What if God was one of us?
Just a slob like one of us
Just a stranger on the bus
Tryin' to make his way home?

If God had a face what would it look like?
And would you want to see, if seeing meant
That you would have to believe in things like heaven
And in Jesus and the saints and all the prophets? . . .

What if God was one of us?
Just a slob like one of us
Just a stranger on the bus
Tryin' to make his way home?

Eric Bazilian, "One of Us"[1]

If God is one of us, then we have a God with whom we can relate.
This is the meaning of the Christian doctrine of the incarnation: in

1. Eric Bazilian, "One of Us," recorded by Joan Osborne, *Relish* (Mercury Records, 1995).

the person of Jesus of Nazareth, God became human and lived among us. This claim is the very foundation on which the rWorld is based. When we think of the Bible or religious faith, we usually think first of rules and regulations, but to do so completely misses the very essence of the Bible. The Bible is effectively an rWorld textbook. It tells us the story of a relational God who has made men and women in his image for the purpose of relating. Cover to cover, Genesis to Revelation, the Bible is primarily about one thing: relationship. It is about the creation of relationship, the destruction of relationship, and the redemption of relationship. When taken as a whole, these concepts are antithetical to the iWorld. Whereas the iWorld focuses on self-fulfillment, the Bible teaches that self-fulfillment is an oxymoron, an impossibility, because it is a denial of our nature. We were created to relate to God and one another, and our personal fulfillment and happiness depend on the health of those two fundamental relationships. Indeed, it is only in these twin relationships that we can understand ourselves. Christianity is not about deciding who we want to be and what makes us happy; it is about learning who we are and how to find not just happiness but fulfillment, in relating to God and one another.

As the reader might infer, I am trying to make a point in a fairly blunt way. My reason for doing so is that this chapter enters "familiarity breeds contempt" territory. Most Americans, along with many others in the West, assume we understand the basic meaning of the Bible and the teachings of Christianity. Consequently, many are strongly tempted not to give these ideas much attention because "after all, we already know what it is going to say."

I've learned from experience that this is likely to happen because I see it every time I give a lecture on religion or preach a sermon. Eyes begin to glaze over, body language indicates withdrawal, and I can tell that the attention of students and parishioners begins to focus on other things:

"Why is he wearing those socks with those clothes?"
"Should I go to Florida or Cancun for spring break?"
"Does God hate the Cubs?"
"Boxers or briefs?"

"Did I turn the oven on?"

"Wow, there are thirteen cracks in the ceiling. I wonder if that's a sign?"

"She really is good looking."

"Why does the pastor say the same thing every week?"

"Did I turn the oven off?"

"Maybe there is such a thing as déjà vu."

"Is this going to be on the test?"

When the lecture is over students simply leave, whereas when the sermon is over parishioners feel compelled to first thank me for preaching such a "nice" sermon before they leave. Since on many Sundays the sermon presents a challenge, the use of the word "nice" is not a hopeful sign.[2]

However, the ideas presented here may be new to you. Until I read an obscure monograph published in England in the 1980s, I was unaware of any serious discussion concerning the relational nature of the Bible.[3] Yet it is not a new argument. It describes the daily experience of most people living in the lower-income world today. It describes the way most Jews and Christians understood life until the twentieth century. The reason so few in the United States and Europe are familiar with this argument is that it was discarded when individualism captured society's imagination. Beginning in the Enlightenment, the relational nature of the Bible began to be ignored in the West. Hence these ideas are not new but represent a way of thinking that modernity had discounted.

Many people still live in something akin to the tWorld, but the iWorld is increasingly reflected in the lives of people everywhere. Given the reach and influence of television and the Internet, this trend may well accelerate. I have two illustrations from my own life about the nature of the transition that is happening globally.

The first image comes from 1990 Berlin. I was attending a conference on the future of Germany shortly after the fall of the Berlin Wall and was having coffee by myself in an outdoor café in the former East

2. The people of Emmanuel Covenant Church of Nashua, NH, are the exception. Really.
3. Michael Schluter and Roy Clements, "Reactivating the Extended Family: From Biblical Norms to Public Policy in Britain," Jubilee Centre, paper no. 1, 1986.

Berlin. A very attractive young woman, a German university student who was also attending the conference, approached and asked if she could sit with me. I said "Sure," and after about fifteen minutes of conversation she asked me with extraordinary innocence, "Would you like to come back to my flat and have sex?" Not seeing this coming, the best response I could muster was, "Why?" to which she replied, "Because we can. Isn't that what this [the fall of the wall and freedom] all means?" I was so surprised, I didn't have the wit or decency to reply, so she said, "I'm not a prostitute; I'm not asking for money." I finally said, "Well, I am married." At that point she sighed and said, "Okay, but I don't see why that should matter." And the former East Berlin is far less innocent today than it was then.

The second image comes from 1994 in an extremely small subsistence-farming village in Costa Rica, about ten miles inland from the Pacific coast. It is a village that has no running water, no electricity, and an extraordinarily meager standard of living. I brought a group of college students to the village for three weeks of work and study. We lived with various families and enjoyed sixty-three straight meals of rice and beans. The town did not have electricity, but it did have a generator, and once a week the town fired up the generator and the people gathered around to watch *Beverly Hills 90210*. Having never seen the show, I was shocked with the iWorld message it was sending. It was more shocking to see and hear the kids of the village mimic the behavior and language of the show in the days that followed. Seeing Tori Spelling's character as an American role model for women gave me a form of reverse culture shock. Later in the trip two of the young men of the village approached me and asked innocently, "What's wrong with the girls you brought on the trip?" I replied, "Nothing as far as I know." "Then why don't they want to have sex? We thought all American women want to have sex." I could not think of any sensible response. Sometimes it's hard to know how to respond to the messages sent by iWorld.

The reach of the iWorld is not merely limited to the West; it is rapidly extending across the planet. This expansion is one of the primary sources of conflict between Islam and the West and between Islam and Christianity. Muslims often equate Christianity with the iWorld and therefore feel threatened by it. There are certainly differences between

Islam and Christianity, but at their core they both stand in opposition to the iWorld.

Given the rate that the planet is embracing the iWorld, can the rWorld stand as a workable alternative? I believe it can. One of the source texts for the rWorld is the Bible. If interpreting the Bible relationally is new to you, please give me a chance to explain. For those familiar with Christianity, this may require taking a fresh look at its very precepts. For those who aren't, hang in there and trust me on this for the moment. Allow me to use an approach employed by Martin Luther to try to get us all to take another look at the meaning of Christian faith. Unlike Luther, who presented *The Ninety-Five Theses* in 1517 for discussion about the meaning of Christianity, I just want to present one: *Christianity is essentially and fundamentally about relationships.*

Jesus makes this exact point when asked to explain what life is all about.

> When the Pharisees heard that he [Jesus] had silenced the Sadducees, they gathered together, and one of them, a lawyer, asked him a question to test him. "Teacher, which commandment in the law is the greatest?" He said to him, "'You shall love the Lord your God with all your heart, and with all your soul, and with all your mind.' This is the greatest and first commandment. And the second is like it: 'You shall love your neighbor as yourself.'" (Matt. 22:34–39)

Christianity is not a religion created by a persnickety God who plays "gotcha" with his creation by creating a maze of countless rules and regulations and then takes pleasure in punishing each and every misstep. Christianity is actually a dramatic love story between God and his creation. While biblical law plays an important role in the love story, it is a supporting role. Even the Ten Commandments are fundamentally about two things: how to love God and how to love one another. Every law in the entire Bible is about one or the other. Why? Men and women were created for the purpose of relating with God and one another. The health of our relationships is the central concern of the law. The story of the Bible is the story of God creating us for relationship, our breaking off that relationship, and God offering to redeem it.

So where's the evidence for this? Where should we begin? As the young man in Joni Mitchell's "Woodstock" says, "We've got to get ourselves back to the garden."

Created for Relationship

The first two chapters of Genesis describe the creation of the universe and the first human home in the Garden of Eden. They provide us with the fundamental meaning of the rWorld—an understanding of who God is, who we are, and how we are meant to live that is very different than the iWorld's. It is as much about *us* as it is about *me*. It tells us who God is, who we are, the meaning of gender, and the meaning of family, marriage, and human relationships.

A Relational God

Then God said, "Let us make humankind in our image, according to our likeness."

Genesis 1:26

Christianity teaches that the nature of God is relational. Note that I did not say it is God's nature to be relational (though I will); what I said is that the very nature of God is relational. The Bible reveals this in the first chapter of Genesis. As the above verse indicates, God possesses a relational nature. It does not say, "God made humankind in his image." It says, "God said, 'Let us make humankind in *our* image.'" This plural reference is rich in relational meaning. While the full picture of the Trinity is not contained here, the passage puts to rest the notion that God has an independent, solitary nature and that being made in the image of God gives us a solitary, independent nature. On the contrary, it tells us that if we are made in the image of God, we may be individuals but we are not complete when we are alone.

The New Testament builds on this in its description of the trinitarian nature of God as being Father, Son, and Holy Spirit. An example of this is seen in Jesus's prayer requesting that we would experience with God and one another the love and relational wholeness that he and the Father enjoy: "I ask not only on behalf of these, but also on behalf of those who will believe in me through their word, that they may all be one. As you, Father, are in me and I in you, may they also be in us" (John 17:20–21). The relational nature of God is found in Genesis, and Jesus reaffirms and expands its meaning in this prayer.

The importance of this to understanding the rWorld cannot be overstated. God did not create humans out of a sense of loneliness or because of his relational need. God is by nature a relational being. Relationships, therefore, are not a product of his creation; they are part of God's very nature. It is for this reason that the concept "God is love" makes sense. Since he is relational by nature, God *knows* love because God *lives* love in the Trinity.

What difference does this make to our self-understanding? If we are made in God's image then we are by nature relational, and by ourselves we are incomplete. "We" is a path to an inclusive wholeness, whereas "me" can all too often be an unfulfilling exercise in narcissism. We were made for fulfillment in something other than the iWorld.

Men and Women: Relational Beings Made in the Image of God

So God created humankind in his image, in the image of God he created them; male and female he created them.

Genesis 1:27

Until now this book has been reasonably noncontroversial. Despite the title and the expectation that the pressures of political correctness would have squashed me several chapters ago, up to this point I hope the book has been interesting and illuminating but relatively straightforward. Here, however, is where the fun begins, things get interesting, and the rWorld begins to take on a shape of its own. Let's talk about gender.

As this passage indicates, we bear the image of God not only in our relational nature but also in our sex, which is important to our understanding of self and to our relationships. In the iWorld gender is not regarded as relevant except for procreation. This verse gives us a sense of how differently Christianity views it. To begin with, Genesis 1:27 implies that our sex (male and female) is a reflection of the nature of God and not merely a distinction for the purpose of procreation. It suggests that our sex has a relational meaning independent of its sexual meaning. This verse tells us that what it means to be male and what it means to be female are different, and they each reflect the image of God in a unique manner. This means there is a second way in which we lack the ability to be whole in and of ourselves. Not only are we relational beings who cannot find wholeness without relating to God and one another, but we are also gendered beings, and we cannot be whole without relating with the other gender. Men and women require the other gender for relational wholeness.

As we have seen, the iWorld seeks to minimize the importance of gender for our lives and relationships. The Bible has a very different understanding of what it means to be human. It shows that our sex provides a depth and nuance to our lives that is of fundamental importance. We need relationships with both genders to be whole. Men need good relationships with men, women need good relationships with women, and men and women need good relationships with each other in order to be relationally whole. It is significant that the creation of gender comes prior to the existence of marriage and any biblical teaching about sexuality. It did not need to be this way. The Bible might have said, "God created human beings in his image, and he made them male and female so they could reproduce." But it doesn't.

Am I suggesting that "male" and "female" are categories that have significance beyond marriage, reproduction, and roles? Absolutely. Gender is an essential part of the biblical teaching on marriage and sexuality. It has to be. It is difficult to have children without the two genders being involved in procreation, and as we will see, the Bible teaches that marriage is a relationship between a man and a woman. I understand that gender matters to marriage and sexual relations, but for now I don't want to dwell on marriage and sexual relations. Why? First, because up to this point Genesis doesn't mention it, and second, there is a depth and richness inherent in the nature of gender that we can easily miss if we are in a hurry to talk about sexual relations and marriage. Understanding the meaning of gender beyond sexual relations is essential in grasping its full importance. The passage from Genesis tells us that our given sex reflects the nature of God, and since we do not regard God to be a sexual being, it is a more than reasonable proposition to infer that when we are created male and female, the distinction goes deeper than the biology and psychology.

Does saying this make me a sexist? If what it means to be a sexist is saying that gender matters, then I am guilty as charged. When it comes to categorizing gender characterizations, there tends to be a great divide, so it's natural and understandable for readers to try to determine where I stand. Do I side with Steven Pinker, the author of *The Blank Slate*, who argues that gender is one aspect of our humanity that is inherent in our nature, or do I side with Rosalind Barnett and Caryl Rivers, the authors of *Same Difference*, who argue there is no innate difference between the genders other than relatively minor differences associated with reproduction and the related hormonal implications? This same divide also exists in theological circles, so readers may wonder if I side with the Christians for Biblical Equality, which supports an essential equality between the genders in matters of Christian ministry and life, or if I side with the Council on Biblical Manhood and Womanhood and those who believe the Bible teaches that men and women have very distinct roles in ministry, marriage, and life. There certainly are a lot of hotly contested viewpoints from which to choose. So, with whom do I stand?

Actually, I'm not going to take a side. Why? Because I believe that each side is missing the primary point of this biblical text and that if I take a side it is likely no one will hear the most important point I'm trying to make, namely that there is a spiritual dimension to gender that the social scientists have understandably missed and theologians shouldn't have missed but did, perhaps because they allowed the social scientists to define the theological debate.

Here is my point:

> *Regardless of whether I know how to resolve the psychobiological debate or the theological variation of it, I don't need to resolve it to know that the biblical text tells us that aside from the biological, genetic, and psychological dimensions, gender also has a spiritual dimension. Hence men and women are not the same nor were they designed to be the same. Rather, they are equal in the fact that they each bear the image of God, and they complement each other in the sense that we need each other to be whole. Period. Full stop.*

Gender matters. No matter what scientists determine about the psychobiological aspects to gender, it does not alter the fact that there is a spiritual dimension to gender. Moreover, theologians would be well served to take note of this and not allow theological debates to become mirror images of the metaphorical brawl in which biologists, geneticists, and psychologists are engaged.

What do I mean by "spiritual dimension"? I mean that if we are made in the image of God, that image extends not merely to our body but also to our soul. Barnett and Rivers acknowledge that men and women are different in terms of reproductive capacity. Hence, even if they are correct about the psychobiological similarities between the genders, in their capacity as social scientists they are not in a position to speak about the spiritual meaning of gender. If we are beings with a spiritual dimension, it would be extremely surprising if gender didn't have a spiritual dimension as well.

In the section that follows, we will examine how understanding the existence of the spiritual aspect to gender helps make the Bible more comprehensible in its teaching about marriage. For example, it gives us a better understanding of Christ's statement that in heaven there will be no marriage (see Matt. 22:30; Mark 12:25). While I am open to other interpretations, I think it is reasonable to infer from this that there will be no sexual relations in heaven. That does not mean, however, there will be no gender in heaven; there will almost certainly be gender in heaven. Why wouldn't there be? As Genesis 1 makes clear, gender is a foundational, creational, human category reflective of the nature of God in us that exists prior to and independent of marriage and sexuality. If we can't see the foundational importance of gender, independent of marriage and sexual relations, then it merely reflects how little we understand and appreciate it. There is a difference on the spiritual level when a man and woman relate to each other compared to when people of the same gender relate to each other. In order to see it we need to look past surface appearance as well as our sexual impulses and gaze deeply into the souls of others to learn what relating to one another truly means both within and between genders. I believe we will find there is much we have missed.

I am of the opinion that there are few people who understand this, and there are almost no examples in contemporary music of anyone who attempts to describe the spiritual dimension of gender. One who does so brilliantly is Bono of U2. There is little question that the following lyrics are from a love song between a man and a woman. Yet this is a song of which the iWorld cannot fully make sense because that requires the acknowledgment that gender matters. To neuter the song would miss the point. To understand it, however, as merely a hetero-sexual love song would miss the point as well. This song describes the dimensions of a relationship between a man and a woman that goes deeper than romance. It plumbs the depths of the spiritual mystery of gender we are seeking to uncover.

> Little sister don't you worry about a thing today
> Take the heat from the sun
> Little sister
> I know that everything is not ok
> But you're like honey on my tongue
>
> True love never can be rent
> But only true love can keep beauty innocent
>
> I could never take a chance
> Of losing love to find romance
> In the mysterious distance
> Between a man and a woman
> No I could never take a chance
> 'Cos I could never understand
> The mysterious distance
> Between a man and a woman
>
> You can run from love
> And if it's really love it will find you
> Catch you by the heel
> But you can't be numb for love
> The only pain is to feel nothing at all
> How can I hurt when I'm holding you?
>
> I could never take a chance
> Of losing love to find romance

In the mysterious distance
Between a man and a woman

And you're the one, there's no one else
You make me want to lose myself
In the mysterious distance
Between a man and a woman

Bono, U2, "A Man and a Woman"[4]

The iWorld is missing out on the distinctiveness of gender. The rWorld, if it is to succeed, needs to take great care to recover it, and should it do so, it will find that many of the differences between the iWorld and the rWorld are rooted in different understandings of gender. To misunderstand gender is to misunderstand humanity, our relationships, and ourselves. Family and marriage is a very useful case in point.

Family and Marriage

Then the Lord God said, "It is not good that the man should be alone: I will make him a helper as his partner" . . . Therefore a man leaves his father and his mother and clings to his wife, and they become one flesh. And the man and his wife were both naked and not ashamed.

Genesis 2:18, 24–25

Honor your father and mother that you may have a long life in the land which the Lord, your God, is giving you.

Exodus 20:12

I have already said that God designed us for relationship. In addition to creating us with a soul and spirit with which we can relate to God, we were created in the image of God, male and female, and thus were created for relating to each other. I do not mean to imply that we lack significance as individuals. Each of us is a unique creation of God deserving of recognition, love, and dignity. What I do wish to say is that we are not made to be alone; we are made for relationship. When we look at the first two chapters of Genesis, we find that God pronounces

4. Bono, "A Man and a Woman," *How to Dismantle an Atomic Bomb*, U2 (Island Records, 2004).

everything that he made as good, with one exception. In Genesis 2:18 he states explicitly, "It is not good that the man should be alone." Men and women can flourish only when we are in relationship with one another and the Creator. The relational order of creation provides us with everything we need for relational fulfillment. The cornerstone of the relational order is the family, and the relationship designated to create families is a marriage between a man and a woman. While the first Scripture passage quoted above speaks directly to marriage, the second speaks, as does the rest of the Bible, to the fundamental importance of family.

Family is an inescapable part of being human. The iWorld, in effect, deconstructs family in favor of individualism and self-fulfillment. It is fascinating, however, that when you put the rhetoric of the iWorld aside and look at behavior, the citizens of the iWorld are not abandoning family. They may redefine it, but they do not want to lose it. In the absence of the traditional family, citizens of the iWorld have bequeathed the name "family" to a wide variety of other relationships. In the iWorld we call two people who are cohabiting a family. We even find single people with a pet calling themselves a family. We find ourselves anointing any reasonably intimate social group with the title "family." Christians often refer to their local church as a family.

Make no mistake: Family matters.

Marriage matters too.

While the iWorld also deconstructs marriage, it still matters. It matters enough to significant segments of the same-sex communities that each seeks to gain the right to marry rather than merely coexist in legal unions. For that matter, those people who endure bad marriages usually want to try again to find a partner with whom long-term commitment can work. Even if two people in a long-term romantic relationship don't marry, they usually develop a reasonable facsimile of a marriage. People want to be in a committed, intimate, nurturing, enduring relationship with another human, and they yearn for it even if they don't ever marry.

Family and marriage matter not because they are social constructions but because they are part of our nature as strongly as are the image of God and gender. Even as the iWorld seeks to free us from every relational commitment, citizens of the iWorld still live as if family and marriage matter. So which—marriage or family, if either—has priority in the rWorld?

Presently the clear answer to this question from most Christian and non-Christian voices is that marriage has priority. People continually emphasize the importance of having strong marriages or committed relationships, and if they have to choose, having a good marriage or its facsimile takes precedence over having a good family. One reason for the priority of marriage is that people believe that the foundation of a good family is a good marriage. But more than that, it is perceived that one of the key elements in human happiness is being in a committed relationship like a marriage. The common perception is that if you want to be whole, you need to be in a committed relationship, and if you are not, you cannot be fully whole. Family is important, but marriage, or a reasonable facsimile, is even more important. This argument concerning the primacy of marriage to human fulfillment has persuasive validity in the culture at large and in the Christian church.

But our culture and the Christian church, insofar as they perceive that marriage is more important than family, are misguided. In the rWorld family has priority. Marriage matters, but family matters more. Biblically, the family is the primary building block of human relational fulfillment, and marriage exists in service of the family. In a world that places such high hopes for relational fulfillment on marriage, any attempt to return marriage to its proper place in service of the family may have the appearance of devaluing its importance. The rWorld values marriage for its intrinsic worth and for its value to the family, but family plays an even more important role in human relational fulfillment. By family, the rWorld is not referring to the nuclear family, as so many evangelical Christians tend to emphasize, but to the three-generation family (3GF—grandparents, parents, children), as well as the extended family.

Genesis 2:18–24 describes both the first marriage and the creation of the first human family. In Adam and Eve's case, but only in their case, marriage had to come first to create the family. But thanks to the family their marriage established, in every subsequent marriage family comes prior to marriage. In verse 24, for instance, the two people marrying come from families (they are leaving their father and mother), as has every married couple ever since.

The reason family has relational priority over marriage is that all of us are born into a family but not all will marry. Being single is not a death sentence or a sign that one is odd. The Old Testament teaches that all humans will be connected to their families of birth unless they marry, and marriage means that the wife leaves her family and is grafted by marriage into her husband's family. If you never marry, you will remain intimately connected to your family of birth for life. Marriage is not a couple's passage out of family. The family ties remain even as new members are brought into it. In the rWorld marriage is an exceedingly important, special, and unique relationship into which most humans will enter, yet it exists in service to the family the couple creates, the extended family from which they come, and the 3GF to which they belong.

This is the meaning of family and marriage described in great detail in the first five books of the Old Testament (the Pentateuch). It is misguided to read the primacy of the nuclear family or legitimization of individualism of the iWorld into the relational teaching of the Bible. In contrast to our society's emphasis on the rights of individuals and nuclear families, the Pentateuch established the 3GF as the primary relational and legal unit of society. It was not a society founded on individual rights or the legal status of the nuclear family; the basic, irreducible legal family unit was the 3GF. Everyone ultimately derived their legal and social identity from their 3GF. Moreover, the 3GF was not an isolated relational unit; the social structure of the Old Testament provided humans with a rich web of interconnected relationships. Members of a 3GF lived in close proximity with their extended family (composed of other 3GFs), their extended families to their clan, their clan to their tribe, and their tribe to the nation.

Extended families lived on adjoining plots of land and shared the various tasks of life: farming, cooking, education, and child rearing. They were legally required to care for one another in the event of death, crime, or poverty. Israel was structured in such a way that everyone existed in an extraordinarily supportive relational matrix, with the 3GF as the center of it all. The 3GF and the extended family did not constitute the only source of relationships for men and women, but it was the center of relational life for everyone. Family was the foundation of human life, and marriage served the family. Whether a person married made little difference in the quality of his or her life because everyone had a place to belong. Everyone had a constellation of relationships in which they found a variety of depth, meaning, and intimacy. Everyone was involved in the care of children, the care of the elderly, and the sick. And everyone was involved in caring for one another. This structure possessed a degree of relational connectedness that is missing from the iWorld.[5]

It is important to note that even though this Old Testament framework contains nowhere near the amount of personal space of the iWorld and does not provide the same amount of individual freedom, it does not ignore the individual. It merely asserts that an individual can best come to understand who he or she is and live the most fulfilling life possible within this framework.

So What Does the Old Testament Have to Do with the rWorld?

Given that this entire chapter introducing the rWorld has been rooted in the Old Testament, it would be easy to draw the erroneous conclusion that the rWorld is simply a twenty-first-century application of the Old Testament social structure. It would also be easy to make the inference, equally untrue, that the tWorld and the rWorld are basically the same. Since the Old Testament forms an important foundation for both the tWorld and the rWorld, there are similarities between them. The relational matrix of both the tWorld and the rWorld is rooted in family and friendship. In addition, both worlds share the belief that our individual happiness and fulfillment are connected to finding relational contentment. But they also differ profoundly. For many the tWorld had an aristocratic, autocratic, and patriarchal quality that was relationally oppressive and degrading to many, especially women. Keeping people in their designated role and station was more important than crossing class, economic, and gender lines for the sake of enjoying the relational gifts people of other classes, races, and genders have to offer. As we will see, love, equality, and mutual respect are central components of relational health in the rWorld and possess an importance often missed in the tWorld. The similarities between the tWorld and the rWorld can

5. Michael Schluter and David Lee, *The R Factor* (London: Hodder and Stoughton, 1993).

primarily be seen in form and structure, with the 3GF framework of family and marriage being a good example.

Hence a full understanding of the Christian conception of the rWorld is based on both Testaments. The Old Testament provides us with a large part of the relational matrix (marriage and family), whereas, thanks to Pentecost, the New Testament provides us with the ability to access love and integrate it into our lives and relationships and gives us a new relational community—the church (see the discussion in chapter 7).

So what will it take to create the rWorld? Many things, but more than anything else it will take love. The rWorld is merely a framework, a noble idea, unless it is fueled by a love so potent that it can bring humans together with God and kindle a profound intimacy between us. Love, which by definition is a relational word because it requires relationship for its very existence, invites us to live in the rWorld. So what is this love? It's time to explore that question.

7

From Hole Hearted to Whole Hearted

A Love Story

Life's ambition occupies my time
Priorities confuse the mind
Happiness one step behind
This inner peace I've yet to find
Rivers flow into the sea
Yet even the sea is not so full of me
If I'm not blind why can't I see
That a circle can't fit
Where a square should be

There's a hole in my heart
That can only be filled by you
And this hole in my heart
Can't be filled with the things I do
Hole hearted
Hole hearted

This heart of stone is where I hide
These feet of clay kept warm inside
Day by day less satisfied
Not fade away before I die

Rivers flow into the sea
Yet even the sea is not so full of me
If I'm not blind why can't I see
That a circle can't fit
Where a square should be

There's a hole in my heart
That can only be filled by you
And this hole in my heart
Can't be filled with the things I do
There's a hole in my heart
That can only be filled by you
Should have known from the start
I'd fall short with the things I do
Hole hearted
Hole hearted
Hole hearted
Hole hearted

Extreme, "Hole Hearted"[1]

Almost everyone is attracted to a good love story. The movie *The Princess Bride* illustrates that even a reluctant young boy can't resist the right love story told well. Probably the last thing you expected when you picked up this book was that there would be a love story buried in the middle. Yet if the rWorld is about relationships, we might be suspicious if it didn't contain something akin to a love story.

This chapter provides an explanation of the rWorld as a Christian might view it, although the rWorld is not the exclusive domain of Christians or people of any particular faith. Building on the relational framework presented in the previous chapter, we now look at a love story that spans both the Old and New Testaments. Were I a poet I would write about this love story in verse and title it "The Love Song from the End of Time." It is a song that transcends time and meets us in every age. Since I am aesthetically challenged, however, there is virtually nothing poetic or artistic about my rendition.

1. Extreme, "Hole Hearted," *Pornograffitti* (A&M, 1990).

We were introduced to this love story in chapter 6. The Bible explains that God made humanity in his image; he created the world so that everyone can enjoy a relationship of love with him and with one another. In the story of the Garden of Eden he invites Adam and Eve and their descendants into this relationship. Unfortunately, Adam and Eve reject God's invitation, are escorted out of the garden, and experience relational dislocation in a manner that impacts us all. It is the story of how we came to have a hole in our hearts and dysfunction in our relationships. Our question is how God can fill the hole and make us relationally whole once again.[2]

Part 1: The Lost Opportunity

And the man and his wife were both naked, and were not ashamed.

Genesis 2:25

The fall depicted in Genesis 3 is the story of broken relationship with God and its impact on all our other relationships. To appreciate what we lost in the fall, we need to understand what kind of relationship Adam and Eve enjoyed with God and each other in the garden and what it meant for Adam and Eve to be naked and unashamed with God and each other.

As we have seen, the first two chapters of Genesis provide a basic understanding of our nature, and in particular our relational nature. It tells that we are made in the image of God, male and female, for relationship with God and each other. Adam and Eve, like all of us, were designed by God but were not made to be equals with God. Since we did not create our nature, our personal and relational health, as well as the development of a healthy personal identity, depends on living in accordance with and respecting the parameters of our nature.

When we live in contradiction to our nature, we put our relationships and essential aspects of our identity at risk. God made us as relational beings, and he constructed a relational network within which we can

2. What follows is a mere summary of the Christian story. A terrific explanation of the rWorld from a Catholic perspective can be found in Pope John Paul II, *The Theology of the Body: Human Love in the Divine Plan* (Boston: Pauline Books and Media, 1997).

flourish. This relational network exists not merely to keep us occupied but is a place for each of us to belong, to live, to love, and to be loved from the day we are born until the day we die. Indeed, we are part of a network that encompasses the entire human race. Understanding our relational nature helps us comprehend who we are meant to be. Deep down we yearn to know others and ourselves.

So what does this look like relationally? Genesis provides a profound glimpse into what relationships are intended to be. As the story begins, we find Adam and Eve living naked and unashamed. It is one of the most evocative pictures of intimacy imaginable, and it goes to the very core of the meaning of innocence. Adam and Eve could be absolutely transparent with each other—no secrets, no lies, no shame—and they could give each other access to their entire being. They were surely sexually engaged with each other, but they enjoyed an intimacy deeper than sex. They knew each other deeply and did not know shame, because they lived truthfully and could trust each other fully. They knew the love of God, and since they knew it in the deepest part of their being, they could literally live naked and unashamed.

Now, it would have been really convenient if the author of Genesis had given us more information about life in Eden before the fall. We know Adam, Eve, and God dwelt in Eden, but we do not know the length of their innocence. For a time the man and woman enjoyed the most profound love relationship with each other and God. Yet love is not love unless it is freely given; hence true love requires the possibility of it being rejected. In loving God, Adam and Eve also had the freedom to reject him. So for a time, we know not how long, they were lovers of God and each other. But then they rejected God and found themselves in need of cover and another garden.

Part 2: Spurning Love

> Now the serpent was more crafty than any other wild animal that the Lord God had made. He said to the woman, "Did God say, 'You shall not eat from any tree in the garden'?" The woman said to the serpent, "We may eat of the fruit of the trees in the garden; but God said, 'You shall not eat of the fruit of the tree that is in the middle of the garden, nor shall you touch it, or you shall die.'" But the serpent said to the woman,

"You will not die; for God knows that when you eat of it your eyes will be opened, and you will be like God, knowing good and evil."

So when the woman saw that the tree was good for food, and that it was a delight to the eyes, and that the tree was to be desired to make one wise, she took of its fruit and ate; and she also gave some to her husband, who was with her, and he ate. Then the eyes of both were opened, and they knew that they were naked; and they sewed fig leaves together and made loincloths for themselves. They heard the sound of the Lord God walking in the garden at the time of the evening breeze, and the man and his wife hid themselves from the presence of the Lord God among the trees of the garden.

But the Lord God called to the man, and said to him, "Where are you?" He said, "I heard the sound of you in the garden, and I was afraid, because I was naked; and I hid myself."

He said, "Who told you that you were naked? Have you eaten from the tree of which I commanded you not to eat?" The man said, "The woman whom you gave to be with me, she gave me fruit from the tree, and I ate." Then the Lord God said to the woman, "What is this that you have done?" The woman said, "The serpent tricked me, and I ate."

The Lord God said to the serpent, "Because you have done this, cursed are you among all animals and among all wild creatures; upon your belly you shall go, and dust you shall eat all the days of your life. I will put enmity between you and the woman, and between your offspring and hers; he will strike your head, and you will strike his heel."

To the woman he said, "I will greatly increase your pangs in child-bearing; in pain you shall bring forth children, yet your desire shall be for your husband, and he shall rule over you."

And to the man he said, "Because you have listened to the voice of your wife, and have eaten of the tree about which I commanded you, 'You shall not eat of it,' cursed is the ground because of you; in toil you shall eat of it all the days of your life; thorns and thistles it shall bring forth for you; and you shall eat the plants of the field. By the sweat of your face you shall eat bread until you return to the ground, for out of it you were taken; you are dust, and to dust you shall return."

Genesis 3:1–19

Genesis 3 is the story of "the fall." Adam and Eve had the opportunity to stay in a love relationship with God and to pass along this gift to their children. But when they rejected God, they chose a different life for all their descendents, right up to the present day.

As we discussed in chapter 5, the issue was not the breaking of a little rule that caused God to overreact. Eating fruit from the Tree of the Knowledge of Good and Evil was the ultimate act of adultery. In doing so Adam and Eve decided to act as God unto themselves, and in so doing they ruptured their relationship with the Almighty and ultimately with each other. Not only did this lead to the loss of their moral compass; it led to the loss of their true identity because when they severed their love relationship with God, they also severed their ability to truly and fully know each other. The effects of their loss are seen immediately. Instantly they became ashamed and felt compelled to clothe themselves, and in so doing they began hiding from God and each other because they lost trust.

The loss of intimacy portrayed in this picture is heartbreaking. Immediately the quality of their relationship with each other became thin and unsatisfying. As soon as they lost touch with their true identity, their behavior became increasingly distorted. What's worse is that they passed this along to their children, which is demonstrated when their son Cain, in a fit of jealousy, murders his brother Abel.

This is not merely the story of Adam and Eve and their family; it has become our story—the story of the human race. There is something about this part of the story that strikes the sensibilities of the iWorld as fundamentally unfair. The fall means that not only are Adam and Eve exiled from Eden, but all of us along with them. To a world that believes so stridently in individual freedom, that anyone should bear the consequences of the choices of others seems patently unjust. It violates the three taboos. We hope that a decent God would at least honor the three taboos. The problem is that this is not the outcome God desired.

God created Eden for us all, yet we now inhabit the place east of Eden to which Adam and Eve were expelled. The sins of the parents are indeed visited on the children (see Exod. 34:7). If we are created to be in a love relationship with God, losing the capacity to relate intimately with God has devastating consequences. When Adam and Eve ceased to feel the love of God, they lost touch with their full identity and began to behave in an inhumane manner not befitting a human created in the image of God. This confusion and the accompanying emotional consequences are what they passed along to their children, and ultimately to us. All of us are born to parents who bear the scars of living in families and a world that has lost touch with the love of God and the knowledge of who we truly are by nature. As a result we are reared in self-misunderstanding and, in even the best circumstances, we do not experience the love for which we yearn. We become acquainted with sorrow and frustration, and we transmit the same to our generation, the next, and so on.

We may wish the universe was not this fragile, but if we understand relationships, we know they are fragile; they must be nurtured and constantly tended. When they are, they are a thing of surpassing beauty and great good, but when they are not, they and the love that goes with them become diseased and wither. Such relationships are unfulfilling and leave us with a hole in our hearts. It is of this longing that Extreme's Gary Cherone sings so passionately in the song "Hole Hearted."

Without being connected to the love God has for us, we cannot properly love others, we cannot be who we were created to be, and we become other than who we are meant to be. Our life becomes the quest to fill the hole in our heart. We often try to fill it by allowing our appetites to guide us. We gorge ourselves with food, sex, alcohol, and drugs, but none provide more than fleeting gratification. We also try to fill the hole with work and the accumulation of things, but that doesn't work either. We grow bored and unfulfilled with each of these because none of them can satisfy our deepest longings. We have a sense that there ought to be more, but we cannot seem to find it no matter what we try. The longer this persists, the deeper the frustration that builds within us, and if this frustration is unchecked, it can become increasingly aggressive or even violent. The tragic irony is that we often vent our frustration on those closest to us. Domestic violence is a consequence of the fall, and it is not limited to our spouse and children.

While it is difficult to say that anything in the area of Christian theology is self-evident, the story of the fall is about as close as it comes. Every human we meet is scarred by relational hurts and frustrations. Moreover, our problems may change but they never seem to go away. The dissonance and alienation that shapes our relationships never dissipates. The persistent sense that we were created for love is deeply ingrained into our nature. Yet by ourselves we can never seem to find a way to fill the hole in our hearts or cure the poverty of intimacy with which we live. By ourselves we can't find our way out of the hole.

Everything about the way we live testifies to the fact that humans by nature are created for relationship, but we can't seem to do it with God or other people. The fact is, in a fallen world all human relationships are against the odds. Yet despite the obstacles, hurt, and frustration, we keep looking. Why? We just can't keep ourselves from hoping. We may be exhausted and discouraged, but a good love story told well still touches us to our core, unless we have become so cynical we recoil. We may profess that we have given up on the human race or God, but such an attitude is merely a defense mechanism we employ until we find a relationship that seems worth pursuing. In moments of hurt, we may declare that we have shut our eyes once and for all to future relationships, but we keep at least one blind eye open in hope that love will find us, even if we can't find love. As frustrating as human relations are, we cannot live without them. We are not self-sufficient. We need other people and they need us. Even Enlightenment liberal Thomas Paine acknowledges this in his book *Common Sense*.[3] We cannot survive or thrive without one another.

So why would a loving God create humans with the capacity to fall in the Garden of Eden, and why would the consequence of the fall be so disastrous? There is an answer: In creating us with the capacity to choose relationship with him (free will), he also gave us the capacity to choose not to relate to him. It should not be surprising that the consequences for electing not to do so would be devastating—one cannot turn the universe on its head and expect all to be well. After all, it's not as though Adam and Eve weren't warned.

While such an explanation answers the question, it does not change the fact that the consequences of Adam and Eve's decision are devastating. Our lives, at worst, take on the quality of a nightmare. As Mick Jagger sings, humans can find nothing on this earth that by itself will bring them satisfaction.[4]

We have lost touch with our true nature and have been deceived by our fallen nature. We seek to develop an identity without understanding the bigger picture; as a result we cannot find anything to satisfy the craving of our heart for true intimacy and love. Our attempts to do so often

3. Thomas Paine, *Common Sense* (London: Penguin Books, 1986), 66.
4. Mick Jagger and Keith Richards, "(I Can't Get No) Satisfaction," *Out of Our Heads*, Rolling Stones (Decca, 1965).

create conflict, alienation, and even war. What's worse, by ourselves we cannot find our way home. No matter what we try sexually, relationally, or chemically, nothing satisfies us. Indeed, the more we depend on these, the less return they provide. The tragedy of the fall is that we get nothing for which we hoped and lose all that we wanted. Instead of freedom, we become enslaved to our senses and impulses and quite literally try to find love in all the wrong places. We live in a world that is reeling from the fallout of pride's triumph. Romans 1 and 7 contain apt descriptions of life after the fall: We don't do the good we know to do and we find ourselves doing the evil we do not want to do. We love what we should not and hide from that which can save us. Like Paul, we cry out, "Who will rescue me from this body of death?" (Rom. 7:24). Thankfully, there is a love song being sung to us.

Part 3: The Invitation

> For God so loved the world that he gave his only Son, so that everyone who believes in him may not perish but may have eternal life. Indeed, God did not send the Son to condemn the world, but in order that the world might be saved through him.
>
> John 3:16–17

> Beloved, let us love one another, because love is from God; everyone who loves is born of God and knows God. Whoever does not love does not know God, for God is love. God's love was revealed among us in this way: God sent his only Son into the world so that we might live through him. In this is love, not that we loved God but that he loved us and sent his Son to be the atoning sacrifice for our sins.
>
> 1 John 4:7–10

If the Christian story has seemed mythological or fanciful up until now, this is where it moves straight out to the edge of believability, which is why living it requires faith. While few people believe in the existence of an actual place called hell, it is easy to imagine. For example, some of us are able to afford a standard of living that provides the means by which we can try to ignore reality. Yet the truth is that for everyone, including the intentionally ignorant, life falls far short of what we want it to be. The longer we live, the more hurt and disappointment we endure, the more we become aware of our own mortality, the more difficult it is to believe that love, let alone heaven, really exists. Yet as unbelievable as it may seem, this particular love story has a happy ending.

Even though Adam and Eve abandoned God and the rest of us were born in this state of abandonment, and even though we have made a pig's breakfast of the world, God has never stopped loving us. His ongoing, unrequited love makes this the most amazing of all love stories. We're talking about God here. The Almighty. The one who is so holy that we are not worthy to utter his name and cannot stand in his presence without perishing. We're talking about a being with the power to ignore or even destroy our corner of the universe, treating us as a failed experiment. Yet God still loves us.

Why? Because he has chosen to. Since it is in God's nature to love, when he made us in his image there was no possibility that he would stop loving us. It is an absolutely arresting truth. There are days when living in this world becomes so bizarre we cannot help but wonder, "If God loves me, he has a really strange way of showing it!" Such a statement may at times feel justified, but it shows a lack of understanding on our part of the consequences of Adam and Eve's decision, to say nothing of our own choices. Yet even though God is not to blame for our situation and the corruption that surrounds us, God wants us back.

So how does God invite us back into relationship? He delivers the invitation in the only way we can fully comprehend it—by literally bringing it in person. God the Son, Jesus Christ, comes to earth, is born to Mary and Joseph, lives a fully human life, and proves his love for us by submitting himself to crucifixion meted out on our behalf. And when he rises from the dead on Easter, he conquers death, making it once again possible for us to live with him forever.

So why did it have to be this way? Two reasons: First, there are consequences to our actions. It is hard to have a relationship with God if we cannot even live with one another. Having rejected God and profaned ourselves, we cannot live in the direct presence of God as Adam and Eve did in the Garden of Eden. Second, we have to have faith that God can do this, and exercising such faith is no small task because believing God actually loves us to this extent pushes the boundaries of plausibility. As a result, for us to believe God's invitation is genuine, he had to deliver it personally and in a manner authentic enough to be believed. In a world filled with men and women scarred by relational abuse and betrayal, it is difficult to trust in a stranger who comes professing love.

As a result, God chose to deliver the invitation the only way love can be authenticated: through self-sacrifice. These words are not empty: "No one has greater love than this, to lay down one's life for one's friends" (John 15:13). It was only when Jesus breathed his last that the Roman centurion saw for himself that this man really was the Son of God. In his death and resurrection God simultaneously delivered his invitation to reconciliation in a way we could see and believe and made it possible for us to live together if we say yes.

It is a fantastic love story, yet it is more than that. It is not merely an invitation to an afterlife in heaven; it is also an opportunity to rediscover our true nature and learn how to mature in our ability to love here and now. God's invitation to us is not to live a holy individualism but to move beyond ourselves and learn how to relate intimately with him and with one another.

Discovering Our True Identity

The iWorld has a very different conception of identity. In the iWorld, identity is something we are instructed to select or create. If we don't like or aren't comfortable with who we are, we are encouraged to remake ourselves in whatever manner we are able to and science will allow. Consequently, in the iWorld the search for meaning and self-understanding can be endless because we are always left to wonder if we could have been happier if we had chosen a different path. Yet according to Genesis we do not design our nature; we discover it by coming to understand who we are as men and women made in the image of God. How do we discover it? By relating to God and each other.

Developmental psychologists have provided us with a rich understanding of the way each of us develop emotionally, physically, and intellectually. They help us see that from an early age our development, identity, and self-understanding are deeply connected to the quality of our relationships, life experiences, and choices. Different experiences affect our identity and self-understanding in profound ways that may not change through the course of our life. When I speak of identity, I am referring to something deeper than just self-understanding. It is something hardwired into our nature as well as something we participate in creating. Our nature is fixed and cannot be altered by our life experiences, even if our life experiences render it difficult to discover.

Identity and self-understanding are very important. We all have various likes and dislikes, different preferences and attractions, different talents and abilities, and different life and relational experiences. There are also aspects of our nature that are fixed. All these factors play an important role in helping us understand who we are.

Identity is arguably the primary focus of the iWorld. It can become the sole focus at the cost of ignoring or denying that we possess a human nature that in some fashion defines or limits us. The question is how we can each come to know ourselves as human beings (our nature and our identity).

The iWorld subjugates nature under identity, whereas the Bible asserts that identity is developed out of our nature. In the latter view, we begin with a given nature from which identity is constructed, maintained, sustained, or destroyed. In the iWorld, however, it is frequently assumed that creating our identity is an intellectual exercise—something we arrive at through deliberation and trial and error. It is a mixed message at best. One message is that we create our identity and the other is that we have to look inside and discover it.

Scripture asserts that accurate self-perception is found in knowing God—his mind and our design. According to Christianity, we come to have a more complete understanding of our nature and identity by first developing a love relationship with God, through his son, Jesus. Indeed, the relationship of primary importance for accurately comprehending who we are is our relationship with God. Misunderstanding of our true nature leads to misconception concerning our identity.

Our relationship with God also has implications for our ability to love and to relate. Since God is love and since we were created by God to love, unless we are able to accept the love of God that alone can fill the hole in our hearts, we can never find spiritual fulfillment. Our attempts to fill that hole with the things we think or hope will satisfy us (including other people) will all fall short. Something will always be missing in our lives, and we will know it even if we don't know what it is.

All of this is not to say that if we do not know God we are necessarily devoid of the ability to love. Since we are all made in God's image, we have the capacity for relating and loving. Moreover, simply knowing God does not in itself create a suave, self-aware, relational lover. There are many who surpass professing Christians in all three categories. Nevertheless, the only way we can fully comprehend who we are, fully relate, and fully love is to know God.

One aspect of the iWorld's perception of love is perfectly summed up by the Beatles: "In the end the love you take is equal to the love you make."[5] This definition of love is a lot like karma—if you want to get it, you've got to give it; conversely, if you don't give it, you won't get it. Christianity has a dramatically different understanding of it: love is not karma; rather, God is the source of all love. As John says, "Beloved, let us love one another, because love is of God; everyone who loves is born of God and knows God. Whoever does not love does not know God, for God is love. . . . God is love, and those who abide in his love abide in God, and God in them. Love has been perfected among us. . . . We love because he first loved us" (1 John 4:7–8, 16–17, 19).

One way we come to know God and his love is by reading Scripture. As we have seen, the Bible can help us become better acquainted with God, and in so doing we can more fully discover our nature and, by extension, our true identity. Now, it's one thing to know God intellectually, but that alone is not enough. We also need to know God spiritually and emotionally. Truthfully, until we also know God spiritually and emotionally, we cannot truly know God. Humans are multidimensional, and we can know who we are only by relating to God with our whole being and receiving his love in all aspects of our being. Spiritually, we know the love of God by relating to him with our soul. While we receive the Holy Spirit at the point of conversion, we then need to go on to develop our spiritual capacity to commune with God.

In the iWorld, spirituality has been lost largely due to its misplaced faith in the adequacy of science to verify the existence of nonmaterial reality. Consequently, many who live in the iWorld have concluded that we

5. Paul McCartney, "The End," *Abbey Road*, The Beatles (Apple Records, 1969).

do not have a spiritual dimension. As a result, just as a muscle atrophies from a lack of use, so also does our soul. Virtually all of us suffer from soul atrophy; we can't live in the iWorld and easily escape it. So how can we redevelop our soul? First, through relating to God, and second, by practicing what are called the spiritual disciplines, such as fasting, prayer, meditation, and silence. These are not magic rituals that are used like an incantation to make God appear; rather, they are practices that help us to quiet ourselves and sharpen our soul's ability to listen to the voice of God and help our spirit to commune with God through the Holy Spirit.

While it is a good thing to know God intellectually and spiritually, these alone are not enough. We also want to feel the love of God emotionally. We are designed to be in relationship; that is part of our nature. It is unhealthy for us to try to live outside relationships. Indeed, this is where our relationships with others enter the equation. It is in relating to our neighbor that we often experience the love of God. Likewise, we can be used to help others experience the love of God. In both the rWorld and Christianity, relationships are not optional—they are essential. We quite literally cannot know love outside relationships, and if we don't know love we will never develop a healthy personal identity.

Let me give an example of the primary role relationships play in our "feeling" the love of God. Christianity teaches us that if we ask God for forgiveness, we are forgiven. The problem is that when we ask God for forgiveness, sometimes we don't feel it even though intellectually we believe we are forgiven. That is why the practice of confession is important to so many. We need to feel forgiven, and until we feel it we have difficulty moving on with our lives. Often we feel the forgiveness of God only after confessing our sin to another and seeing and hearing from him or her that we are forgiven. Conversely, if we do not receive forgiveness from that person, we may not feel it from God.

It is not surprising that Christ tells us we will be forgiven to the same degree we have forgiven others. This is true in forgiveness and in love. It is important to know the love of God intellectually, spiritually, and experientially. Indeed, many times we feel the love of God only when it comes through others. Humans are often the conduits through which the love of God is expressed. Love is not something we make; it is something we receive from God through others, and it is a gift we give from God to others.

This description of love is very different from how it is commonly understood. The language of love we routinely use is completely based in the self. There are three words virtually all of us use: "I love you." If one takes the Christian conception of love to an extreme, it might be said that the only words we should ever speak to one another are: "God loves you." To do so, however, would indicate an impoverished understanding of our role in love. If we are made in the image of God and if God is love, it is certainly the case that, like God, we are made to love. Moreover, the act of love is not limited merely to people who are religious. Indeed, some of the more loving people are not religious. From a Christian point of view this should not be surprising. If we are all made in the image of God, and if God loves us, then we all have love to share whether we know God or not. What is unfortunate is how poorly so many of us love.

Love is not a mere feeling or a self-regarding act. Each one of us has a profound role and responsibility in the administration of love. Because we are made in the image of God, we are made to be lovers, but for us to become the lovers we are meant to be, we need to dwell in the love of God. The more we dwell in that love, the better we can love our fellow humans.

If this conception of love is true, then if we do not know the love of God, we almost certainly will be frustrated lovers. If we do not know the love of God, we will not enjoy the quality of love for which we were made. While we will not live a loveless life, we will never fully understand our true identity and will yearn for a love we will never be able to give or receive. This is the tragedy of what happened in Eden. The consequences of the fall are so profound that it is hard to believe the rWorld can exist in the real world because the world in which we currently reside bears only a shadowy resemblance to Eden.

Confronting the Invitation

The Bible contains a fantastic love story, but is it true? Herein lies the question of faith with which we are confronted. Do we choose to believe and submit ourselves to the God who created us, or do we retain control of our life? That is the question, and the choice is ours.

It is not unlike the choice faced by Thomas Anderson in the *Matrix*. As Morpheus says to Anderson, "Take the blue pill or the red pill. You take the blue pill and you wake up tomorrow in the matrix and all of this is just a dream and you can go on living your own life as if nothing else mattered. You take the red pill and you come with me and you find out just how deep the rabbit hole goes. The choice is yours."[6] And so it is for us.

Christianity is certainly not the only love story; there are many love stories told in our world. We are confronted with many avenues in which it is claimed true love can be found, but the problem is that we do not have time to pursue them all. Our lives on earth are finite and short, hence we have to exercise faith concerning which story, which avenue, is worthy of our trust.

Everyone is invited, but no one has to accept. Accepting the invitation requires faith—believing that God exists and loves us and has provided a way for us to come home. If we accept the invitation, we do so on the basis of his rules, his design, and our need to be rescued from our effort to find satisfaction outside of God. Figuratively speaking, we have to *undo* the impact on our lives of Adam and Eve's decision and give back to God the apple they took from the Tree of the Knowledge of Good and Evil—and in so doing relinquish control of our lives to God.

If we make this commitment we are promised the gift of the Holy Spirit and then we are able to cultivate a relationship with God. We are also joined through the Holy Spirit with the others who have accepted the invitation and made the same commitment. Together, we—God, ourselves, and his church—become an extended family woven together by this love relationship. We can't ever get ourselves *back to the garden*, but we can go forward to the *celebration* God is holding at the end of time. Gradually we will each grow in our ability to become authentic and will come to know the love of God; we will learn how to reflect the love of God to others; and we will feel the love of God through others. While this process won't be completed in this life, the Bible tells us that after death, at the end of time, we will be resurrected perfect and incorruptible, and it will last forever.

6. Wachowski and Wachowski, *The Matrix*.

What's more, the church itself becomes a living invitation from God to the world. One of its purposes is to be the vehicle by which God extends this invitation to everyone. Its persuasive power rests in the quality of love reflected in the lives of its family members. There is room for everyone.

That's the love story. So where does sex fit in?

8

rSex

One is the loneliest number that you'll ever do
Two can be as bad as one
It's the loneliest number since the number one

> Harry Nilsson, "One"[1]

The tragedy of sexual intercourse is the perpetual
virginity of the soul.

> William Yeats

The goal is soul.

> Bono, U2
> *Go Home*[2]

Finally, it's time to talk about sex in the rWorld. The place of sexuality in the broader picture of human fulfillment is arguably the fulcrum of this book. Addressing this matter is the primary reason I decided to write this book, and it may well be the reason you have read this far.

1. Harry Nilsson, "One," recorded by Three Dog Night, *Three Dog Night* (ABC-Dunhill/ MCA Records, 1969).
2. Bono, U2 *Go Home: Live from Slane Castle Ireland*, DVD (Interscope Records, 2003).

Whenever I lecture on this topic in public I can feel the anticipation build with a sense of disbelief as we approach this part of the discussion. People wonder: Are you really going to try to challenge the iWorld's view of sexual freedom? Given the decisive way the sexual revolution overthrew the tWorld, why are you subjecting yourself to almost certain public humiliation? Can't you see that the debate about sexual ethics has already been decided? Nietzsche's shadow is a long one.

Delivering such a lecture would appear to be a modern-day equivalent of the sort of spectacle that took place in the Roman Colosseum centuries ago. People attended wondering not *if* the gladiators would die but *how*. The great curiosity is why I am bothering to try.

Again, people might ask: Do you really believe there is anything left to say that hasn't already been said? Are you really going to try to make the case that the traditional religious teaching about sexuality will provide *everyone* with the possibility of a more fulfilling life? Hasn't Christianity already been discredited on this score? Why add further scorn through such a public spectacle? Why don't you retire the argument to a hospice with some dignity rather than force it to commit suicide in public?

One of the advantages of stating one's case in writing as opposed to doing so via public speaking is that an author is better able to logically build and state his or her case without interruption or diversion. In a public setting, a member of the audience can ask a question in a manner that suddenly pushes the discussion in a different direction. This especially occurs when I am teaching "The Politics of Diversity." It is usually at about this point in the semester that one of my students will ask, "So Professor Kuehne, are you really about to tell us that in the rWorld, if we are not heterosexual and happily married, we're screwed?" That's not what I was going to say, but it is a question I am asked every semester. Before I continue much further another student will ask, "Are you seriously going to try to persuade us that if we forgo consensual sexual relations outside of marriage we can have a fulfilling life, even if that means we never have a sexual relationship?" Well, it will require indulging in a willing suspension of disbelief, but the answer is yes, and explaining why is the purpose of this chapter.

The iWorld has been asking this question of Christianity, Islam, and Judaism since the advent of the sexual revolution, and it is going to keep asking until it gets a satisfactory response. Indeed, it seems virtually everyone is now asking this question, including Christians. While the circumstances may vary widely, the conundrum is the same: people are in a situation in which adherence to traditional teaching appears to stand in the way of their personal fulfillment because the teaching forbids engaging in a consensual sexual relationship outside of marriage, even with someone to whom they are deeply attracted. It seems plainly obvious that Christianity imprisons and/or condemns them whereas the iWorld offers them liberation.

Since Christianity has not recently offered a compelling reason for people not to have merely consensual sexual relationships, fewer and fewer believe that it has one. This is why my students pursue this so persistently by asking me, "Do you seriously believe that following the orthodox Christian teaching about human sexuality and relationships can lead us to a life with more fulfillment than the iWorld offers? Do you really believe you have something to add to the argument that has not been said since the sexual revolution?" Actually, yes and yes.

I'm not claiming I have anything *new* to say, but I do have something to say that seems to have been forgotten, and I believe it is well worth rediscovering. We are presently engaged in a worldwide discussion about the nature of human fulfillment and happiness. The tWorld and its relational matrix disappointed us. There was so much relational dysfunction and so little attention paid to relational healing and growth that the tWorld left millions disillusioned and yearning for more. When the iWorld presented itself with the promise of personal fulfillment and unprecedented individual freedom to pursue it, the attraction was obvious and the response decisive. Yet the iWorld is about much more than sexual freedom. Economic well-being is an important aspect of the iWorld because of the role money plays in providing us the means to do as we please. Still, sexual freedom is paramount in the iWorld.

So decisively has the iWorld triumphed over the tWorld that it seems to have no rival. But does it really deliver the fulfillment for which humans were designed? If we were created for healthy relational intimacy

with one another and our Creator, then no matter how long we live in
accordance with the iWorld, we will never actually find what we seek
in either sexual or financial freedom. The true love and intimacy that
we crave will not be found in sex or money.

Here we come back to the crux of the matter and, in so doing, come
back to the tough questions being asked by the iWorld. Given the disil-
lusionment with the tWorld, what defense can be made that the rWorld
can truly "outperform" the iWorld when it comes to human fulfillment?
More than that, even if the rWorld can make a case for itself beyond
that of the tWorld, what's so bad about consensual sex in the age of
condoms and birth control that we need to bring back the boundaries
the sexual revolution swept away?

As we saw in the previous chapter, the Bible makes the case that
humans are made for relationship and that we crave intimacy and love
more than anything else. The problem with sex is not that it is bad but
that it alone cannot deliver the fulfillment for which we yearn. Worse,
the pursuit of sex can distract us and even rob us of the intimacy and
love for which we yearn. Frankly, until we comprehend the nature of true
intimacy and love we will never really understand the proper place of sex
in our lives. So let's conclude our examination of the Bible by focusing
on what it has to say about sexual relations. In so doing, we won't find
any surprises except that the Bible is just as strict as we expected and
more explicit than we imagined. Indeed, we will have an opportunity
to uncover what has been overlooked and even forgotten by so many:
the rWorld. This relational world provides the basis for an answer to
how we can find true intimacy and love and why the biblical teaching
about sex is part of the solution, not the problem.

Sex and the Old Testament: Leviticus

The Old Testament is very straightforward concerning the place of
sexuality in human life. Professor Jonathan Burnside is not alone in
arguing that the only biblically sanctioned relationship for sex is in a
marriage between a man and a woman.[3] This teaching is supported by
the seventh commandment, "You shall not commit adultery" (Exod.

3. Jonathan Burnside, *God, Justice and Society*, unpublished manuscript.

20:14), and it is fleshed out in the book of Leviticus. Twenty-five of the thirty verses in Leviticus 18 give such straightforward teaching about sexual boundaries that it could be characterized as the "Just Say No" passage.

> The Lord spoke to Moses, saying: Speak to the people of Israel and say to them: I am the Lord your God. You shall not do as they do in the land of Egypt, where you lived, and you shall not do as they do in the land of Canaan, to which I am bringing you. You shall not follow their statutes . . . I am the Lord your God. You shall keep my statutes and my ordinances; by doing so one shall live: I am the Lord.
>
> None of you shall approach anyone near of kin to uncover nakedness: I am the Lord. You shall not uncover the nakedness of your father, which is the nakedness of your mother; she is your mother, you shall not uncover her nakedness. You shall not uncover the nakedness of your father's wife; it is the nakedness of your father. You shall not uncover the nakedness of your sister, your father's daughter or your mother's daughter, whether born at home or born abroad. You shall not uncover the nakedness of your son's daughter or of your daughter's daughter, for their nakedness is your own nakedness. You shall not uncover the nakedness of your father's wife's daughter, begotten by your father, since she is your sister. You shall not uncover the nakedness of your father's sister; she is your father's flesh. You shall not uncover the nakedness of your mother's sister, for she is your mother's flesh. You shall not uncover the nakedness of your father's brother, that is, you shall not approach his wife; she is your aunt. You shall not uncover the nakedness of your daughter-in-law: she is your son's wife; you shall not uncover her nakedness. You shall not uncover the nakedness of your brother's wife; it is your brother's nakedness. You shall not uncover the nakedness of a woman and her daughter, and you shall not take her son's daughter or her daughter's daughter to uncover her nakedness; they are your flesh; it is depravity. And you shall not take a woman as a rival to her sister, uncovering her nakedness while her sister is still alive.
>
> You shall not approach a woman to uncover her nakedness while she is in her menstrual uncleanness. You shall not have sexual relations with your kinsman's wife, and defile yourself with her. You shall not give any of your offspring to sacrifice them to Molech, and so profane the name of your God: I am the Lord. You shall not lie with a male as with a woman; it is an abomination. You shall not have sexual relations with any animal

and defile yourself with it, nor shall any woman give herself to an animal
to have sexual relations with it: it is perversion. Do not defile yourselves
in any of these ways, for by all these practices the nations I am casting
out before you have defiled themselves. Thus the land became defiled;
and I punished it for its iniquity, and the land vomited out its inhabitants.
But you shall keep my statutes and my ordinances and commit none of
these abominations, either the citizen or the alien who resides among
you (for the inhabitants of the land, who were before you, committed
all of these abominations, and the land became defiled); otherwise the
land will vomit you out for defiling it, as it vomited out the nation that
was before you. For whoever commits any of these abominations shall be
cut off from their people. So keep my charge not to commit any of these
abominations that were done before you, and not to defile yourselves by
them: I am the Lord your God. (Lev. 18:1–30)

After reading this passage we cannot accuse God of not having a
sexual imagination. Virtually every conceivable sexual act outside of a
marriage between a man and a woman is prohibited. We also cannot
pretend God does not take sexual offenses seriously. The harm caused
by sexual relations outside of marriage is apparently so significant that
in most cases the penalty attached to sexual misconduct was death (see
Lev. 20).

The iWorld will take exception, if not offense, to Leviticus 18 and
20. From a contemporary perspective these two chapters appear to have
the liberality and sensitivity of Attila the Hun. Leaving aside until the
next chapter a discussion of the criminal sanctions, let us focus on how
this passage helps us understand the differences between the iWorld and
rWorld. Whereas the tWorld advocated capital punishment for these
sexual offenses, the rWorld proposed here does not. More specifically,
why does a sexual act that is not even a misdemeanor in the iWorld
have the seriousness of a capital offense in the tWorld?

The rWorld is interested in engaging the iWorld in a debate about
the fundamental harm caused by sexual relations outside of a marriage
between a man and a woman. As we have seen, the iWorld believes that
so long as it is mutually consensual—and doesn't betray any current
relational commitments—any harm is minimal and limited to those
involved. The rWorld position is that the harm is profound and has
relational consequences that go far beyond the individuals involved in

the sexual act. The iWorld believes any harm caused can be healed with time. The rWorld believes that the harm is devastating—the relational equivalent of the Mutually Assured Destruction policy embraced by the United States and the Soviet Union during the cold war.

The Old Testament consistently supports the sexual boundaries and the gravity attached to them in Leviticus 18 and 20. As soon as Adam and Eve are banished from Eden, the biblical story is of humans engaged in relational genocide. From that moment, human history contains murder, jealousy, envy, lying, theft, and every sexual vice imaginable. Human relational depravity occurs so immediately and acutely that God's response is to send the catastrophic flood that takes the lives of everyone but the family of Noah. The flood, however, doesn't solve the problem because Noah's descendants engage in a bit of déjà vu, and in seemingly no time they find themselves in the same corrupt situation. When God takes the Israelites out of Egypt and instructs them on how they should go into the land of Canaan, he explicitly commands them to execute a floodlike judgment on the Canaanites by annihilating them. The corruption of the Canaanites is so complete that, not only are they beyond recovery, but it is very likely that their corruption is contagious. According to Leviticus 18 the primary source of their corruption is sexual immorality. If any evidence is needed to validate the concerns expressed by God in that chapter, it can be found in the subsequent biblical history of Israel. They did not obey God's injunction to rid the land of the Canaanites, and the Israelites were subsequently corrupted.

Sex and the New Testament

Continuity between Christ and the Law

Sexual boundaries matter greatly in the Old Testament; the teaching is clear and to the point. We could examine additional Old Testament passages, but Leviticus 18 and 20 provide an effective summation. Turning to the New Testament we find continuity in this teaching. Some may infer that sex is a topic of relatively little importance to Christ since, according to the writers of the four Gospels, he spends relatively little time addressing sexuality. When he does address it, however, he clearly reaffirms the Old Testament law in which the Leviticus passages are embedded, and he reaffirms not only the spirit but also the letter of the law.

> Do not think that I have come to abolish the law and the prophets; I have come not to abolish but to fulfill. For truly I tell you, until heaven and earth pass away, not one letter, not one stroke of a letter, will pass away from the law until all is accomplished. Therefore, whoever breaks one of the least of these commandments, and teaches others to do the same, will be called least in the kingdom of heaven; but whoever does them and teaches them will be called great in the kingdom of heaven. For I tell you, unless your righteousness exceeds that of the scribes and Pharisees, you will never enter the kingdom of heaven. (Matt. 5:17–20)

As we read further in this passage, Christ elaborates on the meaning of righteousness in regard to the prohibition against adultery and several other commandments. He consistently teaches that what is required is not merely righteous behavior but also a righteous heart.

> You have heard that it was said to those of ancient times, "You shall not murder"; and "whoever murders shall be liable to judgment." But I say to you that if you are angry with a brother or sister, you will be liable to judgment; and if you insult a brother or sister, you will be liable to the council; and if you say, "You fool," you will be liable to the hell of fire. So when you are offering your gift at the altar, if you remember that your brother or sister has something against you, leave your gift there before the altar and go; first be reconciled to your brother or sister, and then come and offer your gift. . . . You have heard that it was said, "You shall not commit adultery." But I say to you that everyone who looks at a woman with lust has already committed adultery with her in his heart. If your right eye causes you to sin, tear it out and throw it away; it is better for you to lose one of your members than for your whole body to be thrown into hell. . . . And if your right hand causes you to sin, cut it off and throw it away; it is better for you to lose one of your members than for your whole body to go into hell. It was also said, "Whoever divorces his wife, let him give her a certificate of divorce. But I say to you that anyone who divorces his wife, except on the ground of unchastity, causes her to commit adultery; and whoever marries a divorced woman commits adultery. Again, you have heard

that it was said to those of ancient times, "You shall not swear falsely, but carry out the vows you have made to the Lord." But I say to you, Do not swear at all, either by heaven, for it is the throne of God, or by the earth, for it is his footstool, or by Jerusalem, for it is the city of the great King. And do not swear by your head, for you cannot make one hair white or black. Let your word be "Yes, Yes" or "No, No"; anything more than this comes from the evil one. You have heard that it was said, "An eye for an eye and a tooth for a tooth." But I say to you, do not resist an evildoer. But if anyone strikes you on the right cheek, turn the other also; and if anyone wants to sue you and take your coat, give your cloak as well; and if anyone forces you to go one mile, go also the second mile. Give to everyone who begs from you, and do not refuse anyone who wants to borrow from you. . . . You have heard that it was said, "You shall love your neighbor and hate your enemy." But I say to you, Love your enemies and pray for those who persecute you. . . . For if you love those who love you, what reward do you have? Do not even the tax collectors do the same? And if you greet only your brothers and sisters, what more are you doing than others? Do not even the Gentiles do the same? Be perfect, therefore, as your heavenly Father is perfect. (Matt. 5:21–44, 46–48)

While this passage covers many aspects of purity, Jesus goes beyond mere external obedience to the sexual law by emphasizing the importance of spiritual purity. Not only are we to abstain from adultery, but we are not even to lust after a woman in our heart. Lust is considered sinful regardless of our own marital status or the marital status of the object of our lust. Not only are sexual relations outside of marriage wrong, fantasizing about it is equally wrong.

There are those who may argue that the story in John 8:1–11 of the woman caught in adultery is an instance in which Christ relaxed the Old Testament law concerning sexuality. In this passage the Pharisees bring to Jesus a woman caught in adultery, and after telling him that the law of Moses requires that this woman be stoned, they ask Jesus what he orders for a punishment. After a time, Jesus replies, "Let anyone among you who is without sin be the first to throw a stone at her." After everyone leaves, Jesus asks the woman, "Has no one condemned you?" When she replies, "No one," Jesus declares, "Neither do I condemn you. Go your way, and from now on do not sin again" (vv. 7, 10–11).

This story is often cited as an example of Jesus's grace and forgiveness. But it is inaccurate to use this passage to imply that Jesus relaxed or subverted the Old Testament law generally or Leviticus 20 specifically. According to the law, if Jesus was not an eyewitness, he could not condemn the woman. In addition, both the man and woman caught in adultery were supposed to be stoned—not just the woman. This was not a legal stoning, and Jesus did not enable it by providing a false justification for it. Moreover, there is nothing in the story to suggest he relaxed any of the sexual boundaries of the Old Testament. He commanded the woman to leave her sinful lifestyle. Therefore, the grace Jesus showed in his treatment of the woman did not alter the sexual boundaries that he also affirmed.

Jesus did not speak extensively about sexuality and marriage, nor did he specifically address many of the sexual behaviors listed in Leviticus 18 and 20. But when he spoke about marriage, if anything he advocated making divorce even more difficult to obtain. Since he consistently upheld the Old Testament teaching when he did address sexuality and marriage, the most plausible inference to draw from his silence is reaffirmation, not relaxation.[4]

So what do the other New Testament writers say? They reaffirm what Jesus had affirmed, and at no point do they alter the teaching of Leviticus. Paul addresses sexuality in several places in his many letters and reaffirms the sexual boundaries laid out in Leviticus. The clearest example of this is in Romans 1.

> For the wrath of God is revealed from heaven against all ungodliness and wickedness of those who by their wickedness suppress the truth. For what can be known about God is plain to them, because God has shown it to them. Ever since the creation of the world his eternal power and divine nature, invisible though they are, have been understood and seen through the things he has made. So they are without excuse; for though they knew God, they did not honor him as God or give thanks to him, but they became futile in their thinking, and their senseless minds were

4. Robert A. J. Gagnon, *The Bible and Homosexual Practice: Texts and Hermeneutics* (Nashville: Abingdon, 2001), 185–228.

darkened. Claiming to be wise, they became fools; and they exchanged the glory of the immortal God for images resembling a mortal human being or birds or four-footed animals or reptiles. Therefore God gave them up in the lusts of their hearts to impurity, to the degrading of their bodies among themselves, because they exchanged the truth about God for a lie and worshiped and served the creature rather than the Creator, who is blessed forever! Amen. For this reason God gave them up to degrading passions. Their women exchanged natural intercourse for unnatural, and in the same way also the men, giving up natural intercourse with women, were consumed with passion for one another. Men committed shameless acts with men and received in their own persons the due penalty for their error. And since they did not see fit to acknowledge God, God gave them up to a debased mind and to things that should not be done. They were filled with every kind of wickedness, evil, covetousness, malice. Full of envy, murder, strife, deceit, craftiness, they are gossips, slanderers, God-haters, insolent, haughty, boastful, inventors of evil, rebellious toward parents, foolish, faithless, heartless, ruthless. They know God's decree, that those who practice such things deserve to die—yet they not only do them but even applaud others who practice them. (Rom. 1:18–32)

Paul speaks further about sexuality and marriage in his first letter to the Corinthians, reaffirming the sanctity of marriage and the prohibition against sex outside of marriage. He does not devalue marriage or sexuality, but he does argue that one can clearly be whole and fulfilled without being married and engaging in a sexual relationship. He says that it is better to marry than to burn with lust, but he expresses the wish that all could be like him and not need to be married (1 Cor. 7:7–9).

Acknowledging Disagreements

Before I proceed further, I readily concede that there are those who are in very strong disagreement with the summary of the biblical teaching on sexuality presented here. Those who disagree most vociferously, however, are not my friends who identify themselves as gay or lesbian. Interestingly, my experience in dialoguing with those engaged in a homosexual lifestyle is that while they disagree with me, they value an honest, deep, respectful dialogue; if I have something of value to say about sex, love, and intimacy, they're interested in hearing it. When I don't make the case well, I receive their blunt criticism, but I have always sensed their respect. I hope they feel my respect in return. I regard every human I meet as a person created in the image of God, loved by God, and deserving of my love and respect regardless of our differences on the theology or ethics of sexuality.

Still, I believe that Jesus calls me to do something more profound than extend respect to those who disagree with me. Christ calls me not only to respect but to love. If I only respected, I could then choose to dismiss or ignore. Love means I must be willing to engage with, respect, dialogue with, and even die for them. Clearly I have convictions about these issues and I want to discuss them with others, but if in so doing others don't feel love from me, then I will have failed even if I "win" any argument. Questions about sexuality are intensely personal, and the issue of homosexual practice can be highly contentious. Yet I have found that those most interested in these views have been my acquaintances who are engaged, or inclined to engage, in a same-sex sexual relationship. We may not agree, but we are glad to find a safe, respectful group of people to talk with about the things that matter to us. I have certainly found that with them, and I hope they have found the same with me.

Instead, it seems that the people who disagree most stridently are those evangelical Christian theologians, psychologists, and pastors who have interpreted the Bible as saying that for those who do not have the gift of celibacy, a sexual relationship is essential for wholeness and happiness. There tend to be two groups with variations on this theme: One is comprised of those who maintain that the Bible does not condemn monogamous homosexual relations. The other is made up of those who agree that the Bible condemns homosexual relations but argue for an intrinsic link between true relational fulfillment and Christian marriage because of the importance of sexual relations to personal fulfillment for everyone except those with the gift of celibacy.

An example of those in the first group is Dr. Jack Rogers, who in his book *Jesus, the Bible and Homosexuality* argues that the Bible speaks against promiscuity but not against monogamous same-sex marriages. In chapter 5 of his book, Rogers makes the case that the Bible does not condemn homosexual relations per se but only nonmonogamous relations. He argues that when homosexuality is discussed in the Bible, the

prohibitions are culturally biased (Lev. 18, 20) or the homosexual behavior described is condemned because it is not monogamous (Rom. 1).
In chapter 6 of his book, Rogers makes the case that the best scientific
evidence shows that homosexuality is not a choice and that harm can be
done by asking homosexuals to change. He comes close to saying that
since God (or some other factor) made some people to be homosexual,
reading Scripture to say that God restricts sexual relationships to a marriage between a man and a woman is fundamentally unjustified.

I believe the arguments advanced by Rogers are based in part on the
philosophical-psychological inference that sexual preference is prede-
termined and thus no one should be denied the opportunity to be in a
sexual relationship to be whole. Hence, if you are denied the opportunity
to marry because of your sexual preference, you are denied what you
need in order to be whole and to have a fulfilling life. Rogers argues that
sexual relations are an important part of the pathway to experiencing
true love and intimacy. As a result, since God wouldn't have made us
without the possibility of experiencing true love and intimacy, Rogers
concludes that the Bible ought not to be read to prohibit same-sex,
monogamous unions. According to Rogers, such an interpretation is
a mistake of the same magnitude as the historical Christian justifica-
tions for slavery. Thus what is distinctively Christian about the biblical teaching concerning marriage and sexuality is the boundary of no
sexual relations outside of marriage. Rogers believes the debate between
Christianity and the iWorld is primarily a debate about promiscuity.
Given his perspective, the Christian position contends that if you want
to have sex, you should get married to the one person you love and stay
married and sexually faithful to that person, whereas the iWorld argues
for the freedom and right to be promiscuous.

At the very least I'll concede that his argument is culturally easier
to sustain than the one I am putting forth for the rWorld. As we have
seen, the iWorld, for all its talk about freedom and for all its promiscuous sexual activity, finds that its citizens are innately attracted to
monogamous, committed relationships. If same-sex unions are granted
legitimacy, then the debate would simply be about promiscuity rather
than sexual preference.

While Rogers's thesis may be less ambitious and more politically
correct than mine, I still find myself in disagreement with its theo-

logical, philosophical, and scientific reasoning. I will say more about the scientific and philosophical objections to his description of sexual orientation in chapter 10. For now let it suffice to say that David Hume is yelling from the grave, "You cannot derive an ought from an is!"[5] My theological objection, however, is based on a disagreement that the Bible regards sexual relations as an important or essential part of human fulfillment.

Rogers is not alone in this view, nor is his view confined to those who defend same-sex marriage. For decades the American evangelical church has emphasized the importance of marriage to a fulfilling life, and much of this has been driven by some of the same assumptions held by Rogers concerning the importance of a sexual relationship to a fulfilling life. They differ only on the definition of marriage, not its importance. One recent example of the heterosexual version of this view is the 30 Day Sex Challenge issued in February 2008 by Relevant Church of Tampa, Florida.[6] Now, I can affirm with them that the church ought to address all the issues relevant to our world, and to be fair, the curriculum of this challenge goes beyond mere sexual relations. Yet, as this challenge indicates, the challengers regard sex as an important aspect of human relational fulfillment. This understanding of the connection between sex and relational fulfillment has been a largely unquestioned assumption of evangelical psychology, if not theology, for decades. Yet I believe this assumption is not only unjustified but is responsible in large part for the behavioral assimilation of people of faith by the iWorld, especially as it pertains to the divorce, adultery, and promiscuity that has gone along with it. As this reasoning goes, if sex is an essential aspect of human fulfillment, then if Christians, or anyone else, are missing out on sex, and if God wishes us to have the most fulfilling life possible, then that which stands in the way of this fulfillment—divorce, remarriage, or cohabitation—must not be wrong after all. Ironically, the rationalizations used by heterosexuals and homosexuals to justify breaking biblical sexual boundaries are identical: God wants me to be

5. Hume, *Treatise of Human Nature*.
6. "30 Day Sex Challenge Guide," www.youtube.com/watch?v=MOr09AI7Rfk (Feb. 17–Mar. 16, 2008), http://relevantchurch.com. See also the 7-Day Sex Challenge issued by Pastor Ed Wright of Fellowship Church in Grapevine, Texas, www.nytimes.com/2008/11/24/us/24sex.html?bl& ex=1227762000&en=ab700f6adb9c70e5&ei=5087. It will be interesting to see what effect these initiatives have on church growth.

fulfilled; sex is an essential part of relational fulfillment; therefore the Bible can't really mean what it says about sexual boundaries because that would rob me of fulfillment.

So If Sex Doesn't Make Us Happy, What Does?

Although it may be culturally easier to sustain the arguments or approaches of Rogers, the 30 Day Sex Challenge, and others that are based on the assumption of a link between human relational fulfillment and sexuality, they are not actually supported by the Bible. Indeed, if this assumption is removed, the entire teaching of Scripture in regard to sexual boundaries, marriage, divorce, and remarriage takes on an entirely new perspective.

If this is true, then restricting divorce and remarriage does not deny true love and intimacy to people in a difficult marriage because that is not the only or even primary place where true love and intimacy can be found. If this is true, then prohibiting sexual relations between unmarried people does not rob them of the ability to enjoy true love and intimacy now or for a lifetime because sex is not a necessary stop on the pathway to true love and intimacy. If this is true, then the prohibition against homosexual relations does not deny people who are so inclined the experience of true love and happiness. If this is true, then one does not need to engage in hermeneutical contortions to explain why it appears that Christ's words are designed to make people miserable by denying them sex. Instead, in this light, his teaching that he came so that everyone could have life and have it abundantly makes sense. The abundant life is a product of having an intimate love relationship with God and others, and sex has little to do with it.

To be clear, the Bible does not say sex is a bad thing or that there is no place for romantic love. The Song of Solomon is a brilliant book of romantic poetry, and nowhere does the Bible imply that a married couple should discuss household chores while they are having sex. Sex in its place is good. But when it comes to finding and experiencing true love and intimacy, it is not a necessary part of the equation.

This is the clear teaching of Scripture from cover to cover. The Bible tells us that in their youth, David and King Saul's son Jonathan loved each other, but they didn't need to have sex to enhance their relationship. Neither did Jesus and the disciples, nor Jesus and Mary Magdalene. The most plausible explanation for why Jesus didn't address the topic of homosexuality is that no one asked, and no one asked because no one imagined there was a need to ask. The notion that sex was an essential part of human happiness was not in the consciousness of people in that time and place. Sex was considered to be a drive, an appetite, and a necessary means of procreation. If anything, it was seen as something that potentially enslaves us, and the biblical message is to free us from such enslavement. Thus, all that we need to be fulfilled is available to everyone regardless of sexual inclination because it is not found in sex.

So where exactly is this true love and intimacy for which we yearn? It is found in loving both God and neighbor (see Matt. 22:37–40). These commandments do not describe mere behavior; rather, they invite us to a deep, intimate love relationship with God and with others. As we discussed in the previous chapter, when we have a deep, intimate love relationship with God, we are given the ability to love others in the same deep, pure, intimate way. This is how and where we experience true love and intimacy, which is the deepest of all human cravings.

Thus contrary to some contemporary popular evangelical theology, the two great commandments are not to get married and have sex. Being married is not the only means of experiencing true love and intimacy. Marriage is an important institution that exists in service of the family, and God wants those who are married to have great marriages. But the quality of the marriage is connected to the ability of the couple to enjoy true love and intimacy with God, with each other, and with the rest of the people in the extended relational matrix previously described. Sex will sometimes produce children; sex will provide a bond for the marriage that is useful in holding a married couple together. But sex in itself will not be the catalyst for happiness or fulfillment because that is not its innate purpose.

Hence, the notion that sex is an integral part of human fulfillment is an assumption the iWorld brings to the biblical text, but it is not actually found in the text. As a result, the twenty-first century is crossing the threshold into an age in which laws are being established to protect behavior that was morally inconceivable for centuries, including same-

sex marriage. This assumption was given to us by the sexual revolution, and it constitutes a central place in the iWorld. Sexual freedom
is arguably the cornerstone of the iWorld, and it pervades the lives of
every inhabitant regardless of whether they choose to utilize it. This is
why the iWorld and the rWorld have completely different conceptions
of the place of sexuality in human happiness.

The Crux of the Debate

At long last we come to the crux of the debate between the iWorld and
the rWorld: Which world has a more accurate understanding of human
happiness and fulfillment? Now that we know how the rWorld differs
from the iWorld, we can explore the question of whether the rWorld
could offer men and women something not just different but actually
better than the iWorld—not just for some but for *everyone*.

So which of these two worlds will bring the most satisfaction, security, freedom, and fulfillment to its inhabitants? Can the promise of
the sexual revolution be truly realized? Is the iWorld superior to the
rWorld because it does a better job of delivering true happiness by giving
everyone permission to be sexually engaged and the freedom to have a
greater variety and quantity of sexual relationships? Is the iWorld pref-
erable because it allows individuals to tailor their identities and sexual
relationships as they wish, whereas the rWorld would deny this?

The bottom line is that I believe the rWorld offers a quality of love and
intimacy that is more fulfilling than the iWorld at its best. The problem
with the sexual revolution is that we potentially become so focused on
finding happiness in sexuality and a sensual or sensory experience that
we can easily miss the love and intimacy for which our soul craves. We
were created for love and intimacy, not just for sex, and we find fulfillment only when we drink deeply from the well of love and intimacy. One
of the problems with sexual freedom is not that the sex is not pleasurable; it is pleasurable. Rather, it is that unfettered sexual freedom can
inhibit our ability to cultivate and enjoy love and intimacy.

Why is that? It seems counterintuitive when we are dealing with
something so pleasurable. What's so harmful about sexual relations
before or outside of marriage? What credible reason could possibly exist

to believe that sexual relations outside a heterosexual, monogamous marriage are corrupting? For a start, if these warnings are actually true, it would mean that the iWorld itself is not sustainable. It would mean that the sexual behavior the iWorld openly affirms is not only harming us but is also possibly destroying us. Indeed, by a variety of measures a case can be made that this is already beginning to occur. As we have seen (and will see in greater detail in chapter 9), the instability of the iWorld has arguably already wrought some devastating consequences upon the institution of the family and the raising of children. Humanity is in uncharted waters when it comes to the long-term effects of such a relational model, and we're all part of the experiment. As with any paradigm shift of this magnitude, even popular well-intentioned changes can have unforeseen and profoundly undesirable side effects.

Leaving aside such extrapolations for the moment, in practical terms what could be so wrong with sexual relations between a man and a woman outside a marriage relationship? To begin with, there are a couple of obvious problems with which we are all familiar. One is the procreation of children outside of marriage. Condoning this will undermine and weaken the institution of the family, to say nothing about the corresponding impact on the well-being of the children. Another problem is the relational harm of adultery. When two people have pledged themselves to sexual exclusivity and that commitment is then betrayed, the damage to the relationship is profound—so profound that, in some cases, the relationship can never be restored. Crimes of passion related to adultery are not infrequent. The marriage bond is not merely legal; it is one that goes to the very core of the people involved. To break that trust by uncovering the nakedness of someone other than your spouse, to whom you have promised sexual exclusivity, is relational violence of a significant order, to say nothing of violating the second taboo concerning hurting those closest to you.

These two problems—illegitimate children and adultery—are widely agreed to be both morally and practically problematic by many if not most of the inhabitants of the iWorld. But even if we could remove the issue of illegitimacy from the equation through the use of birth control and accept that the three taboos actually prohibit adultery (because unless there is some kind of open marriage agreement, it is profoundly harmful to the spouse who is betrayed), then what's wrong with con-sensual sexual relations between adults who aren't married?

The tWorld response to this question at the advent of the sexual revolution was primarily centered on the argument that there is no such thing as completely safe sex or fail-safe contraception. Hence, sexual relationships outside marriage remained immoral for everyone if for no other reason than the possibility, however remote, of conception or sexually transmitted disease.

It is here that inhabitants of the tWorld looked to their leaders and wondered, "Is that it? Is that the best argument you can make?" Having heard nothing better, the tWorld's migration to the iWorld began with the sexual revolution, and the speed of the exodus is increasing as time goes by. Millions if not billions have broadly accepted the iWorld's contention that since safe sex and effective contraception are widely available, the traditional prohibitions concerning sexual relations no longer apply. The prohibitions have been replaced by the three taboos, and the three taboos have won the day.

The sexual revolution is one of the few aptly named revolutions in human history. Virtually all so-called revolutions fall short of their promise, but the sexual revolution has transformed the West with a speed and power unprecedented in human history. Insofar as the condom is the symbol of both safe sex and contraception, it is not absurd to argue that it is as powerful a transformative tool as any other human invention, including the printing press. Safe sex and contraception constituted the checkmate of traditional sexual ethics, rendering the tWorld irrelevant and coronating the iWorld. If there are no more compelling reasons to restrict consensual sexual relations than illegitimate births, public health, and adultery, then the cultural argument is lost. Christians and non-Christians alike have clearly determined that consensual sex using condoms and respecting the three taboos is not a health or moral hazard. Given the lack of birth control and the close-knit, agrarian family structure of Old Testament Israel, virtually everyone can understand why the tWorld so strictly regulated sexual relations. The conviction exists, however, that the creation of methods of contraception and safe-sex practices has signaled the inauguration of a new sexual millennium, and it is an argument an increasing number of Christians have been willing to accept.

What has been overlooked by virtually everyone is that the erosion of these sexual boundaries has created a relational hazard of the highest order. This lesson can certainly be learned from Leviticus 18, which makes it clear that sexual immorality so polluted the lives of the Canaanites that they provoked the wrath of God, and it infers that their immorality was a clear and present danger to anyone who came in contact with them. Since the sexual offenses listed go beyond merely those acts that would result in procreation, and since sexually transmitted diseases were not listed as a threat, either this is a rather arbitrary prohibition on the part of God or there is additional unseen harm that results from the violation of these boundaries.

Sex and the Soul

So what is this harm? As we have seen, the iWorld's denial of non-material reality has resulted in many denying the existence of the soul. This has led the citizens of the iWorld to neglect the cultivation of their souls and the spiritual dimensions of true love and intimacy that lie at the foundation of every healthy relationship. The iWorld has encouraged us to focus on the sexual and sensual to such a degree that we can easily neglect the maturation and emotional development of our relationships. As a result, in the iWorld we tend to evaluate our relationships by sexual, sensual, and emotional standards. The iWorld redefines the words "love" and "intimacy," giving them a sexual, sensual, and emotional meaning. The consequence of all this is that citizens of the iWorld can easily and completely miss the deeper, more spiritual dimension of our relationships and ourselves. Please understand that I am not saying that all sexual relationships outside of marriage are devoid of love and intimacy. Quite frankly, some have more love and intimacy than many marriages. Nevertheless, the iWorld's obsession with the self is at risk of becoming so in touch with sensual pleasure that awareness of the soul can be lost, and with it, true love and intimacy.

Sex in the iWorld is a profound example of the way the iWorld's assumptions have transformed our understanding of the nature of the sexual experience. In the tWorld, sexual relations were understood to be the exclusive domain of a marriage. The purpose was procreation, and it was not a predominant factor in the overall quality of a marriage relationship.

In many ways the iWorld's understanding of sexual relations can be summed up in the term "iSex," and the iWorld's understanding of relationships can be understood in the term "iRelationship." The iWorld maintains that self-fulfillment is the primary path to happiness and that this is true of every aspect of one's life. In an iWorld relationship it is up to each person to ensure that they are getting what they want, and if they are not, it is their responsibility to find it. Since sexual fulfillment in the iWorld is such an important part of personal fulfillment, it is up to each man and woman to look out for his or her own sexual fulfillment. The same is true for relational fulfillment; we each need to take personal responsibility in looking out for our own fulfillment. That this is true is not necessarily a sign of selfishness. If the truth about ourselves is that we alone can understand who we are or that we alone are responsible for our fulfillment, then it is also the case that no one else can really know what we need or want. The iWorld teaches us that no one can know how to love or fulfill me except me. Hence, iSex and iRelationships exist not because of selfishness but simply because of the belief that there is no one else who can know with certainty what you want or need. Sexual and relational fulfillment is a responsibility that rests with each one of us as individuals.

The iWorld provides an unprecedented feast for the senses and sensuality, and yet its appeal goes even further. As we have seen, the iWorld is pliable. It is a world in which we are free to cultivate consensual relationships in any way we choose. We can explore the sexual dimensions of relationships, or we can leave sexuality out of our relationships and explore other dimensions instead. We can live a sexually promiscuous life so long as we adhere to the three taboos, but if so desired we have the choice to forgo sexual promiscuity and live a tWorld existence right in the midst of the iWorld. Given such a broad freedom of choice, the iWorld appears to be a world for everyone. To paraphrase Voltaire's Dr. Pangloss, it appears the iWorld is the best of all possible worlds.[7] Given

7. Voltaire, *Candide or Optimism*, ed. Norman L. Torrey (Northbrook, IL: AHM Publishing, 1946), 2.

its appeal, it is not surprising that many people, including Christians, have made the iWorld their home.

I understand that there is much that is attractive about the iWorld. Yet for all its promise, for all the sensual pleasure it offers, and for all the individual choice it grants, it does not provide an existence that is deeply satisfying. There is an insatiable quality to the iWorld. It is not that the iWorld is without tenderness, compassion, commitment, love, and intimacy; these can all be found in some fashion. But the iWorld allows people to equate intimacy with sexuality and to believe that relational depth and satisfaction is incomplete without a means of sexual expression.

What iSex, iRelationships, and the iWorld have done is tempt us to remove from our consciousness a sense of the spiritual connection we can have with others. We are left with the notion that the only connection that exists between us is physical and emotional, and to love another means doing something to make him or her feel physical or emotional pleasure. The iWorld renders every category, including love, a fundamentally physical or emotional category. Yet is that an accurate representation of all that we are as humans? The emptiness that so many feel in the heart of the iWorld suggests that it is not.

To reclaim the totality of relational fullness, we need to rediscover the human soul and the spiritual dimension of relationship, and in so doing rediscover the deeper meaning of love and intimacy by gaining an understanding of that which truly fulfills us. In doing so we can discover a new way of understanding sex, love, and intimacy and their role in the happiness and fulfillment that was part of the lived experience of the tWorld, even if it was not clearly articulated or understood. It is a perception of human life that faded with the advent of modernity and the Enlightenment and eventually was lost. It is time to recover it.

The rWorld maintains that humans find our greatest fulfillment and satisfaction in cultivating our soul and our ability to love God and neighbor intimately. Indeed, the major difference between the iWorld and the rWorld comes down to the meaning of "soul." In the television show *Heroes*, geneticist Mohinder Suresh asserts that the soul is ultimately a bodily construct that is contained within the brain. This thesis drives his research on the human genome project and his exploration of the evolution of the human species. Suresh's approach to human understanding is another expression of the modern scientific notion that a human being is nothing more than a complex set of biochemical reactions. When the iWorld speaks of soul or spirituality it is referencing an aspect of our being that is still a mystery. Yet this mystery is presumed to be a product of the physical complexity of humans. In the iWorld, love and intimacy are often understood to be the feelings produced as a result of biochemical reactions caused by, among many things, the interaction of humans with other humans. Hence, if orgasm is one of the most intense biochemical reactions, and if it is associated with relationships we assume are intimate and loving—or wish to be intimate and loving—then it is natural that many people associate sex with love and intimacy. Since it follows that everyone wants an opportunity to partake in the best life has to offer, it is easy to understand why the iWorld would move toward establishing an unfettered *right* to sex.

The rWorld, however, has a very different definition of intimacy and love that is based on the idea that love is not merely the feeling produced by the biochemical reactions of a romantic or sexual relationship but a grace given to our souls. If this is true, our happiness and fulfillment would be ultimately rooted in developing our ability to relate to God and one another through our soul. Humans crave love more than anything else, and the rWorld believes we connect to that love by opening our souls to God and to others. The quality of intimacy we enjoy is based on our ability to do just that. The more open or, to use terminology from Genesis, the more "naked" and "unashamed" we become in our relationship with God and others, the more intimacy we can achieve. The more intimacy we have with God, the more we are able to receive his love and then share that love with others. We receive love spiritually when we are intimately connected with God, and as we grow in the ability to be intimate with him and enjoy his love, we also can grow in our ability to be intimate with and love others. The greater our capacity for intimacy, the greater our capacity to receive love and share love.

Sexuality is not an important part of this equation, not because sex is a bad thing but simply because sex is not an essential aspect of the deepest and most fulfilling relational life that is found in a spiritual connection with God and others. Since we are physical beings, it is not surprising that love and intimacy have a reflection in our physical experience. Neither is it surprising that love and intimacy trigger many drives within us, including our sexual drive. Yet it is important to realize that the thing for which we ultimately yearn is not sexual, and sex is not the means to find it. Indeed, the primary problem with sex in the iWorld is that by mistaking sex for love and intimacy, we can find ourselves in the conundrum William Yeats describes in one of the opening lines of this chapter: "The tragedy of sexual intercourse is the perpetual virginity of the soul." Engaging in sexual intercourse but never developing our capacity to love and be truly spiritually intimate with anyone, including our sexual partner, is a danger for all sexual relationships, including marriage.

In Conclusion: Sex in Context

By this point the reader may be wondering whether I even acknowledge that humans are created with hormones and a sex drive. Absolutely. In my effort to put sex in its proper context I do not wish to infer that we are not sexual creatures. We are, and in our post-puberty years, intensely so. Yet even as we desire sex, what we crave even more deeply is love and intimacy, and the deepest love and intimacy is available to us without sex. Similarly, it is possible to have sex without love and intimacy. If we have a relationship filled with love and intimacy, sex will not make it more relationally fulfilling.

This understanding of intimacy, love, fulfillment, and spirituality is the fundamental point of disagreement between the iWorld and the rWorld. It is here where the road to happiness and fulfillment diverges for the two worlds, and we are faced with the question of which path will come closest to delivering that for which we yearn most deeply.

If the standard used to judge human happiness is the quantity and quality of our sexual experience, the rWorld cannot compete with the iWorld, and anyone who suggests otherwise is simply out of touch with reality. In the rWorld there is no guarantee that you will ever marry and have a sexual relationship, and even if you do marry there is no guarantee that the sexual dimension to your relationship will exceed the pleasure offered by sex in the iWorld. And there are definitely people in the iWorld who enjoy love and intimacy, amidst the uncertainty and transient nature of relationships. The question is, which world offers a greater degree of fulfillment? Which will provide us with the opportunity to satisfy the deepest relational yearnings of our soul? Is the potential for better and deeper relationships and quality of life in the rWorld sufficient to make it worth relinquishing some of the individual freedoms of the iWorld in order to join in? To answer these questions we'll have to look further at how the rWorld would manifest itself in reality.

Having examined relational meaning and the place of sexuality in the rWorld, what would the rWorld actually look like, and what practical and tangible benefits would it bring to our lives? We will now explore that question by examining the public policies and societal initiatives needed to create it.

9

Creating the rWorld

The chief cause of unhappiness is trading what we want
most for what we want at the moment.

Unknown

My child arrived just the other day,
He came to the world in the usual way.
But there were planes to catch, and bills to pay.
He learned to walk while I was away.
And he was talking 'fore I knew it, and as he grew,
He'd say, "I'm gonna be like you, dad.
You know I'm gonna be like you."

And the cat's in the cradle and the silver spoon,
Little boy blue and the man in the moon.
"When you comin' home, dad?"
"I don't know when, but we'll get together then.
You know we'll have a good time then."

My son turned ten just the other day.
He said, "Thanks for the ball, dad, come on let's
    play.
Can you teach me to throw?" I said, "Not today,
I got a lot to do." He said, "That's ok."

And he walked away, but his smile never dimmed,
Said "I'm gonna be like him, yeah.
You know I'm gonna be like him." . . .

Well, he came home from college just the other day,
So much like a man I just had to say,
"Son, I'm proud of you. Can you sit for a while?"
He shook his head, and said with a smile,
"What I'd really like, dad, is to borrow the car keys.
See you later. Can I have them please?" . . .

I've long since retired and my son's moved away.
I called him up just the other day.
I said, "I'd like to see you if you don't mind."
He said, "I'd love to, dad, if I could find the time.
You see, my new job's a hassle and the kid's got the
    flu,
But it's sure nice talking to you, dad.
It's been sure nice talking to you."

And as I hung up the phone, it occurred to me
He'd grown up just like me
My boy was just like me.

Harry Chapin and Sandy Chapin,
"Cat's in the Cradle"[1]

Having explored an alternative meaning of sex and relationship, it is time to consider what it would take to create the rWorld, how it would look in day-to-day life, and some of the numerous benefits it can offer.

As readers are no doubt now aware, much of the focus in describing the rWorld up to this point has been in outlining relational boundaries that put limits on individual freedom. These boundaries serve as the scaffolding on which the rWorld is built. But it is important to recognize that the purpose of this scaffolding is not to gratuitously restrict us but to create a framework that offers a wealth of protections and benefits

1. Harry and Sandy Chapin, "Cat's in the Cradle," *Verities and Balderdash* (Elektra Records, 1974).

that are denied to us in the iWorld. Indeed, the essence of the rWorld is found not in the "rules and regulations" against which Graham Nash and the iWorld rebel, but rather in the protections and quality of life they provide for us all.

"Quality of life": these three small words are critically important in discerning which competing vision offers the greatest tangible benefits for our day-to-day lives. In many respects the differences between the two worlds come down to the distinction between "standard of living" and "quality of life." For the sake of argument I am willing to concede that the iWorld may clearly surpass the rWorld in delivering a wider range of personal choices and a higher standard of living. If our basis of assessment is determined *exclusively* on these factors, then the iWorld will be a better choice than the rWorld.

Unfortunately, however, for a majority of people in the iWorld this victory of choice and wealth comes at the cost of other limitations on their quality of life. Thus when examining the rWorld it is important to consider not only some individual sacrifices of choice and material comfort but also the range of additional benefits and protections that it can provide. As the first epigraph of this chapter explains so well, humans are prone to trade what we most want because of the allure of a moment. It is a story as old as the world. It is Adam and Eve in the garden; it is the tragic story of King Midas; it is the story line of the tragedies played out daily in places with the affluence of Hollywood, as well as in the ghettos of Washington DC. In all likelihood it comprises, in at least some fashion, the life story of everyone reading this book. We all know too well that larger aspirations sacrificed for momentary pleasures can accrue into a life of regret. Thus the purpose of the rWorld's framework is to protect us from our proclivity for excesses, lest we spend our lives in the pursuit of what we want presently, at the cost of missing out on what we actually need for contentment and fulfillment.

Plato ends his *Republic* with the haunting "Myth of Er," which tells the story of Er, a soldier who died in battle but came back to life twelve days later. Er is allowed to travel to the "other world," where he observes that souls are reincarnated and given a choice concerning who they will be in their next life. He witnesses a group of souls ready to be reborn, and they are clearly warned to choose their life carefully by looking deeply at its quality and paying attention to more than simply its power or prestige. When it comes time for the first person to choose, in his haste he disregards the advice and chooses a life that on the surface offered him what he wanted. Only after he had made his choice did he discover that the price he would pay to obtain what he desired would be to commit many evils, not the least of which was to devour his own children.

For too many people the iWorld is a Faustian bargain in which we are free to indulge our desires while carelessly surrendering what we actually need for well-being and fulfillment. Indeed it is this bargain that Harry and Sandy Chapin depict in "Cat's in the Cradle." The song is haunting not only because it so clearly relates how a son learns the Faustian allure of individualism from his father, but also because it provides a chronological portrait of an individualism that leads to isolation and loneliness that replicates itself generationally. It poignantly summarizes the unintended consequences of what happens when we "open up the door" and walk away from the "rules and regulations" that are actually essential to living a fully human life. Hence, the purpose of this chapter is to describe the scaffolding humans need in order to avoid gaining the material and sensual world at the cost of what we crave most deeply— time, space, and freedom for healthy, relational living.

Taking the First Steps Toward the rWorld

One of the reasons public opinion polls can annoy us is not that they are occasionally spurious but that they are so consistently accurate. A well-constructed survey of just a few thousand people can accurately explain the opinion of millions of people simply because humans are creatures of habit. Men and women often talk of change, and many resolutions are made on New Year's Eve, but we rarely change our behavior. How we presently behave and think is connected to how we were raised, and is also predictive of how we are likely to behave and think in the future.

Family and culture shape us profoundly. Their imprint is so deep and lasting that without both personal resolve and the assistance of others, the likelihood of any of us making meaningful change is remote. A risk for each of us is that "Cat's in the Cradle" will become our iWorld lamentation. Yet it doesn't have to be this way. We don't have to live in the iWorld. Opting out of the iWorld will take commitment and effort, as will working with others to establish the rWorld. Yet working to establish the rWorld not only is possible, but it would bring many tangible benefits.

As is by now apparent, we can't choose to live in both worlds at the same time. We can't have the unfettered individual freedom of the iWorld and also get the relational benefits and protections of the rWorld. Neither can the rWorld provide the same amount of individual freedom as does the iWorld. Each world has a different vision of human fulfillment, and to achieve their respective goals requires the creation of a unique cultural milieu. This new world will not be created quickly, but it can be done, and I invite you to consider joining with others and me in doing so.

The first step involves making relationships and not "I" the priority of our lives. It means pausing before we make a decision and asking ourselves whether this decision will strengthen or weaken our relational life. Will working overtime be worth the relational cost? Will going into debt be worth the relational cost? How can I present myself as a gift to someone else, as opposed to giving him or her some material object? How can I receive the gift of someone offering themselves to me?

The second step involves joining with other people to help support one another in this new way of life and to work together to construct the social and political scaffolding that will make this way of life possible. Whereas public policy in the iWorld seeks to relax boundaries in support of the expansion of individual freedom, the distinctive feature of the rWorld's approach to public policy is the creation of a rich relational matrix—a framework that provides the full range of relational benefits in service of human fulfillment. The construction and upkeep of this scaffolding involves personal and community participation, as well as governmental support.

While this chapter focuses primarily on public policy, government alone cannot create the rWorld, since the rWorld cannot be imposed from above. The rWorld will only begin to emerge in a society when enough citizens freely embrace it and government begins to support it. The rWorld cannot be imposed through revolution or emerge solely through individual effort; it can only be created by people working collaboratively with other people, and by citizens working collaboratively with government. Moreover, as Tocqueville so perceptively understood, it is likely that local government and not national government will be most effectual in ushering forth a change such as the rWorld. Process is part of the scaffolding and is as important as outcomes to the emergence of the rWorld. An impersonal process won't yield a positive relational outcome. While national or state government has an important role to play in legally defining the appropriate relational boundaries necessary for the rWorld to exist, implementation will always involve local participation and oversight.

Should there be any doubt, let me reiterate that the rWorld is *not* the tWorld. In endeavoring to create the rWorld we are not going back to the tWorld. There are some similarities between the tWorld and the rWorld, such as the importance of living in accord with the boundaries of a relational matrix and recognizing the importance of the uniqueness of men and women. There are, however, important differences that can especially be seen in the relationships between men and women and the role of family. To start with, the rWorld is not a world of patriarchal coercion. It is not a world in which gender inequities are institutionalized. Gender distinctions are recognized, but in a manner that allows men and women to work together in a complementary way to fashion their family, business, public, and private relationships.

The expansion of individual freedom is a public policy focus in the iWorld. Public policy in the rWorld, however, is concerned with creating appropriate relational boundaries and providing time for people to cultivate healthy relationships, which is the very reason for the rWorld's existence. In the iWorld, government is dedicated to deconstructing as much tWorld scaffolding as possible in order to provide individuals the maximum freedom and space to realize their personal goals and dreams without interference from others. In the rWorld, however, the construction of new relational scaffolding rests not just with government and individual citizens but also with families, neighborhoods, religious institutions, schools, businesses, and the full array of public associations. Government plays a role in defining and enforcing relational boundaries and in helping citizens safeguard their time and space for the cultivation of satisfying and enjoyable relationships.

In truth, the rWorld is a fundamentally different place than the iWorld, and the differences go far beyond sexual ethics. In order to gain a foothold the rWorld will need to bring about a categorical reorientation of citizens away from "me" and "I" to "us" and "we." To do so will require that our first and last thought is no longer "What does it mean for me?" but "What does it mean for us all?" Indeed we will need to more fully understand what is represented by the word "us" and what it is going to take to build "us" up.

The Relational Matrix of the rWorld

In the iWorld we view ourselves so individualistically that we increasingly tend to see the world in terms of either *individuals* or *everyone*. We lose sight of the relational matrix that is essential for our quality of life. In the rWorld every category of relationship that makes up our relational matrix is included, but not in the same way as before. As in the tWorld, the relational matrix recognizes that everyone has relational connections and responsibilities by virtue of birth and that fulfillment is found in recovering and cultivating this matrix.

In the rWorld this matrix is comprised of the following relationships:

3GF
marriage
extended family
friendships
neighborhoods
geographic communities
faith communities
the world as our neighbor

As in the tWorld, marriage is a relationship of permanence between a man and a woman that exists in service to the family. The rWorld recovers the importance and value of the 3GF, marriage, and extended family, as well as our relationships within our neighborhoods, geographic communities, nation, and faith community. In doing so it recovers the mutually shared obligation we have to regard everyone in the world as a neighbor and the importance of taking them into account in our individual and collective decision-making, even while it recognizes that it will not be possible to have relational intimacy with everyone on this side of heaven. It resurrects the mutually shared relationships of obligation from the tWorld even as it keeps friendship as a relationship of choice.

In the rWorld, life is not spent searching for people to make us happy but is instead spent cultivating the relationships we already have. The quality of one's life is largely determined by the quality of one's relationships, and government can assist in this endeavor by helping to provide and safeguard the time, space, and support networks for us to do this well. This will help enable us to focus on those closest to us without neglecting our responsibilities and obligations to each relationship in the matrix.

Effectively cultivating relationships will entail a reorientation and reprioritizing of certain aspects of society to the benefit of all. The word "conversion" aptly describes what will need to take place: we must alter our approach to life so that it is more collective, since such an endeavor cannot be undertaken in isolation. The shift will require perseverance and intentionality. Nietzsche is aware of this: "What is essential 'in heaven and earth' seems to be . . . that there should be obedience over a long period of time and in a single direction."[2]

The rWorld cannot be fully realized as a subset of the iWorld. Hence, for the rWorld to come into existence government will need to be involved. While an entire volume could be devoted to the development of public policy for the rWorld, let us briefly examine some policy directions that can make a significant contribution in establishing boundaries and helping us make time to cultivate relational living.

Healthy Relational Roles and Boundaries

The relational health of a society can be measured by the collective health of its relationships. The focus of the rWorld is on strengthening our relationships by enhancing our ability to love and be intimate.

2. Nietzsche, *Beyond Good and Evil*, 101.

Love and intimacy are key components of human relational fulfillment. Since love and intimacy can be nourished only in a safe place, honoring relational roles and boundaries is essential for relational fulfillment.

To our contemporary sensibilities, the notion of "relational roles and boundaries" may seem restrictive or somehow entrapping. Yet the opposite is true, since they are essential aspects of freedom. Men and women are born into a relational matrix, and our individual and collective fulfillment is based on each of us understanding the various roles within the matrix and the place of each role.

Outlining the full relational structure of the rWorld is beyond the scope of this introduction, but Guy Brandon provides a helpful overview of the importance and meaning of roles.

> With different roles (child, parent, student, friend, spouse, work colleague, boss) come different expectations and responsibilities. Attachment—relationship—is the most basic human need; roles and boundaries secure and protect attachments, enabling them to function as intended. God and culture both ascribe power to people so that they can carry out their various roles. From both a divine and cultural perspective, it is important that we utilize the power associated with the roles we have. There is something chaotic and destructive about a child who rules a house, or a teacher who is subject to a student. Roles have four important components:
>
>   1. Responsibilities
>   2. Prohibitions
>   3. Privileges
>   4. Entitlements
>
> The role of a married person, for example, entails the responsibility to care for the spouse as well as the prohibition of having any other sexual partner. It also includes the privilege of sex and the entitlement to exclusivity. So, too, the privileges of parenthood come with the responsibilities; they cannot be held in isolation—at least, not by a good parent. Abuse of a role is not so much the *mis*use of the power given to it, but the *failure* to take it up in these areas—an absent father, an unfaithful spouse, a cheating student, an ungrateful child. . . . This ideal of roles and what they entail is crucial in understanding the concept

of Relational Order, which poses the question, "Who is responsible to whom for what?"

Understanding the responsibilities, prohibitions, privileges and entitlements of different roles is vital to maintaining relational order. . . . This understanding is a result of healthy psychological development. Hence "the health of the social system is maturation-dependent." It is only when people understand the nature of the roles they are in, along with the purposes, responsibilities and boundaries that those entail, that they can sustain working networks of relationships.

Maturation—healthy psychological development—is indispensable for mutual intimacy between two people. Sex is neither a condition of intimacy nor a route to it. Sex on its own, divorced from this overall context which makes possible "nakedness of the soul," offers a false intimacy which cannot contribute to relational and emotional wholeness. In fact, it tends to do exactly the opposite, because the most intimate physical act of which humans are capable is removed from the broader context of intimacy, undermining individuals' expectations and understanding of what intimacy really means. The goal of public policy that deals with attitudes and behaviour surrounding sex and relationships should therefore be maturation: enabling and nurturing healthy psychological development and ensuring that sex is understood within that framework.[3]

Understanding defined relational roles, appropriate relational boundaries, and how we move toward relational living forms the basis of the public policy directions proposed in this chapter.

It is important to note that we are not talking about creating roles and boundaries that would condemn people to stay in abusive or toxic relationships. To the contrary, the rWorld is constructed to protect victims of such relationships. When roles are abused and boundaries violated we must provide a safe place for the victims, along with assistance in healing. No one should be forced to relate with anyone against his or her will. The relational boundaries and roles of the rWorld exist not to trap us in unhealthy relationships but to protect us from harm and provide the environment best suited to relational health. They provide us with a safe place in which we can relate effectively with each person in our life. These roles and boundaries serve to guide, protect, and

3. Guy Brandon, *Just Sex? Why It's Never Just Sex* (Nottingham, UK: Inter-Varsity, 2009), 32–33.

help mature all of our varied relationships: marriage, family, neighborhood, community, and friendship. They guide our interactions in our religious communities and our professional life. By assisting us in understanding what is appropriate and inappropriate, these relational roles and boundaries provide us with a path to develop healthy relationships with appropriate intimacy. They are created and enforced for the relational health of us all while also helping us come to know who we are as persons. There are numerous roles and boundaries that deserve consideration for public policy, but for our purposes we will examine those relating to persons, gender, sexuality, marriage, and family. In each of these areas, government can use law and public policy to help citizens understand roles and boundaries, to deter people from abusing or crossing them, and to reprimand those that do.

Relational Freedom

There is a fundamental disagreement between the iWorld and the rWorld about the nature of freedom. The iWorld believes that individual freedom is found in the absence of rules, restraint, and structure. The rWorld believes that freedom is found relationally in a multidimensional social structure with rules and boundaries that are anchored in personal and collective self-restraint. We've already pulled back enough of the curtain on the rWorld to understand the contrast. The iWorld asserts that humans can create themselves, change themselves, and live as they wish—so long as they don't violate the three taboos—whereas the rWorld asserts that, like a computer, humans come fully loaded with an operating system that is hardwired into the mechanism, and the world itself functions accordingly. We may do things that damage the hardware or bypass the application software, but we cannot replace the operating system.

With all the talk about relationships, it would be a mistake to ignore or understate the importance of each person in the rWorld. The iWorld is not the only world concerned for us as persons; the rWorld is dedicated to helping each of us move toward fulfillment. A difference between the iWorld and the rWorld has to do with the path we take to fulfillment. In his book *The Political Meaning of Christianity*, Glenn Tinder argues that it is the responsibility of Christians to work with everyone to construct a free society that provides all its citizens with both freedom and functional coherence. As Tinder points out, God gives us freedom to make less than ideal choices, and we need to be able to extend to one another that same freedom.[4] For instance, relationships are ultimately a choice; no one ought to be forced to relate to anyone. Even while some people will choose to forgo relationships to their own detriment, for the well-being of all, they need to have the freedom to make that choice.

Unfortunately, on this side of heaven there is a lot of relational hurt and relational pathology. There are many who are psychologically and spiritually unhealthy, and we all need the freedom to not be involved in relationships that are unhealthy, abusive, or enslaving. We do not have the power to cure anyone else of their relational pathologies, and we can't help people who do not want to be helped. If people with whom we relate refuse to mature, we are limited in what kind of relationship we can have with them. On this side of heaven we cannot have healthy relationships with everyone.

Some relational connections are given to us—such as parents, siblings, and extended family—but if any of these are unhealthy or abusive, we must have the freedom and opportunity to seek safe haven. Yet ideally, we will each have the opportunity to develop healthy, mature relationships with many people both within and outside our extended family. It is through our relationships and our service of each other that we find the intimacy and love for which we yearn. Helping to create the context in which these relationships can be developed is the focus of rWorld public policy.

Gender Distinctiveness

As we have seen, gender matters individually and relationally. If we are to develop and enjoy the fullest range of relational depth, we need relationships with both women and men. In the rWorld government can play a role in maintaining gender distinctiveness. This is not to force men and women to fit into preconceived, socially conditioned gender roles. On the contrary, men and women should be allowed to develop

4. Glenn Tinder, *The Political Meaning of Christianity: The Prophetic Stance* (San Francisco: HarperCollins, 1991).

in every way possible; a person's sex should not be used to hold them back from developing their full potential. If it is the case that God has made men and women with the capacity to do similar things, they should be allowed to do similar things. The purpose of this boundary is to make sure we also recognize that even with the similarities we share as humans, women and men complement each other relationally in ways we may not yet understand. Each provides a richness and depth to our relational lives that must not be sacrificed simply because some of our historical assumptions about gender have been mistaken. Government should strive to keep gender distinctive and should thwart efforts or initiatives to render gender socially meaningless. Correspondingly, government should discourage citizens from attempting to surgically or chemically alter their sex. Government, however, needs to assist parents and others seeking to understand the sex of people born with biological abnormalities that make gender determination ambiguous. This boundary is not about arbitrarily limiting men and women on the basis of sex but is about keeping alive the search for understanding what makes each gender unique and how we can complement each other for the good of all.

Boundaries on Sexual Relations

We are made with a sex drive, but as we have seen, sexual relations are not an essential element of human fulfillment, and when sexual boundaries are violated, the relational and social consequences are significant. The violation of sexual boundaries can inhibit or destroy intimacy by creating hurt and insecurity incompatible with relational health. Moreover, if we channel relational energy disproportionately into the sexual aspect of our relationships, we may neglect other more important aspects of relating. Individual relational deficiencies have social consequences, and we do not function effectively in any aspect of our life when our relationships are deficient or in turmoil.

When children are born to those who are unmarried, the cost to the child and society is significant. There is no question that an unmarried individual or couple can care for and nurture a child, but as we have seen, the statistical reality is that children in such relational settings tend not to do well, and society must bear a significant cost in dealing with the adverse consequences on such children, often throughout their lives. A public policy that establishes a boundary that confines sexual relations to a marriage between a man and a woman could: (1) prevent the physical, emotional, and spiritual harm that comes from engaging in a sexual relationship outside of marriage; (2) remind everyone that love and intimacy are far more essential to human fulfillment than is sex; and (3) prompt us to take the time we currently dedicate to pursuing sexual endeavors and apply it instead to developing ourselves relationally. The time and energy we so often expend in trying to get other people to do and be what we wish, whether sexual or not, could be more constructively channeled into building relationships with those people. Relationships are neither an exercise in manipulation nor a joint enterprise of individual fulfillment; they are a mutual adventure in knowing.

Please be clear that I do not support criminal charges for violating this boundary, as has been the practice in some societies. Instead society should make clear its antipathy to the relational harm caused by sexual relations outside of marriage. Governments need to consider how to ensure that all adults are aware of the full economic cost to society of their sexual behavior, particularly in the areas of child welfare and long-term health costs. It is surely unfair to make one person pay for another's sexual choices. The focus, however, should not be on punitive measures. Outside the fact that policing the bedroom places government where it does not belong, penalties for fornication would be virtually unenforceable. With pregnancy out of wedlock being one of the only obvious ways to detect a breach of the boundary, attempting to punish those involved would likely have the undesirable consequence of leading to an increasing number of abortions. There is a limit to what law can achieve. Not every moral stricture ought to be made part of the criminal code. Laws can regulate behavior to some degree, but they cannot change the heart. Without a change of heart, legal remedies are limited in the extent to which they can bring social change.

Marriage

Society would be well served to recover the understanding of marriage as a lifetime union between a man and a woman, along with the understanding that it exists in service to the family and others. In a good marriage a husband and wife nurture and support each other and their children, as well as parents, relatives, and others in need. The evidence for the positive social impact of this definition of marriage, especially as it pertains to the care of children, is overwhelming.[5] As we have seen, no other arrangement—including polygamous, same-sex, or communal marriages or unions—comes close to providing the necessary care and protection for children that a traditional marriage provides.

The statistical evidence cited in chapter 4 clearly supports the overwhelming benefits of traditional marriage in relation to the rearing and nurturing of children, but certain critics still may not be persuaded. Some will argue that alternative relational models will be just as nurturing once society has accepted them and the people in those relationships no longer need to live with the moral disapproval they presently endure. So rather than get lost in a social argument that cannot be resolved until additional research and longitudinal studies can be done, let me offer my reasoning for not supporting any alternatives to traditional marriage without reference to statistical measures. My three fundamental reasons are: (1) gender matters; (2) people do not need a sexual relationship to be fulfilled; and (3) any union less permanent than marriage is detrimental to children.

Gender Matters

Gender matters to marriage. As we have touched on before, even the supporters of same-sex marriage are amazed at the speed with which society has moved toward support not merely of same-sex unions but also of same-sex marriages. What is it that accounts for the unprecedented and unexpected speed of this transition? I believe it is primarily due to the neutering of male and female designations in contemporary society. If our society believed the distinctiveness of male and female mattered for marriage and family, then initiatives on same-sex marriages or unions would not be under serious consideration. When, however, our society lost sight of the importance of gender distinctiveness, male-female relations were, for all practical purposes, neutered. If

---

5. In addition to the references already cited, see James Q. Wilson, *The Marriage Problem: How Our Culture Has Weakened Families* (New York: HarperCollins, 2002), 170–75; and Hymowitz, *Marriage and Caste*.

we are fundamentally just persons, and if male and female are merely socially constructed categories, then why would gender be relevant in our relational or sexual considerations?

Social revolutions do not occur in an instant. They begin at a moment and they can take a generation or longer to be realized. The point at which we neutered our species provided the tipping point for the social revolution over same-sex marriage. The full impact of what the neutering means won't be immediately apparent, but it will be revealed in time. Indeed, this entire debate may ultimately be reduced to a disagreement over the meaning of gender. Are we by nature men and women or just persons with differing sexual apparatus?

Because gender matters, maintaining marriage as a relationship between one man and one woman is of far reaching importance—in procreation, in the quality of the relationship, and in parenting. Gender is irreducibly significant in all these dimensions. This does not mean that no other factors are important to a good, healthy marriage and family. There are many components to a healthy marriage, but if we lose the qualities gender brings to our relational existence, and to marriage in particular, we are at risk of impoverishing children and families in ways we cannot yet imagine.

People Do Not Need a Sexual Relationship to Be Fulfilled

If our best hope for human fulfillment includes living in a constellation of healthy relationships of which none are necessarily sexual, then no effective purpose will be served by changing the definition of marriage or the boundaries of sexual relations to include same-sex relations. Relaxing the gender boundary of marriage will send the wrong signal about the meaning of relational fulfillment with no discernable societal benefit in return. The potential social cost, however, could be significant.

Any Union Less Permanent Than Marriage Is Detrimental to Children

Even proponents of same-sex marriage, such as Jonathan Rauch, agree that marriage is the best social institution for raising children.[6]

6. Jonathan Rauch, *Gay Marriage: Why It Is Good for Gays, Good for Straights, and Good for America* (New York: Henry Holt, 2004), chap. 6.

Since social science has not yet demonstrated that there is any alternative for child rearing that is superior to traditional marriage, every attempt to do so unnecessarily and irresponsibly involves children in social experimentation or social engineering. Children's lives are too fragile and important to subject them to what could be detrimental experiences.

Civil partnerships and cohabitation are presently less stable and produce demonstrably inferior outcomes for children. Consequently, if gender does matter and if marriage is not essential for human fulfillment, then there is no compelling benefit to engaging in further social experimentation concerning rearing children outside of a marriage between a man and a woman.

As a result of all these factors, public policy should endeavor to support and reinforce traditional marriage and the boundaries that surround it. This includes the elimination of no-fault divorce. Clearly there are cases where divorce is justified, but it ought to be limited to those cases and granted only after every effort at reconciliation has been made. Marriage is a serious business; it is something that ought not to be entered into lightly, and the vows of permanence ought not to be broken lightly. Divorce should not be permitted without just cause and only following a commensurate waiting period designed to give the couple a thorough opportunity to resolve their problems.

Tightening divorce law may seem unnecessary and harsh to an iWorld viewpoint, but that is because the iWorld proceeds under the mistaken assumption that sexual relationships are a primary means of fulfillment. Once individuals are better able to differentiate between sex and relational fulfillment, they can better understand that the source of their unhappiness will be solved, not by another marriage or another liaison, but by seeking to find relational fulfillment within the relational matrix. Discovering what makes for fulfilling relationships may allow their marriage to heal, mature, and become more fulfilling than they now imagine.

This is one example of how public policy can help people find fulfillment. By setting proper boundaries for relationships, everyone will have a greater chance of finding the love and intimacy for which they yearn, regardless of whether they are married.

The rWorld Is about Time

Public policy in the rWorld is not merely about maintaining relational boundaries; it is also about making time to create and sustain healthy relationships. Time is an essential aspect of the scaffolding of the rWorld. As we have seen, sexuality in and of itself is not central to relational fulfillment. After all, there are 168 hours in a week, and for most people sexual relations would occupy only a very small fraction of those hours. So then what is central? Time itself. Time alone won't build healthy relationships, but as the Chapins know, nothing can take its place.

Time matters in every relationship. There is no way to more fully know God and the love of God without spending time with God in prayer, meditation, study, and worship—there are no shortcuts. If it is true that all love comes from God, this is where the journey to relational fulfillment begins, and it requires time and focused attention.

But that is only the beginning of the journey. Time is also an essential component of human relationships. Only by spending time and focused attention with other people can we build healthy, rewarding, loving, and satisfying relationships. It takes time to get to know another person deeply, and it takes time for him or her to get to know you deeply. Relationships require availability. No one can always be there for someone else, but not being available has relational implications. A pattern of non-availability damages or kills relational intimacy and fulfillment.

Time is our scarcest and most valuable commodity, so we need to be very intentional in how we use it. Our use of time indicates what we value and treasure. If we are spending time with others, we have the possibility of growing with them in true love and intimacy; if we are using our time for other purposes, it is almost certain that our life will be lacking in these characteristics and that those who love us will, at a minimum, become frustrated with us.

Time and Money

The single biggest competitor for our time is the pursuit of wealth. If we are going to be serious about making time for healthy relationships, we need to take stock of the lure of money and consider what we can do to resist the temptation to sacrifice our relationships in the pursuit of mammon. Sex and money are both highly prone to idolatry.

Given the unwavering and often vociferous stand the church has historically taken on sexual morality, it would be easy for the casual observer to conclude that sex is the most important moral issue in the Bible. That is simply untrue. Sex is one aspect of purity, but the Old and New Testament writers reserve some of their strongest language for economic justice. Scripture suggests that the two greatest sources of temptation are wealth and sex. Christ explains this teaching in the Sermon on the Mount:

> Do not store up for yourselves treasures on earth, where moth and rust consume and where thieves break in and steal; but store up for yourselves treasures in heaven, where neither moth nor rust consumes and where thieves do not break in and steal. For where your treasure is, there your heart will be also. . . . No one can serve two masters; for a slave will either hate the one and love the other, or be devoted to the one and despise the other. You cannot serve God and wealth. Therefore I tell you, do not worry about your life, what you will eat or what you will drink, or about your body, what you will wear. Is not life more than food, and the body more than clothing? Look at the birds of the air; they neither sow nor reap nor gather into barns, and yet your heavenly Father feeds them. Are you not of more value than they? And can any of you by worrying add a single hour to your span of life? And why do you worry about clothing? Consider the lilies of the field, how they grow; they neither toil nor spin, yet I tell you, even Solomon in all his glory was not clothed like one of these. But if God so clothes the grass of the field, which is alive today and tomorrow is thrown into the oven, will he not much more clothe you—you of little faith? Therefore do not worry, saying, "What will we eat?" or "What will we drink?' or "What will we wear?" For it is the Gentiles who strive for all these things; and indeed your heavenly Father knows that you need all these things. But strive first for the kingdom of God and his righteousness, and all these things will be given to you as well. So do not worry about tomorrow, for tomorrow will bring worries of its own. Today's trouble is enough for today. (Matt. 6:19–21, 24–34)

This passage has much to say about the priorities of our lives and raises an important question about our use of time. How will we invest the time God has given us: in the pursuit of material goods or in obedience to the two great commandments to love God and neighbor?

Ironically, Christ's teaching about wealth and use of time may require as great a change in our lifestyle and societal priorities as will his teaching about sex. The rWorld is focused on the quality of our relationships and not merely sexual boundaries. In Western society we spend so much time working that very few of us reserve enough time to invest in relationship with God or others. A report issued recently in Australia is a damning critique of the way in which Australians are spending their time and what the consequences are for their relationships.

Thirty years ago, the average Australian worker spent less than forty hours a week at work—the vast majority of this time was in steady employment, working on weekdays between the hours of 8 a.m. and 6 p.m. This pattern of working life was shared across the broad community, providing opportunity for most Australians to enjoy consistent patterns of life *outside* work—to spend time on a predictable basis with family and friends, and in other community-related pursuits.

The past three decades have been a time of unambiguous economic prosperity for our country. But this success has come at a price. Working patterns have altered to such an extent that Australia is now the only high-income country in the world that combines:

- average working hours that are at the top end amongst high-income nations
- a strong tendency for work on weeknights and weekends, and
- a relatively large proportion of the working population employed on a casual basis. . . .

A significant body of evidence suggests that those people who work long and unsocial hours spend less quality time with their families and friends and that most Australian families are suffering time pressure resulting from their work.

An emerging body of international research shows that these long and atypical working patterns are associated with dysfunctional family environments, including:

a. Negative health outcomes for those working these times, particularly if they are parents

b. Strained family relationships

c. Parenting marked by anger, inconsistency and ineffectiveness

And, critically, both long/atypical hours and dysfunctional family environments are associated with:

d. Reduced child well-being.

Notably, these associations are evident when either or both parents work atypical schedules, so the timing of fathers' [and] not just mothers' work matters to children. And although low-income members of Australian society are generally more keenly affected by these changes, the impact is shared across all strata in our community.

Unsurprisingly, over the last 30 years in Australia, the decline in family relational health has led to an increased incidence of separation and divorce. And there are now more single parents than ever before. With only a single parent providing care for one or more children, increased time pressure and stress increase the probability of adult ill health, and parenting and child difficulties.

Other trends in the Australian workplace, and society more broadly, exacerbate the relational health problems described here and leave the workforce increasingly vulnerable to an eventual downturn in the economy. These trends include a sustained reduction in job stability, intensification of work responsibilities and increased household debt.[7]

This may be true of Australians, but they are hardly alone. If Australia is ahead of the rest of the West in this regard, it does not lead by much.

So what if anything can we do about it? Given the indebtedness of Western society, the decline in the size of the middle class, the number of families in which both parents work—sometimes multiple jobs—to make ends meet, the problem is not merely one of choice but of survival. It is not clear that many people actually have the discretionary time to give to relationships, even if they are persuaded it is essential. We need help. The rWorld recognizes this, and this is an area where public policy can help.

7. "An Unexpected Tragedy: Evidence for the Connection between Working Patterns and Family Breakdown in Australia," Relationships Forum (2007), 13, www.relationshipsforum.org .au/report/index.html#ut_download.

Making Time for Relationships

As we have seen, one purpose of rWorld public policy is to help establish appropriate boundaries necessary to construct an effective relational framework. Another purpose is to help provide us with the time needed to build and cultivate the healthy mature relationships essential for a fulfilling life.

As the study "An Unexpected Tragedy" makes clear, one of the most profound changes that has occurred in Australia over the past decade is the amount of time devoted to work and its impact on relationships. Yet Australia is not alone in this. Robert Putnam, in his book about the collapse of community in America, *Bowling Alone*, finds a similar story in America:

> Let us sum up what we have learned about the factors that have con- tributed to the decline in civic engagement and social capital. . . . First, pressures of time and money, including the special pressures on two- career families, contributed measurably to the diminution of our social and community involvement. . . . Second, suburbanization, commuting, and sprawl also played a supporting role. . . . Third, the effect of elec- tronic entertainment—above all, television—in privatizing our leisure time has been substantial . . . Finally and most important, generational change—the slow, steady, and ineluctable replacement of the long civic generation by their less involved children and grandchildren—has been a very powerful factor.[8]

We see in Putnam's final factor the impact of the iWorld on our re- lational and social fabric. As the last generation of Americans reared in the tWorld passes on and is replaced by generations reared in the iWorld, we are increasingly faced with the social cost of the individual- ism of the iWorld. There is no easy way to reverse this trend, but doing so will involve prioritizing time for our relationships and not merely for ourselves. This will need to begin with an intentional choice on the part of each of us. But making such a decision will not change the distance we must commute to work, nor does it change the fact that our 3GFs are geographically dispersed, to say nothing of our extended family. In

8. Robert D. Putnam, *Bowling Alone: The Collapse and Revival of American Community* (New York: Simon & Schuster, 2000), 283.

the iWorld parents are increasingly likely to be divorced or geographically separated. We are less likely to know our neighbors beyond a superficial level, and our "closest" friends are often geographically distant. Employers may require us to relocate regularly, and our work schedules may prohibit a family with two working parents from having a common day off each week. There are many factors that contribute to the breakdown of family and community.

Nevertheless, if any change is to come, it must begin with each of us. This will involve not just a personal decision in how we will live but also a decision about what we will ask our government to prioritize. Such a change will require that we value quality of life more highly than standard of living. We need to understand that our quality of life depends largely on the quality of our relationships and that our time is better invested in relationships than merely in the creation of material wealth. Doing so will mean forgoing a standard of living that requires unacceptable relational sacrifice. We will need to curtail certain individual pursuits, such as the time we spend watching television or engaged in electronic games, in order to carve out time that we can spend time together as families, neighbors, and so forth. Absent a change in personal commitment, there is nothing the government can do to improve the relational quality of our lives. Yet if we are willing to make these changes, there are many things government can do to assist us. Let me suggest a few possibilities by way of illustration.

MAKING SUNDAY SPECIAL AGAIN

We tend to regard the freedom to shop on Sunday as a *right*, a freedom everyone in the developed world deserves. The reality is that removing the restrictions on Sunday shopping has had a catastrophic relational impact on our society, and it makes little sense economically. For instance, why should there be incentives for businesses to keep their doors open seven days a week when an across-the-board prohibition on shopping one day a week could save all of them the expense of being open for business on the seventh day? The reality is that removing the restriction on Sunday shopping has made it even more difficult for nuclear families to find time to spend time together, to say nothing of finding time to spend with extended families, neighbors, and friends. With an increasing number of people required to work on Sunday and more community activities, such as children's sports leagues, scheduled for Sunday, it is much harder to find any common time for relationships.

There is a public policy remedy that can be made with no financial cost and that will likely boost profits for businesses and provide all of us with more time for one another: reenact the prohibitions on Sunday shopping and many publicly scheduled activities. The most important reason to do this, apart from any potential financial benefits, is relational. But it will be virtually impossible to achieve this without governmental intervention. As long as Sunday is unregulated, there is an incentive for all stores to stay open so they do not lose their market share. This single change in public policy would do more at less cost to create relational time than anything else we might consider.

There may be those who agree on the importance of a shared day off but would prefer a day other than Sunday. The cultural and political reality, however, is that there will be less resistance to re-regulating Sunday shopping than regulating any other day of the week. If consensus could be built around another day, it would be worth considering, but in the United States, at least, it is hard to imagine any day other than Sunday being protected.

Incentivizing Being Rooted Rather Than Being Transient

We live in a time of extraordinary mobility. We can, with relative ease, travel across town, across the state, across the country, and even around the world. The ability to do this has positive relational benefits, allowing us to visit friends and family who live at a great distance from us. Moreover, it enables us to develop relationships with people of all nations, which is a critical component of the relational matrix—the world as our neighbor. Yet it is also the case that mobility has led to the geographic separation of family and friends, which has devastating relational costs. One cannot develop rewarding relationships without spending time together. Modern technology has allowed for ease of communication, which has relational benefits, but long-distance communication is no substitute for being physically present.

Another way in which mobility has affected us is the increasing number of people who commute to work. As Putnam discovered, "We are spending more and more time alone in the car. . . . The car and the commute, however, are demonstrably bad for community life. In round numbers the evidence suggests that *each additional ten minutes in daily commuting time cuts involvement in community affairs by 10 percent.*"[9] While developments in technology have certainly made this possible, public policy has been a major contributor to the development of mobility. The government has spent billions of dollars on roads, thus enabling increasing sprawl and commuting. In contrast, so little has been invested in public transportation that we have built our economy on mobility. In addition to the environmental impact, the relational impact of this is profound.

The government is doing this even as it spends more and more money dealing with the social problems caused, at least in part, by mobility, such as the deterioration in the relational connectedness of neighborhoods and the cost of caring for the elderly who do not live in geographic proximity to their children.

It doesn't have to be this way. Just as the government incentivized mobility, so it can incentivize rootedness. Without being overly intrusive, government can change public policy to promote geographic stability. Through changes in taxation and in transportation policy, it can give incentives to businesses to relocate in neighborhoods rather than in commercial centers that require its employees to engage in long commutes. In addition, development of public transportation at the expense of the automobile will encourage people to conduct their business locally, enabling more people to work locally. On a related note, the government could give larger tax breaks to families who have elderly parents living with them and to children who relocate to live close to elderly relatives. Doing so would take significant pressure off of public services, which in turn can save substantial financial resources. These are just a few examples of what the government can do to revitalize families and neighborhoods, not only economically but also relationally.

Relational Schools

The government can also use public policy to introduce a relational curriculum into the educational system. The likelihood is that those who are suffering the most from the iWorld are children, and we have yet to

9. Ibid., 213.

see the full impact of what this will mean when they become adults.[10] A decreasing number of children are raised by their biological parents, grow up in relationally healthy neighborhoods, or even live in the same location throughout their childhood. All these factors directly impact the relational connectedness of children. More and more kids have, in essence, become iChildren, and as a result do not know what they are missing. Society bemoans the fact that children are not as active and do not play together as they once did, but is this simply because they do not know any differently? Living in the iWorld may be a choice for their parents, but the children themselves haven't had a say in the matter. That is why, even in the name of choice, a relational curriculum in the school is of vital importance.

Presently public schools specialize in a curriculum that is rooted in the language of individual choice. A child is taught the values of the iWorld from the outset. At the very least we owe children an education that makes them aware of a completely different way of looking at the world that includes hallmarks of moral and relational responsibility. It would be even better to be able to give parents the opportunity to have their children educated in a school that is fashioned by a relational framework so that healthy relational living is modeled rather than merely taught.

What would such an education look like? The framework of this book is suggestive, but groups all over the world—such as the Institute for American Values in the United States, the Relationships Foundation in England, and the Relationships Forum in Australia—have already conducted significant research and have much to offer regarding the specifics of such an approach.

We have merely scratched the surface of what might be done in public policy to prioritize, promote, and create time for relationship. The point of this overview is simply to suggest that government can do much to help us make time for relationships. A broader view of such matters would include the benefits society would accrue from the introduction

10. Bibliographical evidence for this statement can be found in virtually every developed nation. For examples, see *Breakthrough Britain*, written by the Social Policy Group of the Conservative Party in Britain; the previously referenced "An Unexpected Tragedy"; and virtually everything published by the Institute for American Values (www.americanvalues.org) and the Relationships Foundation in Cambridge, England (www.relationshipsfoundation.org).

of relational business structures, relational forms of finance, relational justice, relational health care, and relational lifestyles. It is evident that government has a pivotal role to play if we are to prioritize relational values for the future well-being of our families and our children.

While much more could be written on the subject of public policy and the rWorld, we have at least taken a cursory glimpse at ways in which life would differ between the iWorld and the rWorld. Now it is time to compare and contrast the two worlds and consider which is a more effective model for our lives and our world.

10

Where Then Shall We Live?
The iWorld or the rWorld?

Can you see the real me?

> Pete Townsend,
> "The Real Me"[1]

I firmly believed that I didn't need anyone but me
I sincerely thought I was so complete
Look how wrong you can be

> Rod Stewart, "Every Picture Tells a Story"[2]

Now that the competing models of the iWorld and the rWorld have been set forth, we have an opportunity to consider which world is best suited for our lives. Each model has benefits and limitations but we cannot successfully attempt to live in both simultaneously. We have to make a choice that will affect our life and our world.

1. Pete Townsend, "The Real Me," *Quadrophenia*, The Who (Track Polydor, 1973).
2. Rod Stewart, "Every Picture Tells a Story," *Every Picture Tells a Story* (Mercury Records, 1971).

For many people this will not be an easy choice. Moving toward the rWorld may be a daunting prospect for those who have grown up in (or grown accustomed to) the iWorld and value its remarkable personal autonomy, even if it is something that they infrequently exercise. On an individual level, however, there is much more to be gained than lost in such a realignment of society. Many people are quietly concerned about where the iWorld is leading us, but they have been willing to follow along as a result of their belief in progress and modernity, even in spite of severe misgivings about the relational cost and the detrimental impact the policies of the iWorld have on their quality of life.

Many people have placed an inordinately high value on the iWorld freedoms that the vast majority of people fail to exercise most of the time, despite costs that profoundly impact them on a day-to-day level. Indeed, the iWorld can be said to be the embodiment of a philosophy that we know to be false in our everyday lives—namely, that getting what we want at the moment often comes at the cost of what we most want. Examples abound: cheating on a diet, indulging in impulse spending, and quitting the race before the finish, among others. Such a modus operandi can lead to a deeply unhappy and unfulfilling life on both a personal and a collective level; its pleasures are fleeting, but its regrets linger on. Even in the iWorld it can be difficult to dispute that *the chief cause of unhappiness is trading what we want most for what we want at the moment.* Many have taken such a path by default because of the belief that there is no effective alternative to the iWorld. But a genuine alternative exists in the rWorld.

Still, there are those who resist the idea that a choice must be made between the two. The difficulty with this is that the iWorld and the rWorld are fundamentally incompatible. In reality, the iWorld offers choice but is not neutral; it does not allow people with competing worldviews to uncompromisingly reside within it. The iWorld and rWorld are each ruled by a different set of fundamental assumptions about the meaning of life that profoundly shape the lives of everyone who dwells therein. If you live in the iWorld, you can try to live in accordance with the moral framework of the rWorld, but you will miss out on many of its fundamental relational benefits—such as the relational matrix, the moral structure, and the incentives and assistance that boundaries provide in nurturing healthy, rewarding relationships. Many who live in the iWorld assert that it is enough to give people who are favorably inclined to the rWorld the freedom to live in accordance with its moral framework. Unfortunately, such thinking demonstrates that the iWorld does not fully understand its limitations. The relational benefits of the rWorld cannot be fully realized without the social and moral boundaries that make those benefits possible. You can no more fully live the rWorld within the iWorld than you can fully live the iWorld within the rWorld. The aims of the two worlds are mutually exclusive.

The tension between the Amish community and the iWorld is an illustration of the limits of the iWorld. The iWorld provides the Amish with some space and freedom to live in accordance with their religious faith, but they still have to live in a society that is profoundly at odds with the Christian pacifism that is a foundational element of their faith. Moreover, the iWorld makes it difficult for the Amish to pass along their worldview to their children, because their children do not get to see the full picture of what their worldview produces, since the Amish community is constrained by the iWorld from living it fully.

At this point the iWorld might protest that it has given the Amish the most it can give. Precisely. The most it can give is not the same as giving enough. The iWorld cannot be all things to all people.

The same is true of the rWorld. If we decide the rWorld is the world for us, then we will need to invest the time and effort of a generation to begin to construct it. The predominance of the iWorld has come about as the result of billions of choices made by billions of people. The iWorld was not built in a day, and neither will the rWorld be. As we have seen, the rWorld cannot be created from the top down; it must be built from the bottom up. We must recognize that even if enough of us are persuaded to begin to transition from the iWorld to the rWorld, the transition will require time as well as focused effort, commitment, and vision.

Since the choice impacts everyone, wouldn't it be radical if we were to choose the world that brings about the maximum benefit for all rather than one based on self-centered motivations? That's what I recommend we do. But how can we determine what is best for everyone? In order to do this we as a society will need to resolve one of the most significant disagreements we presently face in the public square: understanding who we are as humans. Are we created with a common nature such that we can discover, even with our individual differences, what will bring us all health and fulfillment? Or do we differ by nature to such a degree that we will not be able to discover a common avenue to happiness and fulfillment?

Who Are We and How Do We Know?

The central questions of this book are: "Who are we?" and "How do we come to know who we are?" In asking these questions we connect the epigraph from Nietzsche, used to open this book, and the one from Pete Townsend at the beginning of this chapter. Both deal with the difficulty we have answering the question, "Who are we?" These questions frame the commencement of this book because how we each choose to answer these questions will, as Robert Frost discovered, "make all the difference" in the road we choose to travel.

Historically two primary approaches to understanding who we are have developed. According to the *Oxford English Dictionary*, the concept of personal identity doesn't show up in the English language until modern philosophers first used it in the seventeenth century. Prior to that point in Western history, the fundamental assumption was that humans shared a common nature and that the individual search for fulfillment was focused on comprehending and living in accordance with who humans are by nature. Understanding human nature was believed to be of greater importance in knowing ourselves than was awareness of our individual characteristics. Beginning with the Enlightenment, the search for self-understanding became a more individualistic quest. Understanding individual characteristics became more important than human nature in seeking to answer the question of who we are. In other words, beginning with the Enlightenment we became less likely to ask, "Who are we?" but more likely to ask, "Who am I?" This emphasis on asking an individualistic question about identity has only increased since the Enlightenment.

This shift in our understanding of who we are is the primary reason for the transition that eventually took place between the tWorld and the iWorld. The tWorld was based on the assumption that we come to understand who we are as humans by living in the relational matrix with the men and women with whom we share a common nature. The iWorld is based on the assumption that it is our individual differences, rather than what we share in common with other individuals, that are most important in knowing who we are. Consequently, the iWorld is constructed to honor our individuality more than our common humanity.

The rWorld, like the tWorld, is based on a shared conception of the importance of understanding human nature in determining our identity. Like the tWorld, the rWorld and the iWorld are engaged in a debate about how best to understand who we are and how we as individuals are developed, sustained, and nurtured. If this is best determined by each of us individually, then the iWorld is almost certainly better suited to the process than is the rWorld. But if this is best done in the context of the relational matrix, then the rWorld is better suited to the process than is the iWorld.

While it is not possible to resolve this debate in the pages that remain, the terms of the debate can be clarified. Science and philosophy can be of assistance in this endeavor. However, since many contradictory points are claimed in the name of both, we will need to examine both with an eye toward understanding what each can and cannot contribute to the debate.

Modern Science, Sexual Orientation, and Self-Understanding

One point of divergence between the iWorld and the rWorld concerns the extent to which sexual orientation is considered a fundamental component of personal identity. In other words, is a person's sexual orientation a more important factor in understanding that person's identity than shared aspects of their humanity? The rWorld doesn't actually define people by their inclinations or attractions, sexual or otherwise. The rWorld recognizes we may each have different sexual desires, impulses, and interests, but believes the deepest answer to the question of who we are is found not in our sexual orientation or attractions but in our common human nature. A Christian might argue that the deepest truth about who we are is that each of us is a male or female made in the image of God, loved by God, and deserving of the dignity that comes with this love. The rWorld maintains that the fundamental truth about who we are is found in our common human nature, not in different attributes persons may possess.

The iWorld disagrees. Rather than looking for self-understanding in what we have in common with each other, it encourages each of us to focus on what we each desire. Since for many, if not virtually all of us, our sex drive is one of our most powerful sensual components, it is not surprising that freeing us to try and satisfy ourselves sexually became one of the highest values of the iWorld. With sexuality being so highly regarded, it is easy to understand why sexual preference is one of the more important aspects of self-understanding in the iWorld. In the iWorld more and more people do not centrally identify themselves as human in a common sense, but as human in a particular sense, with sexual preference becoming one of the chief markers. Before we are human we are gay, lesbian, bisexual, transgendered, heterosexual, and so on.

This is a critical distinction between the rWorld and the iWorld. To what degree should sexual preference be determinative of our fundamental identity? Clearly each of us can live as if it is or is not our fundamental identity, yet we need to realize that equating sexual orientation with our core identity is a choice, not destiny. There are many who operate under the assumption that sexual preference, whatever it may be, is fixed and so should be a component of identity. The reality is, however, that sexual preference is not fixed for everyone, and even if it were, it does not necessarily follow that sexual preference needs to be a core factor in determining our identity. People often reference *The Science of Desire* by Dean Hamer and Peter Copeland as scientific research that demonstrates the existence of a gay gene and, by extension, that homosexual behavior is biologically or genetically determined and therefore morally justified. Aside from the fact that people making such an assertion did not carefully read the book—the authors do not claim that what they have discovered is determinative of behavior or morally justifies behavior—it shows, as Hamer and Copeland point out, a baseline misunderstanding of what modern science can and cannot do. As the authors say, "Concepts like 'good' and 'bad' or 'right' and 'wrong' do not appear in biology textbooks. Nevertheless, there seems to be an almost irresistible urge for people to try and use biology to either condemn or justify homosexuality and similar human behaviors. They talk about what's 'natural' and what's not, or what makes evolutionary 'sense.' None of the arguments really resolve the issue, however."[3]

First, there are a lot of unanswered scientific questions about human sexuality; hence the dogma that accompanies most contemporary discourse about sexual preference is, at best, not yet justified. Second, even if a scientific understanding of human sexual attraction were clear and precise, the scientific method is not in a position to resolve moral questions about sexual behavior and identity, either in favor or opposition. It is here that we again visit David Hume. Since we cannot derive an "ought" from an "is," the existence of sexual attraction does not in itself justify any particular sexual behavior, nor does it mandate or prohibit a link to identity. One cannot derive a moral or theological imperative merely from a scientific observation.

The factors that determine sexual orientation are complex and are still being unraveled by scientists. "Sexual orientation typically refers to the directionality of a person's experience of sexual attraction. Sexual orientation refers to a person's sexual predispositions, and these may come from a variety of sources: *nature* (biological antecedents) or *nurture* (environmental or psychological factors) or, most likely, some combination of both."[4]

On the nature side, scientists are exploring the possible existence of a genetic, biochemical, or hormonal component to sexual preference. On the nurture side, scientists are exploring the degree to which a person's life experiences may contribute toward sexual preference. Even if it were possible to unravel the mystery of sexual attraction, such empirical evidence would be unable to provide a moral basis for actions based on those attractions. For instance, we do not know what leads to alcoholism. Like sexual attraction, alcoholism is probably triggered

3. Dean Hamer and Peter Copeland, *The Science of Desire: The Search for the Gay Gene and the Biology of Behavior* (New York: Simon & Schuster, 1994), 213.
4. Stanton L. Jones and Mark A. Yarhouse, *Ex-Gays? A Longitudinal Study of Religiously Mediated Change in Sexual Orientation* (Downers Grove, IL: IVP Academic, 2007), 27. See also Simon Burton, *The Causes of Homosexuality* (Cambridge, UK: Jubilee Centre, 2006).

by a combination of natural and social causes. While the existence of these factors may explain what happens, such an explanation does not provide a basis for behavioral justification; it merely explains the inclination and attraction.

It is important to note that for many if not most people, sexual attraction is not a choice. We can exercise choice over our actions but not our attractions. In addition, the object (person) of our attractions can change, as can the direction (gender) of those attractions. Most people are fixed in the gender direction of their sexual preference for their life, even though some might desire it to change. But there are also some people whose sexual preference has changed unintentionally or who have been able to choose to change the gender direction of their affections.[5]

The point is that modern science is agnostic about the connection between human sexual attractions, the morality of human behavior, and our understanding of who we are. While political correctness may dictate enforcement of respect for sexual preference and identity politics, the reality is that this pressure comes from iWorld societal mores rather than from science or objective reason.

The study of modern science leaves the iWorld and the rWorld on an even playing field; it does not give an advantage to either. The questions of human identity and morality are left unresolved by modern science, which is precisely what Hume has been trying to tell us all along. This is why it is useful to also bring philosophy to bear in the quest to understand identity.

The Identity Conundrum: Philosophically Speaking

If science cannot conclusively tell us who we are, what assistance can philosophy offer? While Charles Taylor can't resolve the question in a final way, he can help us understand philosophically why the question of our identity has become such a conundrum in the present.[6] In his book *Multiculturalism*, Taylor traces the history of identity by examining the

5. Jones and Yarhouse, *Ex-Gays?* 42.
6. I acknowledge that there is a chasm between the ways philosophers and psychologists, particularly developmental psychologists, understand identity. While I attempt to bridge the gap between them, where I fail, I am speaking as a philosopher and not a psychologist.

shift that has occurred in human self-understanding and identity in the West since the Enlightenment. As we have seen, prior to the Enlightenment the question of identity was not an issue of concern. Rather than engaging in a quest to establish a personal identity, humans focused on making the most of the life they had been given. Personal identity was of little importance relative to its role in today's society.

This changed with the Enlightenment. We see a shift in many early Enlightenment authors, especially Rousseau, who communicate a sense that human identity is not something we derive from a common nature but is rather a product of an individual's quest for self-understanding. Taylor chronicles this transition. In what he calls the *monological* turn in the construction of human identity, people are encouraged to look within to find their true self and live lives that authentically reflect who they discover themselves to be. Self-discovery and authenticity, not birth and nature, become the new source of human identity. Rather than blindly accepting identity in the traditional manner, each of us is exhorted to find it for ourselves. In this quest, we can find companions to support us, but we cannot find anyone to do it for us, nor can we take as normative the discoveries other people have made about themselves. Finding our personal identity is perhaps the most important quest of our life, and it is a solitary venture.

The problem with the self-contained monological quest for self-identity is that it doesn't work. As Taylor points out, later Enlightenment thinkers, such as Herder, recognize that humans are incapable of understanding themselves without a reference point outside of themselves. Why? Humans on the monological quest can never achieve certainty about who they are, because they will never know if there are aspects of themselves that have been left undeveloped or undiscovered. Yet, rather than discard the individualistic quest for self-understanding and return to the pre-enlightened tWorld approach, the later Enlightenment authors replaced the monological quest (finding our identity by ourselves within ourselves) with the *dialogical* quest (finding our identity in dialogue with others).

In the dialogical quest, humans look to other humans to authenticate the discoveries they believe they are making about themselves. People become reference points for one another. The quest for self-discovery is still individually based, but it can be pursued only with the assistance of others, recognizing that we need the help of others to authenticate what we believe we have discovered about ourselves. The dialogical quest is still a subjective endeavor. But since no other approach to self-understanding is regarded as legitimate and authentic, a certain level of uncertainty and insecurity becomes a fixed feature of the identity of the inhabitants of what becomes the iWorld.

On a societal level, what the dialogical approach tends to produce are groups composed of people with similar identities who serve to affirm the identity of the others in the group. These groups are as varied and numerous as the number of possible identities people may perceive they possess. The problem is that even the dialogical quest cannot tell us with certainty who we are. If no one can know who they are without the aid of others, and if even with the aid of others we cannot be sure others see us for who we really are, none of us can use this approach to find certainty about who we are.

The dialogical approach creates a dynamic with significant political implications. If it is true that we need others to help us get a sense of who we are, then in a very real sense our well-being is dependent on the affirmation of others. Consequently, the iWorld asks the government to go to every length possible to make sure we are affirmed in the manner we wish to be and to restrict those who might deny us this reassurance. Taylor argues that this is why politics in the iWorld has become focused on authenticity and affirmation. It has become a political imperative that everyone receive as much social affirmation as possible in their quest to have their perceived identity authenticated. This has provided the impetus for governments to expand and enforce nondiscrimination laws, and to see to it that the lifestyles and identities of its citizens are affirmed to the greatest degree possible, so long as they do not violate the three taboos. The political importance of affirmation in the iWorld is second only to sexual freedom.

While this is a useful way to understand how society and politics are developing in the iWorld, it also demonstrates its identity conundrum. Uncertainty about who we are and who we might have been will exist for many, if not most, inhabitants of the iWorld, because no one will ever be able to know with certainty if they have chosen the identity, spouse, or career path that will maximize their happiness.

Tocqueville captures the essence of the dilemma of the iWorld:

In America I saw the freest and most enlightened men placed in the happiest circumstances that the world affords, it seemed to me as if a cloud habitually hung upon their brow, and I thought them serious and almost sad, even in their pleasures.

The chief reason for this contrast is that [they are] forever brooding over advantages they do not possess. It is strange to see with what feverish ardor the Americans pursue their own welfare, and to watch the vague dread that constantly torments them lest they should not have chosen the shortest path which may lead to it.

A native of the United States clings to this world's goods as if he were certain never to die; and he is so hasty in grasping at all within his reach that one would suppose he was constantly afraid of not living long enough to enjoy them. He clutches everything, he holds nothing fast, but soon loosens his grasp to pursue fresh gratifications.

In the United States a man builds a house in which to spend his old age, and he sells it before the roof is on; he plants a garden and lets it just as the trees are coming into bearing; he brings a field into tillage and leaves other men to gather the crops; he embraces a profession and gives it up; he settles in a place, which he soon afterwards leaves to carry his changeable longings elsewhere. If his private affairs leave him any leisure, he instantly plunges into the vortex of politics; and if at the end of a year of unremitting labor he finds he has a few days' vacation, his eager curiosity whirls him over the vast extent of the United States, and he will travel fifteen hundred miles in a few days to shake off his happiness. Death at length overtakes him, but it is before he is weary of his bootless chase of that complete felicity which forever escapes him.

At first sight there is something surprising in this strange unrest of so many happy men, restless in the midst of abundance. The spectacle itself, however, is as old as the world; the novelty is to see a whole people furnish an exemplification of it.

Their taste for physical gratifications must be regarded as the original source of that secret disquietude which the actions of the Americans betray and of that inconstancy of which they daily afford fresh examples. He who has set his heart exclusively upon the pursuit of worldly welfare is always in a hurry, for he has but a limited time at his disposal to reach, to grasp, and to enjoy it.

The recollection of the shortness of life is a constant spur to him. Besides the good things that he possesses, he every instant fancies a thousand others that death will prevent him from trying if he does not try them soon. This thought fills him with anxiety, fear, and regret and keeps his mind in ceaseless trepidation, which leads him perpetually to change his plans and his abode.

If in addition to the taste for physical well-being a social condition is added in which neither laws nor customs retain any person in his place, there is a great additional stimulant to this restlessness of temper. Men will then be seen continually to change their track for fear of missing the shortest cut to happiness.[7]

Tocqueville understands the sociology of the iWorld, which profoundly impacts its perception of the meaning of life and happiness. This is particularly true of self-understanding. The iWorld and the rWorld have divergent views of the way we come to understand who we are. The iWorld sees the formation of self-understanding as primarily an individualistic enterprise, whether, to use Taylor's terminology, it is approached monologically or dialogically. The rWorld, however, believes that we come to know who we are only by first coming to know our true human nature through relating with God and other persons. Then we can make sense of our individual characteristics. While the distinction between the two approaches may appear slight, it is profound. A primarily individualistic approach to self-understanding is fundamentally different from a relational approach. In the former, the individual *uses* self or others to discover what can only be their individual identity. In the latter, persons come to understand themselves by first coming to understand who we are as humans. We come to this understanding through relating to ("knowing") others and God. Only then can we make sense of the unique aspects of who we are.

This is where the two worlds diverge. The rWorld maintains that everyone possesses a common nature and reference point, which is a view that stands in opposition to the iWorld's monological and dialogical approaches. As a result, the rWorld is unable to morally affirm the varieties of human behavior and perceptions of identity that the iWorld believes humans deserve as a right to be protected.

This doesn't resolve the difference between the two worlds, but it does help us understand why the differences are so emotionally charged and intractable. When the rWorld cannot affirm that someone's self-identity ought to be found in his or her sexuality, material resources,

7. Tocqueville, *Democracy in America*, vol. 2, bk. 2, chap. 13.

marriage, pets, and so forth, it challenges what is for the iWorld not merely an ethical or philosophical point for discussion but core issues of identity that are deeply held, strongly reinforced by peer groups, and increasingly protected by government mandate and law. The key to deciding which world we want hinges on how we determine who we are.

Parting Questions

After all that has been written in these pages, there remain a few questions to be asked of the three "worlds" we have discussed. They are questions that we need to consider in trying to determine which world would serve us best.

Questioning the iWorld

There is much about which the iWorld can be justifiably proud. It has provided an era of unprecedented freedom and believes that it will also produce an era of unprecedented economic prosperity. Its embrace of equality has given the fight for equity a moral quality that has rarely existed in human history. Its embrace of toleration has allowed coexistence to reign in a manner only rarely realized. Even as a critic, I must acknowledge the marvels it has achieved. Despite my misgivings, I am aware that we could do worse than the iWorld, and history is replete with examples.

The major question that concerns me about the iWorld is its sustainability. Can this level of individualism and freedom, with only the three taboos serving as its moral guide, provide an effective, self-sustaining, long-term societal structure? Does the iWorld possess enough coherence to continue to hold itself together, or will its citizens, in their individual pursuits, find themselves diverging ever further from any shared interests with their fellow citizens? Will the iWorld be able to avoid the social, societal, and political fragmentation that would lead to its disintegration? Will it be able to find a way to sustain itself economically without the societal cohesiveness and moral capital upon which capitalism was built? Is it the case that the iWorld is a destination, or might it someday be viewed as a political and social accident of time and place in the transition from modernity to post-modernity? As we have seen, the iWorld already has struggles with identity, personal insecurity, societal instability, and third-party consequences of individual choices. Will, however, its devotion to virtually boundless personal freedom without regard for possible consequences be its undoing? How long can such a world be sustained?

Questioning the rWorld

The major question facing the rWorld concerns the credibility of the model and how such a societal structure could be implemented. Both supporters and critics of the rWorld may wonder whether it is merely a world of words, or whether *r* can also stand for "real." Social change is very difficult, revolutions often make things worse, and humans have a poor track record when it comes to well-intentioned, logically conceived schemes falling prey to the law of unintended consequences. Our efforts to stimulate the economy can undermine it. Our efforts to end poverty can exacerbate it. Our programs to end racism can make it endemic. I believe in the rWorld, but I also believe that without the thoughtful help of supporters and critics alike it can never be successfully created. If the rWorld becomes an ideology that lacks the ability to critique itself, accept criticism, or adjust to changing realities, it will fail like every other ideology. If it develops into a movement that everyone is invited to participate in and contribute toward, we can find out just how real it can be.

Questioning the tWorld

Some might be surprised that there are still questions for the tWorld at this point, but they persist. There are no doubt readers who remain persuaded that what is necessary for humanity to thrive is for us to reengage with ancient wisdom, revelation, natural law, and the tradition. There is increasing interest on the part of many people, especially young people, to look for roots in the past and search for meaning in long-standing religious traditions and communities. The world today shares a pervasive sense that something is missing. We are all on a quest for fulfillment, but we still haven't found what we are looking for. While I am not persuaded that we can go back to the tWorld, it was too substantial for too long for us to ignore what it may still offer. As a Christian, I believe that God created time itself and that Christ stands at the end of history calling us home. I do not have a problem drawing on the past, but I am persuaded we must go forward. If we cannot find the answer in *i*, perhaps we will discover it in *r*.

Afterword

It's Déjà Vu All Over Again

And you may ask yourself
What is that beautiful house?
And you may ask yourself
Where does that highway go?
And you may ask yourself
Am I right? . . . am I wrong?
And you may tell yourself
My god! . . . what have I done?

> Talking Heads,
> "Once in a Lifetime"[1]

We stand only on the threshold of an inconceivable age.

> Perry Miller, "The Insecurity of Nature"[2]

It is perhaps surprising that any relevant link exists between this book and my first, *Massachusetts Congregationalist Political Thought, 1760–1790: The Design of Heaven*. But Perry Miller, in his Harvard lecture cited in the epigraph above, makes the link between the two. The

---

1. Talking Heads, "Once in a Lifetime," *Remain in Light* (Sire Records, 1980).
2. Perry Miller, "The Insecurity of Nature," in *Nature's Nation* (Cambridge, MA: Harvard University Press, 1967), 121–33.

eighteenth-century Massachusetts Congregationalist clergy made two notable mistakes that we would be well served not to repeat.

Their first mistake was to underestimate the challenge with which they and their society were faced. The Congregationalists were aware of the Enlightenment and of the fact that it was entertaining ideas that, if embraced, would radically change and undermine the world the Congregationalists had so carefully constructed. Yet because the implications of the ideas seemed too fantastic to be believed, they chose to ignore them and assumed that rational people would never embrace them. They chose to look back and ignore the challenges that lay ahead.

The second mistake was to expect modern science to support their moral reasoning. The Congregationalist clergy believed in natural theology, an approach to theology based on the assumption that Christian theology and the study of nature are in harmony. Harvard University's Dudleian Lecture, its oldest endowed lectureship, was founded in 1750 in part to reinforce the belief that modern science and divine revelation were fundamentally harmonious. The clergy believed deeply in the synthesis they developed in the eighteenth century between science and theology, and they believed that the self-evident truth of both would forever mutually reinforce the other. The problem, as they could have plainly seen if they had fully understood modern science, is that the scientific method does not support moral conclusions. As Miller points out, the history of the Dudleian Lecture on natural theology is a historical, real-world demonstration that science and nature cannot ultimately take the place of philosophy and theology because science does not answer moral questions and nature requires interpretation. The study of science and the natural world provides information in the service of moral reasoning, but nothing more. Miller illustrates the failure of these Congregationalist assumptions by pointing out that many of the twentieth-century Dudleian lecturers presented arguments in the name of science and nature that completely contradict the theological beliefs of the Dudley family, who endowed the lecture series. As Miller writes, quoting Pascal, "There is nothing man cannot make natural and there is nothing natural than man cannot make unnatural."[3]

3. Perry Miller, "The Insecurity of Nature," Dudleian Lecture for the Academic Year 1952–1953, Harvard University, Cambridge, MA, 36.

Using Miller's imagery, we either stand at or are crossing the threshold into an age that until recently was inconceivable. None of us know with certainty where the iWorld is going. And rather than pretend everything will be all right or ask science to put things right, we would be well served to learn from the mistaken assumptions of the Congregationalist clergy. Rather than look at the world with our eyes shut tight, we need to open them and take responsibility to be proactive in directing the future and live in the real world as opposed to being passive observers and potential victims of change.

Even though we may find it hard to "change the world," none of us can be released from the responsibility to be engaged in directing the future. It is certainly tempting to disengage from the challenge by putting on our headsets, turning up the volume of our iPods, and trying to ignore what's going on all around us in a world that is rapidly changing. It is also tempting to convince ourselves that modern science will be our teacher and our guide. Unfortunately, both responses are incomplete and ineffective. The task of moral reasoning is a fundamental human responsibility, as is the responsibility to do our part to shape the future. We don't have to accept the responsibility, but neither should we complain when things unfold in a manner we do not like. Modern science provides us with knowledge and power, nothing more, and it does not come with a handbook on how they should be used.

We live at a moment when we still have time to choose what kind of society we are constructing. The iWorld and the rWorld offer profoundly different alternatives. Will we proceed as though modern science can release us from the task of having to make a moral choice? Or will we, either with fear or with assurance, choose our path? We have come out of the woods into the iWorld and, like Robert Frost, are at a fork in the road; the direction we choose will make all the difference. The question for each of us is whether we will continue on the road to the iWorld or decide that something is missing and choose the path toward constructing the rWorld.

Since poets and songwriters express my thoughts and feelings better than I am able, I'd like to conclude with Procol Harum's "Pilgrim's Progress." The song captures the essence of the pilgrimage on which I find myself.

I sat me down to write a simple story
which maybe in the end became a song
In trying to find the words which might begin it
I found these were the thoughts I brought along

At first I took my weight to be an anchor
I gathered up my fears to guide me round
but then I clearly saw my own delusion
and found my struggles further bogged me down

In starting out I thought to go exploring
and set my foot upon the nearest road
In vain I looked to find the promised turning
but only saw how far I was from home

In searching I forsook the paths of learning
and sought instead to find some pirate's gold
In fighting I did hurt those dearest to me
and still no hidden truths could I unfold

I sat me down to write a simple story
which maybe in the end became a song
The words have all been writ by one before me
We're taking turns in trying to pass them on
Oh, we're taking turns in trying to pass them on[4]

4. Procol Harum, "Pilgrim's Progress," *A Salty Dog* (A&M, 1969).

Bibliography

Amaechi, John. "John Amaechi Busts Out." *ESPN the Magazine*, February 26, 2007, 68–74.

Aristotle. *Nicomachean Ethics*. Translated by Terence Irwin. Indianapolis: Hackett, 1985.

Ash, Christopher. *Marriage: Sex in the Service of God*. Vancouver: Regent College Publishing, 2003.

Atkins, Anne. *Split Image: Male and Female after God's Likeness*. Grand Rapids: Eerdmans, 1987.

Bahnsen, Greg L. *Homosexuality: A Biblical View*. Grand Rapids: Baker Books, 1978.

Bainton, Roland H. *What Christianity Says about Sex, Love and Marriage*. New York: Association Press, 1957.

Barger, Lilian Calles. *Eve's Revenge: Women and a Spirituality of the Body*. Grand Rapids: Brazos, 2003.

Barna, George. *Revolution*. Carol Stream, IL: Tyndale House, 2005.

———. *Think Like Jesus: Make the Right Decision Every Time*. Nashville: Integrity Publishers, 2003.

Barna Group. "American Lifestyles Mix Compassion and Self-Oriented Behavior." *Barna Update*. February 5, 2007. www.barna.org/FlexPage.aspx?Page=Barna UpdateNarrow&BarnaUpdateID=264.

———. "Born Again Christians Just As Likely to Divorce As Are Non-Christians." *Barna Update*. September 8, 2004. www.barna.org/FlexPage.aspx?Page=Barna UpdateNarrow&BarnaUpdateID=170.

———. "A New Generation of Adults Bends Moral and Sexual Rules to Their Liking." *Barna Update*. October 31, 2006. http://www.barna.org/FlexPage.aspx ?Page=BarnaUpdate&BarnaUpdateID=249.

Barnett, Rosalind, and Caryl Rivers. *Same Difference: How Gender Myths Are Hurting Our Relationships, Our Children, and Our Jobs*. New York: Basic Books, 2004.

Barrow, John. *Theories of Everything*. Oxford: Oxford University Press, 1991.

Baum, Frank. *The Wizard of Oz*. Screenplay by Noel Langley, Florence Ryerson, and Edgar Allan Woolf. Loew's Incorporated, 1939.

Beall, Anne E., and Robert J. Sternberg, eds. *The Psychology of Gender*. New York: Guilford Press, 1993.

Becker, Carl L. *The Heavenly City of the Eighteenth Century Philosophers*. New Haven: Yale University Press, 1932.

Bellah, Robert N., Richard Madsen, William M. Sullivan, Ann Swidler, and Steven M. Tipton. *The Good Society*. New York: Vintage Books, 1992.

———. *Habits of the Heart: Individualism and Commitment in American Life*. Berkeley: University of California Press, 1985.

Blackburn, Simon. *Truth: A Guide*. Oxford: Oxford University Press, 2005.

Blankenhorn, David. *The Future of Marriage*. New York: Encounter Books, 2007.

Bloom, Allan. *The Republic of Plato*. 2nd ed. New York: Basic Books, 1991.

Boswell, John. *Christianity, Social Tolerance, and Homosexuality*. Chicago: University of Chicago, 1980.

———. *Same-Sex Unions in Premodern Europe*. New York: Villard Books, 1994.

Brandon, Guy. *Just Sex? Why It's Never Just Sex*. Nottingham, UK: Inter-Varsity, 2009.

Brown, Montague. *Restoration of Reason: The Eclipse and Recovery of Truth, Goodness, and Beauty*. Grand Rapids: Baker Academic, 2006.

Browning, Don S., M. Christian Green, and John Witte Jr., eds. *Sex, Marriage, and Family in World Religions*. New York: Columbia University Press, 2006.

Burke, Edmund. *Reflections on the Revolution in France*. Edited by J. G. A. Pocock. Indianapolis: Hackett, 1987.

Burnside, Jonathan. *God, Justice and Society*. Unpublished manuscript.

Burton, Simon. *The Causes of Homosexuality*. Cambridge, UK: Jubilee Centre, 2006.

Cere, Dan. *The Future of Family Law: Law and Marriage Crisis in North America*. A Report from the Council on Family Law. New York: Institute for American Values, 2005.

Chesterton, G. K. *Orthodoxy*. Garden City, NY: Image Books, 1959.

———. *What's Wrong with the World*. New York: Dodd, Mead, 1927.

Comiskey, Andrew. *Strength in Weakness: Healing Sexual and Relational Brokenness*. Downers Grove, IL: InterVarsity, 2003.

Crompton, Louis. *Homosexuality and Civilization*. Cambridge, MA: Belknap Press of Harvard University Press, 2003.

Dallas, Joe. *A Strong Delusion: Confronting the "Gay Christian" Movement*. Eugene, OR: Harvest House, 1996.

Davies, Bob, and Lori Rentzel. *Coming Out of Homosexuality: New Freedom for Men and Women*. Downers Grove, IL: InterVarsity, 1993.

"Dutch 'marriage': 1 man, 2 women: Trio becomes 1st officially to tie the knots." *World Net Daily,* September 30, 2005. www.worldnetdaily.com/news/article .asp?ARTICLE_ID=46583.

Edgar, Brian, and Gordon Preece, eds. *Whose Homosexuality? Which Authority? Homosexual Practice, Marriage, Ordination and the Church.* Adelaide, Australia: ATF, 2006.

Edsall, Nicholas C. *Toward Stonewall: Homosexuality and Society in the Modern Western World.* Charlottesville: University of Virginia Press, 2003.

Elshtain, Jean Bethke. *Public Man, Private Woman: Women in Social and Political Thought.* Princeton, NJ: Princeton University Press, 1981.

Eskridge, William N., and Darren R. Spedale. *Gay Marriage: For Better or for Worse: What We've Learned from the Evidence.* Oxford: Oxford University Press, 2006.

Fausto-Sterling, Anne. *Sexing the Body: Gender Politics and the Construction of Sexuality.* New York: Basic Books, 2000.

"4% Fall in UK Marriages." National Statistics. www.statistics.gov.uk/CCI/nugget .asp?ID=322.

Fox-Genovese, Elizabeth. *Marriage: The Dream That Refuses to Die.* Wilmington, DE: ISI Books, 2008.

Frost, Robert. "The Road Not Taken." In *Mountain Interval.* New York: H. Holt, 1916.

Gagnon, Robert A. J. *The Bible and Homosexual Practice: Texts and Hermeneutics.* Nashville: Abingdon, 2001.

"Gay Marriage." Pew Forum on Religion and Public Life. http://pewforum.org/ gay-marriage.

George, Robert P. *The Clash of Orthodoxies: Law, Religion, and Morality in Crisis.* Wilmington, DE: ISI Books, 2001.

George, Robert P., and Jean Bethke Elshtain, eds. *The Meaning of Marriage: Family, State, Market, and Morals.* Dallas: Spence, 2006.

Giddens, Anthony. *Modernity and Self-Identity: Self and Society in the Late Modern Age.* Stanford, CA: Stanford University Press, 1991.

Grant, Michael, trans. *Tacitus: The Annals of Imperial Rome.* Rev. ed. London: Penguin Books, 1971.

Greenberg, David F. *The Construction of Homosexuality.* Chicago: University of Chicago Press, 1988.

Hamer, Dean, and Peter Copeland. *The Science of Desire: The Search for the Gay Gene and the Biology of Behavior.* New York: Simon & Schuster, 1994.

Hanigan, James P. *Homosexuality: The Test Case for Christian Sexual Ethics.* New York: Paulist Press, 1988.

Hawthorne, Nathaniel. *The Celestial Rail-Road.* Washington DC: Trinity Forum Reading, 2003.

Hays, Richard B. *The Moral Vision of the New Testament: A Contemporary Introduction to New Testament Ethics.* San Francisco: HarperSanFrancisco, 1996.

Heimbach, Daniel R. *True Sexual Morality: Recovering Biblical Standards for a Culture in Crisis*. Wheaton: Crossway Books, 2004.

Helminiak, Daniel A. *What the Bible Really Says about Homosexuality*. San Francisco: Alamo Square Press, 1995.

Höpfl, Harro. *The Christian Polity of John Calvin*. Edited by Maurice Cowling, G. R. Elton, E. Kedourie, J. G. A. Pocock, J. R. Pole, and Walter Ulmann. Cambridge, UK: Cambridge University Press, 1982.

Hume, David. *A Treatise of Human Nature*. 2nd ed. Edited by L. A. Selby-Bigge and P. H. Nidditch. Oxford: Clarendon, 1978.

Hymowitz, Kay S. *Marriage and Caste in America: Separate and Unequal Families in a Post-Marital Age*. Chicago: Ivan R. Dee, 2006.

"An Illegitimate Argument." *Spectator*, December 12, 2007. www.spectator.co.uk/coffeehouse/399431/an-illegitimate-argument.thtml.

Instone-Brewer, David. *Divorce and Remarriage in the Bible: The Social and Literary Context*. Grand Rapids: Eerdmans, 2002.

Jaki, Stanley L. *Bible and Science*. Front Royal, VA: Christendom, 1996.

James, Carolyn Custis. *Lost Women of the Bible: Finding Strength and Significance through Their Stories*. Grand Rapids: Zondervan, 2005.

————. *When Life and Beliefs Collide: How Knowing God Makes a Difference*. Grand Rapids: Zondervan, 2001.

Jefferson, Thomas. *The Life and Morals of Jesus of Nazareth: Extracted Textually from the Gospels, Together with a Comparison of His Doctrines with Those of Others*. St. Louis: N. D. Thompson, 1902.

————. *Selected Writings*. Edited by Harvey C. Mansfield Jr. 1979. Reprint, Arlington Heights, IL: Harlan Davidson, 1987.

Jones, E. Michael. *Degenerate Moderns: Modernity as Rationalized Sexual Misbehavior*. San Francisco: Ignatius, 1993.

Jones, Stanton L., and Mark A. Yarhouse. *Ex-gays? A Longitudinal Study of Religiously Mediated Change in Sexual Orientation*. Downers Grove, IL: IVP Academic, 2007.

————. *Homosexuality: The Use of Scientific Research in the Church's Moral Debate*. Downers Grove, IL: InterVarsity, 2000.

Kinnaman, David, and Gabe Lyons. *UnChristian: What a New Generation Really Thinks about Christianity . . . and Why It Matters*. Grand Rapids: Baker Books, 2007.

Lewis, C. S. *The Abolition of Man; or, Reflections on Education with Special Reference to the Teaching of English in the Upper Forms of Schools*. New York: Macmillan, 1955.

————. *The Four Loves*. New York: Harcourt Brace Jovanovich, 1960.

Lord, Charles. *Aristotle: The Politics*. Chicago: University of Chicago Press, 1984.

Lovelace, Richard F. *Dynamics of Spiritual Life: An Evangelical Theology of Renewal*. Downers Grove, IL: InterVarsity, 1979.

Machacek, David W., and Adrienne Fulco. "The Courts and Public Discourse: The Case of Gay Marriage." *Journal of Church and State* 46, no. 4 (2004): 767–86.

MacIntyre, Alasdair. *After Virtue: A Study in Moral Theory.* 2nd ed. Notre Dame, IN: University of Notre Dame Press, 1984.

Marquardt, Elizabeth. "When 3 Really Is a Crowd." *New York Times*, July 16, 2007. www.nytimes.com/2007/07/16/opinion/16marquardt.html?adxnnl =1&adxnnlx=1185202864–E43yMY4/Iit5/TTsWQlPZA.

Marriage and the Law: A Statement of Principles; A Call to the Nation from Family and Legal Scholars. New York: Institute for American Values, 2006.

McCourt, James. *Queer Street: Rise and Fall of an American Culture, 1947–1985.* New York: W. W. Norton, 2004.

Mill, John Stuart. *On Liberty.* Edited by Elizabeth Rapaport. Indianapolis: Hackett, 1978.

———. *Utilitarianism.* Indianapolis: Hackett, 1979.

Miller, Perry. "The Insecurity of Nature." Dudleian Lecture for the Academic Year 1952–1953, Harvard University, Cambridge, MA.

———. "The Insecurity of Nature." In *Nature's Nation*, 121–33. Cambridge, MA: Harvard University Press, 1967.

Mitchell, R. B. *Castaway Kid: One Man's Search for Hope and Home.* Carol Stream, IL: Tyndale House, 2007.

National Association of Secretaries of State. "American Youth Attitudes on Politics, Citizenship, Government and Voting." *New Millennium Project*, part 1, 1999.

Nietzsche, Friedrich. *Beyond Good and Evil: Prelude to the Philosophy of the Future.* Edited by Rolf-Peter Horstmann and Judith Norman. Cambridge, UK: Cambridge University Press, 2002.

———. *The Will to Power.* Edited by Walter Kaufmann and R. J. Hollingdale. New York: Vintage Books, 1967.

Nouwen, Henri J. M. *Life of the Beloved: Spiritual Living in a Secular World.* 10th anniversary ed. New York: Crossroad, 1992.

Nozick, Robert. *Anarchy, State, and Utopia.* New York: Basic Books, 1974.

O'Donovan, Oliver. *Resurrection and Moral Order: An Outline for Evangelical Ethics.* 2nd ed. Leicester, UK: Apollos, 1994.

Olson, David T. *The American Church in Crisis: Groundbreaking Research Based on a National Database of Over 200,000 Churches.* Grand Rapids: Zondervan, 2008.

Paine, Thomas. *Common Sense.* London: Penguin Books, 1986.

Pangle, Thomas, trans. *The Laws of Plato.* Chicago: University of Chicago Press, 1980.

Peck, M. Scott. *The Road Less Traveled: A New Psychology of Love, Traditional Values and Spiritual Growth.* New York: Touchstone, Simon & Schuster, 1978.

Peterson, David, ed. *Holiness and Sexuality: Homosexuality in a Biblical Context.* Carlisle, UK: Paternoster, 2004.

Phillips, Melanie. *The Sex-Change Society: Feminised Britain and the Neutered Male.* London: Social Market Foundation, 1999.

Pinello, Daniel R. *America's Struggle for Same-Sex Marriage*. Cambridge, UK: Cambridge University Press, 2006.

Pinker, Steven. *The Blank Slate: The Modern Denial of Human Nature*. New York: Viking, 2002.

Piper, John. *What's the Difference? Manhood and Womanhood Defined according to the Bible*. Wheaton: Crossway Books, 1990.

Piper, John, and Wayne Grudem, eds. *Recovering Biblical Manhood and Womanhood: A Response to Evangelical Feminism*. Wheaton: Crossway Books, 1991.

Pope John Paul II. *The Theology of the Body: Human Love in the Divine Plan*. Boston: Pauline Books and Media, 1997.

Popenoe, David. "Essay: The Future of Marriage in America." In *The State of Our Unions 2007: The Social Health of Marriage in America*. National Marriage Project at Rutgers State University, 2007. http://marriage.rutgers.edu/Publications/SOOU/TEXTSOOU2007.htm.

Preece, Gordon. "(Homo)Sex and the City of God." *Interface* 9, nos. 1 and 2 (May and October 2006): 187–216.

Putnam, Robert D. *Bowling Alone: The Collapse and Revival of American Community*. New York: Simon & Schuster, 2000.

Rauch, Jonathan. *Gay Marriage: Why It Is Good for Gays, Good for Straights, and Good for America*. New York: Owl Books, Henry Holt, 2004.

Rawls, John. *A Theory of Justice*. Rev. ed. Cambridge, MA: Belknap Press of Harvard University Press, 1999.

Regnerus, Mark D. *Forbidden Fruit: Sex and Religion in the Lives of American Teenagers*. Oxford: Oxford University Press, 2007.

"Resolution in Support of Equal Marriage Rights for All for General Synod 25 of the United Church of Christ." United Church of Christ. www.ucc.org/synod/resolutions/RESOLUTION-IN-SUPPORT-OF-EQUAL-MARRIAGE-RIGHTS-FOR-ALL-FOR-GENERAL-SYNOD-25.pdf.

Ridgeway, Stephan. "Sexuality and Modernity: The Sexual Revolution of the 60s." Annadale, Australia: Isis Creations, 1997. www.isis.aust.com/stephan/writings/sexuality/revo.htm.

Rimmerman, Craig A. *From Identity to Politics: The Lesbian and Gay Movements in the United States*. Philadelphia: Temple University Press, 2002.

Rogers, Jack. *Jesus, the Bible, and Homosexuality: Explode the Myths, Heal the Church*. Louisville: Westminster John Knox, 2006.

Saltzman, Russell E., ed. *Christian Sexuality: Normative and Pastoral Principles*. Minneapolis: Kirk House, 2002.

"Same-Sex Unions and Civil Unions." Ontario Consultants on Religious Tolerance. www.religioustolerance.org/hom_marp.htm.

Sarup, Madan. *An Introductory Guide to Post-structuralism and Postmodernism*. 2nd ed. Athens: University of Georgia Press, 1988.

Satinover, Jeffrey. *Homosexuality and the Politics of Truth*. Grand Rapids: Baker Academic, 1996.

Schluter, Michael, and John Ashcroft, eds. *Jubilee Manifesto: A Framework, Agenda and Strategy for Christian Social Reform*. Leicester, UK: Inter-Varsity, 2005.

Schluter, Michael, and Cambridge Papers Group. *Christianity in a Changing World: Biblical Insight on Contemporary Issues*. London: Marshall Pickering, 2000.

Schluter, Michael, and Roy Clements. "Reactivating the Extended Family: From Biblical Norms to Public Policy in Britain." Jubilee Centre, paper no. 1, 1986.

Schluter, Michael, and David Lee. *The R Factor*. London: Hodder and Stoughton, 1993.

———. *The R Option: Building Relationships as a Better Way of Life*. Cambridge, UK: Relationships Foundation, 2003.

Schmidt, Thomas E. *Straight and Narrow: Compassion and Clarity in the Homosexuality Debate*. Downers Grove, IL: InterVarsity, 1995.

Schumacher, E. F. *A Guide for the Perplexed*. New York: Harper and Row, 1977.

Shalit, Wendy. *A Return to Modesty: Discovering the Lost Virtue*. New York: Touchstone Books, Simon & Schuster, 1999.

Sider, Ronald J. *The Scandal of the Evangelical Conscience: Why Are Christians Living Just Like the Rest of the World?* Grand Rapids: Baker Academic, 2005.

Siegel, Daniel J. *The Developing Mind: Toward a Neurobiology of Interpersonal Experience*. New York: Guilford Press, 1999.

Smith, James K. A. *Who's Afraid of Postmodernism? Taking Derrida, Lyotard, and Foucault to Church*. Grand Rapids: Baker Academic, 2006.

Spaeth, Harold J., ed. *The Predicament of Modern Politics*. Detroit: University of Detroit Press, 1964.

Storey, John. *An Introductory Guide to Cultural Theory and Popular Culture*. Athens: University of Georgia Press, 1993.

Storkey, Elaine. *The Search for Intimacy*. Grand Rapids: Eerdmans, 1995.

Stott, John. *Homosexual Partnerships? Why Same-Sex Relationships Are Not a Christian Option*. Downers Grove, IL: InterVarsity, 1987.

Strauss, Leo. "The Crisis of Our Time." In *The Predicament of Modern Politics*, 41–53. Edited by Harold J. Spaeth. Detroit: University of Detroit Press, 1964.

Sullivan, Andrew, ed. *Same-Sex Marriage: Pro and Con; A Reader*. Rev. ed. New York: Vintage Books, 2004.

———. *Virtually Normal: An Argument about Homosexuality*. New York: Vintage Books, 1995.

"A Symposium on the Politics of Same-Sex Marriage." *PS: Political Science and Politics* 38, no. 2 (2005): 189–239.

Tanner, Lindsay. *Crowded Lives*. Melbourne, Australia: Pluto, 2003.

Taylor, Charles, K. Anthony Appiah, Jürgen Habermas, Steven C. Rockefeller, Michael Walzer, and Susan Wolf. *Multiculturalism: Examining the Politics of Recognition*. Edited by Amy Gutmann. Princeton, NJ: Princeton University Press, 1994.

"30 Day Sex Challenge Guide." February 17–March 16, 2008. www.youtube.com/watch?v=MOr09AI7Rfk. Additional information is available at http://relevant church.com.

Thompson, Chad W. *Loving Homosexuals as Jesus Would: A Fresh Christian Approach*. Grand Rapids: Brazos, 2004.

Tinder, Glenn. *The Political Meaning of Christianity: The Prophetic Stance*. San Francisco: HarperCollins, 1991.

Tipton, Steven M., and John Witte Jr., eds. *Family Transformed: Religion, Values, and Society in American Life*. Washington DC: Georgetown University Press, 2005.

Tocqueville, Alexis de. *Democracy in America*. 2 vols. Edited by Phillips Bradley. New York: Vintage Books, 1990.

Tripp, C. A. *The Homosexual Matrix*. New York: McGraw-Hill, 1975.

"An Unexpected Tragedy: Evidence for the Connection between Working Patterns and Family Breakdown in Australia." Relationships Forum, 2007. www.relationships forum.org.au/report/index.html#ut_download.

Van Domelan, Bob. *The Church, the Sex Offender, and Reconciliation*. Resource Series: Church and Theology. n.p.: Exodus International-North America, n.d.

Van Leeuwen, Mary Stewart. *Gender and Grace: Love, Work and Parenting in a Changing World*. Downers Grove, IL: InterVarsity, 1990.

Vernon, Mark. *The Philosophy of Friendship*. New York: Palgrave Macmillan, 2005.

Via, Dan O., and Robert A. Gagnon. *Homosexuality and the Bible: Two Views*. Minneapolis: Fortress, 2003.

Voltaire. *Candide or Optimism*. Edited by Norman L. Torrey. Northbrook, IL: AHM Publishing, 1946.

Wardle, Lynn D., Mark Strasser, William C. Duncan, and David Orgon Coolidge, eds. *Marriage and Same-Sex Unions: A Debate*. Westport, CT: Praeger, 2003.

Wells, David F. *God in the Wasteland*. Grand Rapids: Eerdmans, 1994.

———. *No Place for Truth, or, Whatever Happened to Evangelical Theology?* Leicester, UK: Inter-Varsity, 1993.

West, Christopher. *Introduction to Theology of the Body*. 4 CD-ROMs. West Chester, PA: Ascension, 2004.

———. *Introduction to Theology of the Body: Discovering God's Glorious Plan for Your Life*. An Adult Faith Formation Study Guide. West Chester, PA: Ascension, 2003.

———. *Theology of the Body for Beginners: A Basic Introduction to Pope John Paul II's Sexual Revolution*. West Chester, PA: Ascension, 2004.

White, Heath. *Postmodernism 101: A First Course for the Curious Christian*. Grand Rapids: Brazos, 2006.

"Why Fireman Sperm Donor MUST Pay to Raise Our Children, by Lesbian Mother." Mail Online, November 4, 2008. www.dailymail.co.uk/news/article-499342/Why -fireman-sperm-donor-MUST-pay-raise-children-lesbian-mother.html.

Why Marriage Matters: Twenty-Six Conclusions from the Social Sciences. 2nd ed. A report from Family Scholars. New York: Institute for American Values, 2005.

Wilson, James Q. *The Marriage Problem: How Our Culture Has Weakened Families*. New York: HarperCollins, 2002.

Wilson, Robin Fretwell, ed. *Reconceiving the Family: Critique on the American Law Institute's Principles of the Law of Family Dissolution.* Cambridge, UK: Cambridge University Press, 2006.

Winner, Lauren F. *Real Sex: The Naked Truth about Chastity.* Grand Rapids: Brazos, 2005.

Wolfs, Frank. "Introduction to the Scientific Method." http://teacher.pas.rochester .edu/phy_labs/AppendixE/AppendixE.html.

Wolfson, Evan. *Why Marriage Matters: America, Equality, and Gay People's Right to Marry.* New York: Simon & Schuster, 2004.

Discography

Note: *Readers who would like to listen to the songs discussed in this book will find almost all of them in an iTunes iMix list at http://tinyurl.com/dh6scj.*

Bazilian, Eric. "One of Us." Recorded by Joan Osborne on *Relish*. Compact disc. Mercury Records, 1995.

Bono. "A Man and a Woman." *How to Dismantle an Atomic Bomb*. U2. Compact disc. Island Records, 2004.

———. *U2 Go Home: Live from Slane Castle, Ireland*. DVD. Interscope Records, 2003.

Bono with The Edge. "Vertigo." *How to Dismantle an Atomic Bomb*. U2. Compact disc. Island Records, 2004.

Bonoff, Karla. "Someone to Lay Down Beside Me." *Karla Bonoff*. Compact disc. Sky Harbor Music, 1976.

Chapin, Harry, and Sandy Chapin. "Cat's in the Cradle." *Verities and Balderdash*. Compact disc. Elektra Records, 1974.

Crimes and Misdemeanors. DVD. Directed by Woody Allen. Produced by Robert Greenhut. New York: Orion Pictures, 1989.

Dada. "Puzzle." *Puzzle*. Compact disc. Blue Cave Records, 1992.

The Doobie Brothers. *What Were Once Vices Are Now Habits*. Compact disc. Warner Brothers Records, 1974.

Extreme. "Hole Hearted." *Pornograffitti*. Compact disc. A&M, 1990.

Jagger, Mick, and Keith Richards. "(I Can't Get No) Satisfaction." *Out of Our Heads*. Compact disc. Rolling Stones. Decca, 1965.

Joseph, Martyn, and Stewart Henderson. "Whoever It Was That Brought Me Here Will Have to Take Me Home." *Whoever It Was That Brought Me Here Will Have to Take Me Home*. Compact disc. Pipe Records, 2003.

The Matrix. DVD. Directed by Andy Wachowski and Larry Wachowski. Warner Brothers Pictures, 1999.

McCartney, Paul. "The End." *Abbey Road*. The Beatles. Compact disc. Apple Records, 1969.

Mitchell, Joni. "Woodstock." *Ladies of the Canyon*. Compact disc. Warner Brothers Records, 1970.

Nash, Graham. "Chicago." *Songs for Beginners*. Compact disc. Atlantic Records, 1971.

Procol Harum. "Pilgrim's Progress." *A Salty Dog*. Compact disc. A&M, 1969.

Roland, Ed, and Ross Childress. "The World I Know." *Collective Soul*. Compact disc. Atlantic Records, 1995.

Stewart, Rod. "Every Picture Tells a Story." *Every Picture Tells a Story*. Compact disc. Mercury Records, 1971.

Stills, Stephen. *Love the One You're With*. Compact disc. Atlantic Records, 1970.

Talking Heads. "Once in a Lifetime." *Remain in Light*. Compact disc. Sire Records, 1980.

Townsend, Pete. "The Real Me." *Quadrophenia*. The Who. Compact disc. Track Polydor, 1973.

Index

For more information about *Sex and the iWorld*,
visit www.therworld.com.

To download a study guide for *Sex and the iWorld*,
go to www.bakeracademic.com/sexandtheiworld
and follow the link under Resources.